29.95

MANAGING
INTERDISCIPLINARY
RESEARCH

MANAGING INTERDISCIPLINARY RESEARCH

Edited by

S. R. Epton
R & D Research Unit,
Manchester Business School,
University of Manchester

R. L. Payne
M. R. C./S. S. R. C., Social and Applied Psychology Unit,
University of Sheffield

A. W. Pearson
R & D Research Unit,
Manchester Business School,
University of Manchester

JOHN WILEY & SONS
Chichester · New York · Brisbane · Toronto · Singapore

Copyright © 1983 by John Wiley & Sons Ltd.

All rights reserved.

No part of this book may be reproduced by any means, nor transmitted, nor translated into a machine language without the written permission of the publisher.

British Library Cataloguing in Publication Data:
Managing interdisciplinary research.
  1. Research—Congresses
  I. Epton, S. R.   II. Payne, R. L.
  III. Pearson, A. W.
  001.4'068   Q180
  ISBN 0 471 90317 5

Library of Congress Cataloging in Publication Data:
Main entry under title:
Managing interdisciplinary research.
  'Second International Conference on the Management of Interdisciplinary Research held at the Manchester Business School, Manchester, England in July 1981'—Foreword.
  Bibliography: p.
  1. Research—Management. 2. Research, Industrial—Management. I. Epton, S. R. II. Payne, Roy.
III. Pearson, A. W. IV. International Conference on the Management of Interdisciplinary Research (2nd: 1981: Manchester Business School)
Q180.55.M3M36   1984   001.4'068   83-17048

ISBN 0 471 90317 5

Phototypeset by Dobbie Typesetting Service, Plymouth, Devon.
Printed by Pitman Press Ltd, Bath, Avon.

Contents

Foreword	ix
1 Introduction	1
2 Multidisciplinary, Interdisciplinary— What is the Difference?	3
3 Cross-disciplinarity in Action	10
4 Cross-disciplinarity and Organizational Forms	21
5 The Implications for Management	38

Papers presented at the Second International Conference on the Management of Interdisciplinary Research

Leadership by Objectives in R & D *S. A. Bergen*	46
Predictors of Long-term Research Performance *P. H. Birnbaum*	47
Noise Control R & D in the United Kingdom *J. Butler*	59
Indicators of Interdisciplinary Research: A Blueprint for Analysis *D. E. Chubin, A. L. Porter,* *T. Connolly, and F. A. Rossini*	66
The Tendency of Fields of Science to Form Interdisciplinary Relationships *G. Darvas and A. Haraszthy*	66

Management, Planning, and Organization in Initiating, Supporting, and Coordinating an Ongoing Freshwater Diversion Project 71
   D. J. Etzold

The Marine Technology Directorate and Interdisciplinary Research 78
   G. Ford and M. Gibbons

Some Elements of a Model to Improve Productivity of Interdisciplinary Groups 86
   S. E. Gold and H. J. Gold

University-based Technology Transfer 102
   R. D. Handscombe

Motivation: A Diagnostic Approach 107
   J. Holman

Peer Assessments in Industrial R & D Departments: Some Considerations and Implications for Future Research Based on a Review of Recent Literature 108
   E. Jochum, M. Domsch, and T. Gerpott

The Shirley Institute—An Interdisciplinary Contract Research Establishment 117
   D. Jones

Adaptors and Innovators: The Way People Approach Problems 121
   M. J. Kirton

Management of Scientific Staff at the Harwell Laboratory of the UK Atomic Energy Authority 122
   G. G. E. Low

The Interdisciplinary Impact 122
   A. R. Michaelis

Genetic Engineering—Is There a Need for More Interdisciplinarity? 123
   D. Miller, A. W. Pearson, and D. F. Ball

Relations between Decision-makers and Research Workers on Environmental Problems: The Case of French Research on Noise 127
   G. Moser and C. Levy-Leboyer

Team-building and Group Process Analysis in Interdisciplinary Research Teams A. W. Pearson	136
Managerial and Organizational Determinants of Efficiency in Biomedical Research Teams C. Pineau and C. Levy-Leboyer	141
Divide and Ruin—A Pathological Approach to Fragmenting Resarch N. K. Powell	163
The Interdisciplinary Researcher: Some Psychological Aspects I. T. Robertson	164
Cross-disciplinarity in the Biomedical Sciences: A Preliminary Analysis of Anatomy F. Rossini, A. L. Porter, D. E. Chubin, and T. Connolly	176
Peer Review in Interdisciplinary Research: Flexibility and Responsiveness M. G. Russell	184
Interdisciplinary Research in the University: Need for Managerial Leadership B. O. Saxberg and W. T. Newell	202
A Method for Peer Group Appraisal and Interpretation of Data Developed in Interdisciplinary Research Programs J. M. Sharp	211
Development of a Special Purpose, Interdisciplinary Research Institute in an Academic Setting: A Case Study R. J. Trybus	219
Interdisciplinary In-service Training in the Urban Realm F. Vidor	228
Futures Research as a Framework for Transdisciplinary Research R. Waśniowski	228
List of Papers Presented at the First International Conference on Interdisciplinary Research	236
Bibliography	239
Subject Index	241

Foreword

The event that prompted the writing of this volume was the Second International Conference on the Management of Interdisciplinary Research held at the Manchester Business School, Manchester, England, in July 1981. The First Conference had taken place in Schloss Reisensburg in the Federal Republic of Germany in April 1979. The growing importance of the interdisciplinary approach to problem-solving had then been recognized by a small group of practitioners and management scientists, which inspired them to call the conference. Their aim was to identify and discuss the key issues affecting the management of this kind of research.

Papers from the First Conference have been collected together in a book entitled *Interdisciplinary Research Groups: Their Management and Organization*, edited by Richard Barth and Rudy Steck. As might have been expected, the Conference revealed the existence of a large number of problems, which caused it to take two concrete decisions. One was to set up an international association to foster the study of interdisciplinary problem-solving groups to be known as Interstudy. This has provided an effective channel for disseminating information and maintaining contact between the interested parties. It is responsible for the publication of *Interstudy Bulletin*, a newsletter edited by Don Baldwin of the University of Washington, Seattle, USA.

The other decision was to plan a series of working conferences to be held at about two-year intervals, designed to permit the regular exchange of views and experience relevant to any of the issues of concern to those involved in interdisciplinary activities. The first fruit of this decision was the convening of the Second International Conference in Manchester.

This was attended by forty-two people from academic, government, and industrial environments from eight countries. Some had attended the first conference; they provided a useful degree of continuity, confirming incidentally that this area has staying power and can be treated seriously as a stable field for investigation.

The Conference strongly encouraged us, the editors, to compile this book. It is not to be read as a formal record of the proceedings. Its aim is rather to use the papers presented at the Conference and the informal discussions which took place around them to capture the main themes and to illustrate the variety of activity in the field.

The choice of material for inclusion was left to us. This has been a difficult task — as has been the putting together of the short introductory chapters which are designed to highlight the points we believe to be the key to the successful management of interdisciplinary research. Inevitably reasons of space have forced us to omit much of the Conference material. We have tried to compensate for this omission in three ways: we make frequent reference to the valuable information contained in the published proceedings of the First Conference; especially in Chapter 4, we make use of the literature on group dynamics; and we provide a generous amount of bibliographical material.

Perhaps our hardest task was to decide which of the twenty-nine papers to reprint in full, given the amount of space available to us. We found this not to be a matter of winnowing the wheat from the chaff but rather one of crude butchery. We applied as uniformly as possible the same criteria as those used for selecting the topics for discussion in the prefatory chapters. We also include a complete list of all papers submitted and a short summary prepared by ourselves of the content of those we have been unable to reprint in full.

Much needed help has come from many people. Our special thanks go to Don Baldwin, who is the leader of this enterprise, as far as an interdisciplinary group such as ours will permit him; to Shirley and Harvey Gold who made many helpful comments and helped to sustain our efforts; to the several authors who abridged their papers or repaired the damage inflicted by our surgery; to all those who participated in the Conference and who recognize their ideas as being included in the book but without explicit acknowledgement; and above all, to Kathleen Eatough who besides acting during the Conference as major-domo uncomplainingly typed and re-typed and re-re-typed the indecipherable drafts of the book with which we liberally provided her.

Manchester 1982

CHAPTER 1

Introduction

Examples of research projects where all parts are undertaken and completed by a single person alone and unaided are hard to come by. Some kind of interaction with other people is always necessary during all phases of a project— at the start, during its execution, and for the implementation of its results. It comes as no surprise, therefore, to find that a good deal of effort has been put into searching for ways of making such interactions as effective as possible. The main conclusion that can be drawn from the search so far is that probably much more remains to be learnt about the process, the task, the situation, and the interactions among the individuals concerned than the search has so far revealed.

Nowhere is there more need for learning than when the scientific content of the task needs inputs from different disciplines and the execution of the task demands that the individuals providing the inputs work together closely and continuously, i.e. in what has come to be known as interdisciplinary research.

The First Interdisciplinary Research Management Conference in 1979 showed that such research was of growing importance but that many barriers to its introduction and efficient use were being encountered. Most of them were a matter of getting people coming from diverse disciplinary backgrounds to overcome institutional obstacles and personal inhibitions which prevented them from working together in a mutually supportive manner. The difficulties were in fact intensifying because more and more projects required not only collaboration between practitioners of different scientific and technical disciplines but also collaboration over the cognitively greater distances such as separate these as a group from, say, economists, behavioural scientists, and politicians.

A reading of the selection of papers which were presented at the Second Conference on Interdisciplinary Research, held in Manchester, England, in 1981, and which are appended to this volume will show that they tell the same story and add much circumstantial detail needed to confirm its truth. They also provide a number of examples where interdisciplinary approaches have been successfully used and others where one was greatly needed. The purpose of the prefatory chapters of this book is to present, as we see it, a brief and coherent overview of the scene as depicted by the Conference, where necessary supplemented by material from the proceedings of the First Conference and by information derived from the literature of the subject.

We have organized our overview as follows:

Chapter 2 is a discussion of the question of nomenclature. This turns out not to be a matter of mere semantics but to reveal a methodological point of some importance. Current usage imposes an evaluative tone to some of the words frequently met which can get in the way of communication. The key to clarity of thought is to use different terms to describe the content of a task and the form of organization needed to carry it out. Specifically we argue that a task requiring a combination of disciplines should be known as cross-disciplinary while the terms multi- and inter-disciplinary should be reserved to describe how the practitioners are organized to make their several contributions.

Chapter 3 is intended to illustrate the variety of areas in which interdisciplinary problem-solving has a claim to be the best approach to obtaining research results of lasting value. Examples taken from the conference papers show the contribution that interdisciplinary working can make to the solution of technology assessment problems, to basic research, including the formation of new disciplines, to mission-oriented R & D, and to innovation. There is also a brief discussion of the role of the interdisciplinary individual.

Chapter 4 lies at the heart of the subject for it consists of a consideration of the barriers, institutional and personal, that prevent the setting up of interdisciplinary teams and inhibit the achievement of the needed integration of thought and action. It provides a taxonomy of the setting of interdisciplinary working in terms of group size and institutional location. It is here that we have had the most frequent recourse to the wider literature of the subject and we make extensive use of the analytical concepts developed by Mintzberg. The main message of this chapter is that the means that have to be adopted to get the high degree of cooperation necessary to produce effective interdisciplinary working differ markedly from one setting to another.

Chapter 5 extracts the lessons for management that lie buried in all the material presented at the Conference, in the papers and the ideas floated in the preceding chapters. It introduces some new material and draws attention to one paper that supplies evidence that the interdisciplinary groups are not the best for all occasions. It is perhaps this part of the book that will most interest those readers who are at the sharp end of all this activity, i.e. those whose daily task it is to run this most demanding form of research activity.

Finally, there are appendices containing a selection of papers presented at the Conference in alphabetical order of first authors' names, brief summaries of papers that could not be reproduced in full, and a bibliography. For completeness we also append a list of papers which were included in the proceedings of the First Conference.

CHAPTER 2

Multidisciplinary, Interdisciplinary— What is the Difference?

(In this and the following chapters references quoting authors' names followed by the symbol (1) will be found in the List of Papers presented at the First International Conference; those followed by a date (e.g. 1980) are in the Bibliography; and those followed by neither are included or summarized in the present volume.)

In the introduction we referred briefly to the distinction between multidisciplinarity and interdisciplinarity. We have found that making the distinction more specific, i.e. casting it in a form in which it could be used to decide whether a particular project or project group was or was not interdisciplinary, was not as straightforward as it might seem. In fact, the attempt revealed the possibility of methodological problems if the distinction was not carefully formulated. Therefore, arriving at a clear understanding of the meaning of the two terms is not merely an exercise in semantics.

Interdisciplinary: is it multidisciplinary plus integration?

The following extracts taken from papers presented at both the First and Second Conferences represent different expressions of the consensus view of the differences between multi- and interdisciplinary activities:

Birnbaum
Interdisciplinary as opposed to multidisciplinary research refers to research teams in which the effort is integrated into a unified whole. Multidisciplinary research refers to research in which scholars from different disciplines work independently and are joined together externally through editorial linkages.

Michaelis
Interdisciplinary work results from the joint and continuously integrated effort of two or more specialists having a different disciplinary background.

Rossini, Chubin, Porter, and Connolly
Multidisciplinarity is the result of the inter-relation of disciplinary components when they are linked externally only . . . interdisciplinarity involves the internal and substantive interlinking of the various disciplinary analyses so that each considers the results of the others in its own development.

Lindas[1]
IDR implies joint co-ordinated and continuously integrated research conducted by experts with different disciplinary backgrounds working together and producing joint reports and papers in which the specific contributions of each researcher tend to be obscured by the joint product.

The thinking behind these and other formulations to be found in the papers implies the following propositions:

Proposition 1

There are tasks that require for their effective completion contributions from more than one discipline. In the literature such tasks are sometimes referred to as multidisciplinary, sometimes as interdisciplinary.

Proposition 2

Such tasks can be carried out using either of two different organizational forms:

2.1 The 'pure' *multidisciplinary* form in which the portions of the task are carried out by organizationally separate units each of which includes practitioners of only one discipline. The products of their activities are combined into a coherent whole by a task coordinator who bears ultimate responsibility for so doing.

The task coordinator may be a member of one of the units or he may stand apart from all of them; he may or may not have a supervisory relationship to any or all of them. It is also possible for the project coordinating responsibility to be carried out not by an individual but by a group bearing a similar relationship to the operating units.

2.2 The 'pure' *interdisciplinary* form in which the elements of the task are carried out within a single organizational unit consisting of the practitioners of the disciplines necessary for the completion of the task. The members of the unit share the responsibility for combining their individual products into a coherent whole.

These two propositions are objective and non-evaluative. If the only difference between the multi- and interdisciplinary collaborative forms were that between 2.1 and 2.2, it would be possible to decide on this basis alone whether a given task was being implemented in a multi- or interdisciplinary manner.

Unfortunately this is not the end of the story for the quoted definitions imply another distinction between the terms multi- and interdisciplinary. According to them it is possible for a unit to purport to be working in an interdisciplinary manner yet not fulfil its responsibility for self-integration. In such a case there is an implication that the group should be referred to as multidisciplinary. As a result, the terms lose their objective status and become evaluative—interdisciplinary, good; multidisciplinary, bad.

Quite apart from the possibility that empirical data may not always support this proposition (cf. Birnbaum's paper in this volume) it is methodologically unsound to employ terms which have two different meanings, one of them objectively value-free and the other subjectively value-laden, especially when the context does not provide a clue as to which meaning is being employed in that moment.

In fact, the value-laden meaning of these terms imposes a real methodological problem. The characteristic, i.e. actual self-integration, which is said to distinguish the multi- from the interdisciplinary style can be observed only on the unit in action or when its task is completed. A unit must therefore be deemed to be multidisciplinary until observation of its actions and results proves it to be interdisciplinary. To make matters worse, any measures of integration are certain to be continuous; therefore an arbitrary degree of integration would have to be set (by whom?) before a unit could be allowed to call itself interdisciplinary.

More precision is clearly necessary to avoid ambiguity and confusion. Some suggestions about how to achieve it are made in the next section.

Distinguishing task, organization, and performance: the key to precision

The key that opens the door to precision is to keep three matters separate: the task, the organizational framework within which the task is carried out, and the evaluation process which measures how well it has been done.

To preserve this distinction we need to modify the terminology. This is done reluctantly, for the subjective already has an overabundance of terms. Nevertheless, the changes suggested in the following seem to be a necessary minimum if the objective of clarification is to be achieved. They have the merit of neither introducing new polysyllabics nor altering the meaning of commonly used words.

We rephrase Proposition 1 as follows:

Proposition 3

There are *tasks* that require for their objective completion contributions from more than one discipline. Such tasks are defined as *cross-disciplinary*.

A valuable precedent for using the word cross-disciplinary in this sense is that it is so used by Rossini *et al.* in their paper in this volume. To clarify matters further, we note that it would be correct to employ the word as a qualifier of terms such as 'study', 'mission', or 'project', but not of terms such as 'unit', 'team', or 'group'. In other words, 'cross-disciplinary' should refer exclusively to the *content* of a task.

We now turn to the question of describing the organizational form. The proposal is to use the words multidisciplinary and interdisciplinary only as qualifiers to terms that refer to the *manner* or style in which a task is being carried out. The problem is to define them descriptively and not normatively and in a way that does not require postponement of a judgement about which one to apply until the unit in question has been observed at work or has completed its business.

The necessary distinction can be made relatively easily provided that users are ready to accept an *intention* to work in an interdisciplinary manner (later to be defined) as the distinguishing characteristic rather than how far the intention is translated into practice. In making this proposal more concrete we draw on the paper in this volume by Gold and Gold. This proposes a model of collaborative working that focuses on the nature of transactions between members of the group in question.

Gold and Gold's analysis starts from a consideration of the nature of transactions between the members A and B of a minimal collaborative group. A has the capability to produce a desired output from inputs elicited from B. The mode of the collaboration between A and B then depends on how the responsibility for specifying, producing, and using the output is shared between them.

Two extreme modes are defined: the contractual and the partnership modes. In the contractual mode, A plays the role of a customer and is entirely responsible for the specification of the input, which B, playing the role of a contractor, uncritically accepts; B is then entirely responsible for producing the input which A will accept and use, provided only that it fulfils the specification. At the other extreme, in the partnership mode, A and B share equally the responsibility for all three operations. They jointly define the specification, jointly produce the input, and jointly use it to produce the output.

Between these extremes Gold and Gold describe a third form, referred to as the consulting mode. Here A plays the role of a client and B that of a consultant. A takes the lead in specifying the input but B can view the specification critically and suggest a redefinition. B will have the lead responsibility for producing the redefined input, but A may intervene in B's production process to suggest a modification into some more appropriate direction, and so on. Unlike the contracting mode A and B do not operate at arm's length and unlike the partnership mode A and B retain their disciplinary identities.

The *contractual* mode describes very satisfactorily in formal terms the relationship we would expect between the IDR coordinator referred to in Proposition 2.1 above and the members of the satellite units that supply him with inputs. On the other hand, the *consulting* mode is apt for describing the relationship expected (and aimed for) between members of a group functioning in an interdisciplinary manner as defined in 2.2.

Let us now put these proposals more formally as an amendment to Proposition 2:

Proposition 4

Cross-disciplinary tasks can be carried out using either of two different organizational forms:

4.1 The 'pure' *multidisciplinary* form — in which portions of the task are carried out by organizationally separate units each of which includes practitioners of only one discipline. The responsibility for ensuring that their outputs are compounded into a coherent whole lies with a task coordinator whose relationship with members of the contributing units may be described as 'contractual', in the sense used by Gold and Gold.

4.2 The 'pure' *interdisciplinary* form — in which the elements of the task are carried out within a single unit that:
   (a) Includes practitioners of all the disciplines necessary for the completion of the task.
   (b) Has an internal structure such that transactions between the members can take the form described by Gold and Gold as 'consulting'.

The essential difference between 2.2 and 4.2 is the responsibility it puts on the designers of the interdisciplinary unit to set it up in such a way that interdisciplinary working is possible. In this case, to establish whether a cross-disciplinary task was being tackled in a multi- or interdisciplinary manner one would look for data on the size of group, geographical separation between its members, existence of formal procedural instruments devised to make the consulting mode of collaboration a practical possibility, evidence of team-building activities, absence of any circumstances that could confer higher status on a particular discipline (though this does not rule out status differentiation on other grounds), etc. The essential point is that the distinction is made on the intended situation rather than the actual process.

A new problem of nomenclature is created by the adoption of these definitions. In many cases reported in the literature, and perhaps some cited in this volume, the papers do not make it clear or do not provide sufficient evidence whether the terms inter- and multidisciplinary are being used in the senses defined in the chapter. To allow us to discuss such cases we need a neutral description of the organizational form. To avoid bringing in yet another word we shall use 'cross-disciplinary' for this purpose, in addition to the one given to it by Proposition 3, but we do not think that this will cause any confusion.

Complexities of the R & D process

The preceding discussion gives the impression that any cross-disciplinary task can be carried out either in a pure interdisciplinary or pure multidisciplinary form. But a task as complex as the average cross-disciplinary project is always divisible into sub-tasks, each of which in principle could be managed in a multi- or interdisciplinary manner. Furthermore, an interdisciplinary group may obtain some of its information by sub-contracting part of its work to external specialist units.

The situation is made more complex still when consideration is given to the whole R & D process rather than only that part in which the actual research task is executed. The total process consists of at least three separate stages which we can call project initiation, project execution, and results implementation.

The initiation stage is that in which the task objectives and resourcing are decided, usually across an interface and in collaboration with sponsors and other potential beneficiaries from the results. The execution stage consists of the professional research operations properly within the internal world of R & D. The implementation stage is the one during which the R & D results are transferred across another interface and into the keeping of the sponsor/user.

Each stage is a separate task with its own objectives and problems to be solved. Not all are necessarily cross-disciplinary, and not all of those that are need to be always carried out in a multi-disciplinary manner. For example, Sharp's paper describes a project whose object was to forecast the environmental effects of offshore drilling for oil in the Texas Gulf. This was recognized as a cross-disciplinary problem. An interdisciplinary group was set up to manage project execution and integrate the data, the acquisition of which was sub-contracted to separate specialist groups. Another example is provided by Moser and Levy-Leboyer in their paper. They describe the operations of an interdisciplinary research-funding committee (i.e. project initiation stage) which sponsored many projects that were carried out by single-disciplinary groups.

The existence of such complexities provides a further reason for avoiding the use of the terms in question in an evaluative manner. The message is that task comes before organization and evalution should relate to the appropriateness of the form chosen to the task undertaken.

Conclusion

This discussion has led to the following conclusions:

1. To avoid methodological problems the terms multidisciplinary and interdisciplinary should not be used evaluatively.
2. A task requiring a combination of disciplines for its achievement should be described as cross-disciplinary; the terms multi- and interdisciplinary should be used only to describe the organizational form used to carry out a cross-disciplinary task. However, when the exact organizational form is not then the term 'cross-disciplinary' can be used as a general term to describe the form as well as the content of the task.
3. Different organizational forms may be needed for different stages of tasks as complex as the average cross-disciplinary R & D projects. In such a case no single description may be appropriate to define the organizational form.

CHAPTER 3

Cross-disciplinarity in Action

Introduction

Some form of cross-disciplinary problem-solving has for long been advocated as the most effective way to deploy professional manpower resources in the pursuit of many types of scientific research. Papers presented to the Conference marshalled old and new evidence in support of this view, including several reporting first-hand experience of cross-disciplinary teams. The purpose of this chapter is to summarize these contributions, which has been done under five headings. These are respectively the role of cross-disciplinary problem-solving in basic research, especially in the evolution of new disciplines; in mission-oriented applied research; in the encouragement of innovation; in the study of the impact of technological developments on society, i.e. in what is usually referred to as technology assessment; and the role of the interdisciplinary individual.

Cross-disciplinarity and basic research

None of the papers submitted to the Conference reported any specific examples of the contribution of cross-disciplinarity to the advancement of pure scientific knowledge. However, several were concerned with its implications for this field.

Darvas and Haraszthy are interested in the problem of furthering scientific progress through the combination of disciplines. They have therefore tried to identify the fields of science that are most likely to form cross-disciplinary conglomerations. They were able to use as their data base the information collected in the monumental UNESCO project which investigated the productivity of research groups in six European countries. To do this they selected data on groups whose activities covered several fields of science and produced a correlation matrix showing the frequency of links between one field and another. Data were adequate only for investigating the interlinking of twelve subjects—mathematics, physics, chemistry, life sciences, earth sciences, agriculture, medicine, technological sciences, economics, law, and sociology. They find that interdisciplinary links are concentrated into relatively few pairs of sciences. The tendency is for other sciences to establish links with chemistry, life sciences, and engineering.

The authors admit that their analysis is incomplete and few conclusions can be drawn. In any case the evidence is purely situational. In their paper to the 1979 Conference Pearson, Payne, and Gunz[1] use a classification of disciplines originally proposed by Whitley which has potential as a means of structuring disciplinary interactions. Disciplines are characterized as restricted (R) or configurational (C). R-sciences deal with highly specific objects with a restricted set of relevant properties (e.g. the so-called 'hard' sciences such as physics and chemistry) whereas C-sciences deal with more complex objects exhibiting a broad range of features (e.g. the soft sciences such as psychology and sociology). It is likely *a priori* that R-sciences will combine better with R-sciences and C with C; attempts to combine C with R will meet with considerable communication and value barriers.

However, this is a speculation requiring confirmation. In fact, work reported by Rossini and collaborators[1] to the 1979 Conference in which they were able to construct an index of 'distances' between disciplines showed that if anything the greater the distance between disciplines the easier was their integration. They ascribe this to the possibility that the larger the gap between disciplines the more obvious it is to managers that integration is something to be managed rather than left to look after itself. This raises the question of the role of management in team development which is dealt with in another part of this report.

Rossini and collaborators in their 1981 paper draw attention to an intriguing problem that is having to be faced by those concerned with the training of medical doctors. Every doctor must have a thorough knowledge of the subject of human anatomy. But anatomy as a subject for research is virtually worked out. The situation is being dealt with by tying up anatomy with the associated discipline of neuroscience. The authors have come to this conclusion through a study of advertisements for anatomists, the qualifications expected of applicants, and the composition of anatomy departments. They found that non-anatomists made up 45 per cent. of the staff and 75 per cent. of postdoctoral students of the faculties investigated.

This tendency is leading to an increasingly familiar situation—the contradiction between pedagogic and research needs. The intellectual driving challenge is cross-disciplinary—away from pure anatomy towards anatomical aspects of neuroscience. If this tendency deprives the faculty of anyone able or willing to teach the indispensable but intellectually moribund subject of anatomy, how are medical students to learn their anatomy? This question is left unanswered.

This leads on to the question of the evolution of new scientific disciplines. Darvas and Haraszthy[1] pointed out that in the history of science growth of knowledge has been the result both of differentiation and integration among disciplines. This theme is developed by Russell in a paper to the present

Conference. While disciplinary differentiation grew out of the profession of learning, its objective being to advance and transmit knowledge, interdisciplinary research arose from pressure to solve problems. However, if a particular interdisciplinary group is able to maintain its composition over time, say because it is presented with a succession of problems to which its collective wisdom is relevant, then it may grow into a new discipline.

The birth of a new discipline is a painful process, the daughter discipline tending to be rejected by its parents. The new discipline has to develop its own criteria for judging the quality of its outputs as a preliminary to their acceptance as valid new knowledge. These criteria may differ from those accepted by parents. When the process is eventually completed, the new discipline stands up on its own feet. Then, paradoxically, a new boundary has been created, a new specialization evolved. Russell, therefore, points out the need to encourage interdisciplinary collaboration by exposure to practical problems as a means of ensuring both vitality in research and making good the losses resulting from disciplinary consolidation.

How new disciplines begin and whether prior interdisciplinary combination or collaboration is necessary is strictly a matter for deep historical study. As is frequently the case in historical investigation, it may turn out that each existing discipline is a product of unique historical circumstances, such as a chance combination of the autonomous development of one of the parent disciplines with an externally imposed practical necessity, or the presence on the scene of a person of polymathic genius. Whether creation of a new discipline is something else—like team integration that can be managed—therefore remains an open question.

The cross-disciplinary approach to applied R & D

By the term 'applied' we mean R & D carried out to achieve an externally imposed and tangible technological objective, as distinct from basic research aimed at extending or deepening scientific knowledge. Such activities are also commonly referred to as mission-oriented R & D. More and more frequently their solution necessitates cross-disciplinary inputs from diverse professions. More frequently, too, is it becoming the practice to integrate their varied activities into interdisciplinary teams.

Teams of this kind are common in industrial R & D, so common that their existence is not recognized as something worthy of remark. Their members would be surprised to learn that their group had a special name. On the other hand, such teams are rarely a feature of academic research and the necessity to work in them has come as something of a shock to Academia. Indeed, one may speculate that the main reason for the academic interest in the subject, the existence of organizations such as Interstudy, and even the convening of this Conference, are the difficulties that beset would-be organizers of university interdisciplinarity groups when they try to introduce it into their institutions.

Among the papers presented to the conference, several bear on the theme of mission-oriented R & D. Michaelis remarks upon historical examples of successful collaborative research of this kind. He cites particularly the Manhattan Project as a case where cross-disciplinarity triumphed, for the Western Allies combined all the scientific and technological talent available to produce an atomic bomb. The rigidity of the German scientific establishment obstructed cross-disciplinary cooperation, and the rest is history.

It is then interesting to learn that the very large UK Atomic Energy Authority laboratory at Harwell in Southern England, which was a world pioneer in its field, is having to diversify its activities away from exclusively nuclear interests, but in doing so it is preserving the interdisciplinary tradition. Low's paper describes how Harwell now deploys its skill and knowledge originally built up on the needs of nuclear science and technology as a service to UK industry generally. Its capability is very diverse. Staff have to be assembled into interdisciplinary teams, disassembled, and reassembled depending on clients' needs. The paper describes in some detail how this flexibility is achieved through a form of the matrix management system. The laboratory is thriving and no serious operational difficulties have been encountered.

The emphasis of Low's paper is more on the functioning of the matrix than on the day-to-day matters of interdisciplinary working. It is worth recalling, as a comment, the view put by Stucki[1] in his 1979 Conference paper that 'a matrix or multiple command system . . . is a stressful solution to complex problems and not one which should be lightly adopted'. One wonders, given the stress resulting from the very fact of interdisciplinary working, whether the stress added on by the inbuilt role-ambiguity of matrix working could in fact inhibit the achievement of team integration. This is especially the case if the lifetime of a team is so short that there is no time to make the necessary interpersonal adjustments needed to achieve integration. Relevant to this issue, and a matter discussed at the 1979 Conference, is the Pearson–Davies–Gunz characterization of management roles in matrix a system (leadership versus coordination) and its interaction with the urgency and predictability of the problem in hand. A case can be made out that the matrix system tends to destroy team cohesion and that the best environment for interdisciplinary working is the project organization (using J. Galbraith's terminology). Pearson considered some of the issues in his paper on process analysis. He argues that the nature of many R & D establishments is such that team-building for each project on its own may be less valuable than building through training programmes an awareness among all the individuals of the importance of the understanding of interpersonal relationships and their critical effects on project and team performance. Clearly this issue deserves further discussion.

Encouragement of cross-disciplinary problem-solving in universities is advocated as a means of increasing the value for public money spent in supporting research in these institutions. More positively, this form of working is seen as a way of concentrating the formidable array of talent to be found in universities on complex and important technological problems. Initially their form of collaboration had virtually to be imposed on the universities by sponsors as a condition for receiving grants. To some extent, coercion is still needed but many academic institutions, feeling the way the wind blows relative to survival, are organizing themselves in an interdisciplinary manner when required.

Handscombe describes some of the ways in which a university could make its resources of know-how, skill, and facilities available to carry out or supplement industrial research. Of the many possibilities he comes down in favour of the autonomous university company, with ultimate control on policy and performance being exerted by a board on which senior university staff are strongly represented. He describes the origin and current set-up of one such company with which he is concerned—part of the UK University of Salford. It possesses a permanent complement of staff and can call on other university staff if need be. Of the projects recently undertaken he draws special attention to one aimed at developing a computer-aided manufacturing system. The special feature of this project was that the sponsor, the US Air Force, insisted both on a cross-disciplinary approach and on the combination of the talents of Salford with those of the neighbouring University of Manchester Institute of Science and Technology.

Ford and Gibbons described another way and another field in which university resources are being combined in a cross-disciplinary way. Their paper deals with research into the exploitation of marine resources with emphasis on the mining and extraction of ocean-bed mineral ores. This field is ripe for broad cross-disciplinary attack as its formidable technological problems are aggravated by national rivalries, international legal difficulties, multinational companies' aspirations, and environmentalists' pressures.

The group with which Ford and Gibbons are associated is carrying out investigations to help to formulate public policy. In this case the UK Government has put money into a consortium of universities in North-West England to form a self-managing group of academics from diverse disciplines whose task is to produce a package of research proposals. This area is considered to be one of national importance, whence the availability of public money.

Ford and Gibbons take the view that the difficulties of interdisciplinary working will be overcome as the individuals involved come together as a result of day-to-day necessity. They go further than this since they believe such interaction will, over time, result in consolidating the varied groups involved in different projects into a stable academic community. The projects which are put forward for funding must satisfy two criteria—academic quality needed to sustain the interest of the faculty members and industrial relevance demanded by the sponsors.

Two further papers on mission-oriented interdisciplinary problem-solving drew attention to a need for it in specific fields. Butler has investigated the situation in the United Kingdom of research into noise control, a particularly complex area. Noise is undoubtedly a product of technology but whether or not it constitutes a problem is a highly subjective, even emotional, matter. Intense noise will produce actual physical effects on the human subject, but at lower levels what constitutes noise is individually or even socially defined. Technically, a small amount of energy will produce a large amount of noise. Unfortunately, because of the way the ear registers sound, halving the amount of energy going into noise produces noise reduction which is only just perceptible. Noise control is, therefore, technically very difficult, expensive, and dysfunctional to the noise producer. Hence any basic research into noise requires the active interest of engineers, physicists, human biologists, psychologists, economists, and sociologists.

Butler points out the need for cross-disciplinary contacts within the engineering disciplines in which further specialization has also taken place. The facts in general are that noise control research is greatly neglected in the United Kingdom and he advocates, as an initial step towards progress, the formation of an interdisciplinary noise research support unit to investigate the field and make research proposals.

Miller, Pearson, and Ball point out the urgent need for a cross-disciplinary attack on genetic engineering, a branch of biotechnology. It deals with research into the manipulation of the genetic material in reproductive cells to alter the nature of the descendant organisms or their metabolic products. Biotechnology is not new to the human species — we have used it for millennia to make bread, cheese, alcohol, and many other products — but genetic engineering is something quite new and brings with it totally new problems. Firstly, and foremost in the public mind, there is the question of safety. The possibility of accidentally producing a pathogenic bacterium with no natural antagonists or, more likely, of deliberately producing frightful germ-warfare agents has produced an antipathy to the subject which at one time almost succeeded in stopping research into it. Secondly, conversion of the laboratory findings into practice, taking into account the peculiarities of biotechnological processes and the safety aspects, may well cause a revolution in chemical engineering; indeed, it may demand the evolution of a new discipline altogether. Already novel forms of industrial enterprise are emerging, notably in the United States, to obtain the right combination of state-of-the-art science and technology with economics and entrepreneurship.

The authors point out the vital necessity of an interdisciplinary approach to this area and show particular concern with its neglect in Europe.

Cross-disciplinarity and innovation

It is a commonplace of technological history that radically new advances in specialized fields are often made by persons outside the speciality. The general belief is that such outsiders are less constrained by boundary demarcation and professional inhibitions than are the specialists. Consequently they have available to them a greater number of possibilities.

A built-in advantage of interdisciplinary problem-solving is that it is a way of ensuring, through the adoption of a relatively simple organizational form, that problems are simultaneously exposed to insider and outsider views. The pay-off is expected to be a significantly greater group creativity. The paper by

Moser and Levy-Leboyer presented some interesting evidence to support this contention. They were able to investigate the group dynamics of two French government-sponsored R & D funding committees. One, concerned with supporting R & D into atmospheric pollution, was made up entirely of pollution experts; the other, which supported R & D into noise control, was interdisciplinary, numbering among its members physicists, engineers, acoustic scientists, economists, and an ethnologist.

The authors studied the content of the meetings of these committees, specifically apportioning the time among the activities of scientific discussion, proposal evaluation, and organizational matters. It seems that the noise committee spent more of its time on organizational matters (wrangling about internal politics perhaps?) than did the atmospheric pollution committee, but when it discussed scientific matters it spent much more time considering new information and novel ideas. The noise committee usually proceeded from generalities to particularities and frequently changed its goals, while the pollution committee aimed at getting deeper and deeper knowledge of a restricted field.

The authors conclude that the noise committee will identify more areas for innovation than its counterpart because of its interdisciplinarity, though this is also the reason it spends more time on internal politics.

At the Conference, Jones described the way the Shirley Institute of Manchester, England, has moved over the years from being a research association serving the UK textile industry to an institution offering a wide variety of scientific and technical expertise on a world-wide basis. A significant part of its work is carried out in an interdisciplinary manner. The need to move in this direction was stimulated initially by external pressures but the changes that had to be made to methods of working, though not easily affected, produced many benefits. Some of the projects are interinstitutional (see Chapter 4) and many opportunities have been opened up for collaborative working in new technological as well as geographical areas. Jones's paper describes a case which illustrates the potential value of such interinstitutional collaboration.

Cross-disciplinarity and technology assessment

A major public issue of the late twentieth century is the impact of new applications of science and technology on the quality of life—if not to the continued existence of life on our planet. Science and technology are seen by many to be implicated in, if not totally responsible for, the development of weapons of mass-destruction, the desecration of the environment, the destruction of jobs, and even the increase of population. A demand therefore arose in the seventies that the possible community impact of proposed large-scale applications of technology should be assessed before the work to develop them was put in hand. This process became known as Technology Assessment, or TA.

At first TA was looked upon as a thing apart—an operation to be carried on at arm's length from the project itself; the relationship between the two was adversarial and therefore divisive. Fortunately in recent years the atmosphere has become more constructive. TA has in a sense lost its separate identity and is now looked on as an essential part of a project, especially in the early stages when the alternative pathways for the development are being formulated and weighed.

The point about such an assessment is that it must not be carried out by technologists and experts alone; representatives of other sections of society should also be involved. This is not only to put to rest suspicions that the technicians may be *parti pris*, but more importantly to ensure that all relevant inputs are received from all groups who are influential in the community upon which the development will impact. This has the added advantage that these groups often include the very people who will have to implement or authorize the implementation of the results of the project when it is completed.

In this situation we are dealing with a new kind of interdisciplinary group and a new concept of what is meant by a discipline. Not only does it contain a mix of disciplines from the hard sciences and technologies but it may also include sociologists, economists, businessmen, pressure-group representatives, and politicians. (Implications for the management of such groups are taken up in Chapter 4 below.)

Two examples were described at the Conference by Etzold and Sharp respectively. They reported instances of cross-disciplinary projects with strong political and economic overtones. In both cases the sponsors took elaborate steps to ensure an interdisciplinary collaboration among the diverse interest groups involved.

Etzold was involved in a very large project to improve the productivity of the fishery industry in the Louisiana/Mississippi estuarine waters. Productivity had fallen over the years largely because the solution to an earlier problem—flooding—had entailed as a measure of flood control the diversion of fresh water into the sea; in consequence the estuarine waters had become saline and unproductive.

The technological solution proposed for solving the problem was to dilute the salinity by diverting back a controlled supply of fresh water into the estuarine area. An interdisciplinary task-force was set up to plan and initiate the project. Its members recognized from the start that the job was certain to be multifaceted and lengthy; consideration would have to be given as early as possible to finding out the likely impact of the means proposed, the diversion of river flows, on all aspects of life in the region. To this end the major focal points of community interests in the region were identified and brought into the task of reviewing and reformulating the technical objectives proposed by the task-force. These focal points included national, state, interstate, industrial, conservationist, recreational interests, and, of course, the funding agencies. As a result the preliminary plans were considerably modified. The pay-off is that the degree of social acceptance of the need for the project and commitment to its completion, which will not be until 1990, are now high and stable.

Sharp's interuniversity–industrial project of a somewhat similar kind has already been referred to in Chapter 2. The public issue was the leasing of public offshore land for private sector development of petroleum resources. One of the public anxieties related to how far such a development would damage the marine ecosystem, particularly by the discharge of effluents from the technical operations. In such a situation a valid interpretation of the data requires the combined efforts of disciplinary specialists, ecosystem generalists, and non-scientific managers. In this project such contributors were organized formally into a so-called peer group which commissioned, integrated, and interpreted the data produced by appropriate experts.

Two facets of this process are of special interest. The author notes the reluctance of the scientifically trained to give a straight 'yes' or 'no' answer to any question in a field as complex as this and the equal reluctance of lay public to be convinced by any answer that is not a straight 'yes' or 'no'. In this instance the method of assessment by an interdisciplinary peer group with its wide spectrum of knowledge, culture, values, and shared responsibility ensured that the risk assessment was based on the best possible appraisal of all the data available. The scientists were able to face the public with a greater degree of unanimity and conviction than would otherwise have been possible. Sharp doubts whether any consensus at all would have been reached had they worked at their problems and intepreted their data in disciplinary isolation.

The second facet illustrates the impact of modern technology on the achievement of consensus. Computer technology enabled the participant interests to interrogate all the data available almost instantaneously. Here we have a technological development which facilitated or even made possible the completion of a complex social process, that of consensus development. Many would see this process as a vital issue for the future of mankind and it is comforting to know that a technology exists to lower one of the barriers to it.

Another project with similar large-scale social implications, and which arrived at a similar *modus operandi*, was described by Bents and Horsmann[1] at the 1979 Conference. Its purpose was to define a project proposal and operating plan for the introduction of a computer-based traffic management system into a major German city. A very large number of interests and technologies had to be involved.

The main strategic management problem which had to be solved was how to achieve true integration of all the interests, technologies, and knowledge areas involved in the investigation without making the managing body unwieldy. The solution ultimately adopted was to set up a three-tier organization. This consisted of a permanent interdisciplinary working team of experts in the key knowledge areas to supervise the day-to-day activities of specialists whose opinions or services were required only intermittently. The working group reported to a management group whose main functions were to undertake necessary administrative activities and to monitor, progress, and resolve any differences within the working team. External relations, such as liaison with the sponsors and political contacts, were handled by a board of advisers to the management team, consisting of representatives of the supplying industries and traffic authorities.

The authors remark that a major problem in this kind of activity is to motivate the sponsors, in this case the local political authority, to make a constructive input into the project and to remain committed to its aims. This matter was dealt with by holding interim report-back meetings between the board of management and the sponsors. As a result it was possible to adjust the programme to take care of any new requirements of the sponsors and to ensure that decisions on matters outside the scope of the study but needed for its steady progress could be made by the sponsors, besides keeping them interested in the success of the project as a whole.

The interdisciplinary individual

A good deal has been made of the intellectually fertilizing role of the polymath, a person who has been able to master and creatively combine two or more disciplines. How frequently this has happened is a matter for historical research but clearly the timely advent of such a person is not an event to be counted upon. Nevertheless, Sharp draws attention in his paper to the value of having in an interdisciplinary team a lesser mortal, whom he calls a bridge-scientist. The ideal bridge-scientist must have acquired a familiarity with a number of sciences or technologies, their basic paradigms, methodologies, and ways of working; moreover, he or she must be sensitive to the motivations, aspirations, and value orientations of people in the several disciplines. Such an ability Sharp says 'enables the bridge-scientist particularly to assist in the crucial matter of problem definition because he can facilitate communication between the specialists, for example, by rapid diagnosis of the causes of points of difference and the detection of cross-purposes'.

Wilpert[1] in the 1979 Conference observed that the second stage of research, programme design, is even more difficult than problem definition since it deals with concrete action rather than abstract analysis. Here again a bridge-scientist would undoubtedly have a role to play. Further consideration of the role of such persons, how they can be identified, and how trained deserve concentrated attention. They obviously have much in common with the 'technological gatekeepers' identified by communications theorists.

In this connection we draw attention again to the paper by Ford and Gibbons. Gibbons is head of the department of Liberal Studies in Science at Manchester University on which the main responsibility for implementation of the mineral resources project described above has been placed. He is using the existence of the project to further an aim to produce an output of scientific generalists— persons who combined a knowledge of science with a high degree of literacy and communication abilities. The cross-disciplinarity of the Marine Resources Project and the Department's polymathic aspirations match particularly well for achieving this purpose.

For similar reasons we draw attention to the paper by Robertson where he refers to the existence at the University of Aston in Birmingham, England, of its interdisciplinary higher degrees scheme. Postgraduates can study for a higher degree by carrying out a project in an area where several disciplines overlap including, if possible, one from the behavioural sciences.

The student has the dual status of a temporary employee of a manufacturing firm and a student. The project is always chosen as one that could have immediate practical value to the firm if it were to be completed successfully. The work is supervised by a team, with one member from the firm and two from the university, the last always being from different disciplines. The scheme has two features to commend it as a model—its fostering of interdisciplinarity and collaboration with industry. It has already had a number of successes.

Robertson has conducted studies to correlate success with the character of the total situation, student, task methodology, and environment. He related personal traits such as proneness to anxiety, reasoning ability, and cognitive complexity to degree of success. An interesting finding is that high success is correlated with moderate levels of cognitive complexity. Translated into everyday language this means that students who oversimplified a situation or who overcomplicated it were less successful as researchers in this situation than those who settled for a moderate level of complexity. Robertson speculates that in cybernetic terms this result in some way reflects the optimal matching of the variety in the environment with the variety of the response.

Since the more disciplines which are needed to execute a task the more complex the project organization must be, then we may suppose that a researcher whose complexity is optimal for a project requiring inputs from, say, two disciplines may not be the best person to carry out another requiring say, four.

Robertson is cautious in his interpretation of his findings but they are obviously worthy of consideration in team-building and might throw some light on the desirable personality of the bridge-scientist.

Conclusion

Most of the participants in the Conference started from the conviction that for the types of problem-solving with which they were concerned a cross-disciplinary approach was indispensable to a solution. The real difficulty lay in getting the operation under way, for many obstacles stood in the path. The nature and origin of these obstacles and possibilities for removing them are discussed in the next chapter, but we must conclude with a warning that there was at least one dissentient from the majority point of view. Birnbaum produced in his paper some empirical evidence that interdisciplinary integration was not always necessary or even desirable: it depends on the exact form of the desired output of the project. This paper could have important practical consequences and for this reason its review is deferred until Chapter 5 where the practical implications of all our discussions for management are brought together.

CHAPTER 4

Cross-disciplinarity and Organizational Forms

Introduction

An organization and the social environment in which it exists live in a state of mutual dependence. What the organization can do for the environment depends on what the environment is prepared to do for the organization. The environment supplies the organization with resources of money, technology, information, machines, materials, and people but if the environment restricts their supply then the achievement of the organization will be constrained.

But achievement is also constrained by the internal workings of the organization itself, by the way its members relate to one another, by the perception that each member has of the possibilities for self-fulfilment, by the way rewards are distributed among them, and by the skill of the leadership in controlling, coordinating, and motivating.

How far these two forms of constraint, external and internal, operate in cross-disciplinary research depends on a number of factors, of which institutional setting and size are the most important. Therefore in the rest of this chapter we look at the problem of how to make such research most effective in the face of the constraints and within this two-dimensional framework. The following section contains a description of this framework.

A Taxonomy of Organizational Forms

Group size

A major determinant of the complexity and degree of structuring of activities in task-oriented groups is the number of people they employ. More people means more departments; more departments means more rules spelling out who does what, and when, and how (Pugh *et al.*, 1968). There is no reason why cross-disciplinary organizations should not also be subject to this tendency, even though research organizations are usually not large in the way that their government and industrial counterparts can be. Nevertheless, research groups range in size from two or three up to hundreds or occasionally to thousands of members.

Social psychology recognizes that the nature of social relationships changes when a group becomes too large for a member to know most of the others well and to identify with the total group that makes up the organization. Sociologists have traditionally distinguished between primary groups, where there is intimacy and identification with the group (e.g. the family, the clan, the work group), and secondary groups, where such intimacy is unlikely (e.g. schools, work organizations) (see Cooley, 1902).

Although size is not the only factor that distinguishes a primary from a secondary group it is of major importance. How large a group can be and remain primary is impossible to say, but we shall assume that in an industrial context a group is unlikely to be primary if it has more than twenty-five to thirty members. Certainly above this size it is difficult to regulate people's behaviour without formal rules and standard procedures. In contrast, behaviour in primary groups is regulated informally by implicit agreement among members as to who is entitled to exert authority and have power over the others.

Institutional setting

The second element in our taxonomy likely to influence the structure of a cross-disciplinary group is its location relative to particular social organizations. This location is often coterminous with the client organization it serves. We shall use the following simple classification of such reference organizations:

University-based research units
Industry or government-based research units
Interinstitutional units

The last group are those units that are set up to serve several social institutions.

Table 1 summarizes the elements of our taxonomy and provides examples of each sub-division. We distinguish between primary and secondary groups (small versus large) and the three institutional locations. Together these generate six potential settings for the execution of cross-disciplinary problem-solving which can be expected to call into being different organizational forms.

This classification is perhaps rough-and-ready but it has a precedent in a study by Aimetti *et al.* (1979) who carried out typological examinations of a large number of research groups. Although this work produced a finer classification than ours, we believe that the coarser breakdown is adequate to make the point, as we show below, that cross-disciplinary research in different institutional settings faces different kinds of difficulties. (Note that Aimetti *et al.* call our

Table 1. The organizational setting of interdisciplinary problem-solving groups
(examples are taken from Conference papers)

Institutional location	(Size)/Psychological nature of the group	
	(Small)/Primary: <25	(Large)/Secondary: >25
University/and other academic	Futures Research Group (Wasniowski)	Institute for Research into the Education of the Deaf (Trybus) University-based industrial company (Handscombe)
Industry or government	Small consultancy groups (no examples from Conference)	UK Atomic Energy Authority (Low) Shirley Institute (Jones)
Interinstitutional	Interdisciplinary Higher Degree Scheme (Robertson) Policy Research in Engineering, Science and Technology (Gibbons)	Gulf Universities Research Consortium (Sharp) Fishery management in the Gulf of Mexico (Etzold)

industrial/government groups applied-scientific groups and our interinstitutional groups cooperative groups.)

We can now return to our main theme which is to examine how the constraints discussed in the first section of this chapter apply to the six settings of interdisciplinary problem-solving groupings and to offer some suggestions on how their effects may be overcome.

Small, University-based Groups

Financial resources

These groups typically consist of university teachers who have found a problem which crosses their disciplinary boundaries and who then find some resources, usually from outside the university, to enable them to work on the problem. Thus, the project leaders are often part-time leaders. They may have some full-time researchers working for them and some full- or part-time technicians. Technical facilities are often obtained from the host institution when it has the capacity to spare.

Since the services of the full-time research assistants and the technicians are commonly paid for by grants to the university teachers they are often employed on short-term contracts. This has the effect of increasing turnover among such personnel, because they become anxious about their career prospects during the final year of a grant allocation (Pugh and Hickson, 1976). Restriction of financial resources and uncertainty about their continuation are major environmental constraints upon staffing these small problem-solving groups.

It is also possible, though the evidence is scarce, that the poor career prospects offered by such employment discourage the very best people from accepting them. This may be particularly exacerbated when the problem is cross-disciplinary, for there are clear career risks for people who stray from the well-defined career paths of the established disciplines. This theme was strongly presented at the First International Conference by Teich[1] who described such individuals as the 'unfaculty', to emphasize their different status from the normal university faculty.

The limited financial resources also cause other problems. It has been shown several times (e.g. Allen and Cohen, 1969; Tushman, 1977) that successful research/innovation depends on having good linking with sources of information outside the group. These information-providing activities take up much time in scanning and contacting the environment. The contacting is best effected by personal contacts at conferences or by direct visits to other institutions. This involves much travelling, not always easy to schedule if the researchers spend much of their time teaching. Extensive travelling requires extensive funds. They are frequently not adequate since a small group of researchers may need to do almost as much travelling as a much larger group, but the travel grant may be calculated as a proportion of the total grant. When the research problem requires inputs of information from several disciplines these difficulties increase in severity.

On the other hand, one of the advantages of locating a cross-disciplinary problem-solving activity in a university is that a wide range of expertise is readily at hand to help speed up the identification of relevant sources of knowledge and skills. The university's library and computing resources are also easily available, and relatively cheap.

Even here the question of adequate resourcing is important. The paper by Pineau and Levy-Leboyer in this volume shows that small size is quite strongly correlated with lower levels of performance or effectiveness. Stankiewicz (1979), looking at university research groups in Sweden, found that very small groups (five or less) were less effective. Moch and Morse (1977) found that size was the single best predictor of innovation in a sample of one thousand hospitals, but they also detected an interaction between size and decentralized structure, which meant that large, decentralized organizations innovated most of all. The organizations in the Moch and Morse study are much larger than the research groups at present under consideration, but their findings reinforce the point that size, and the resources that accompany it, has a considerable effect on group effectiveness. The removal of this constraint is easy, but only if the resources are available.

The removal of the resource barrier usually depends on the generosity of funding bodies, but in times of economic recession they tend to strive even harder to get value for money. Outside pressure to meet deadlines in an activity as uncertain as cross-disciplinary problem-solving can lead to poorer research, or to the failure to apply careful 'polishing' which can transform the quality of the finished product. This is particularly true when that product is a written publication rather than a patent. On the other hand, the evidence that moderate levels of pressure lead to improved performance is too powerful to ignore (McGrath, 1976) and this positive function of the client–customer contract must be taken into account. However, where pressure is excessive its effects may be negative since quantity is less valued than quality by university-based researchers (French and Caplan, 1973).

Cultural factors

As Gold and Gold in this volume and Birnbaum (1981) point out, differences in values and training create major problems of cooperation and coordination for people from different disciplines. These within-system problems, however, are possibly least troublesome in small university groups. This is because there is very little compulsion in the university for people to work on projects they do not like. Thus the choice of projects and the choice of collaborators is largely free. This does not mean that such conflicts are absent, but it does mean there is more often than not a prior commitment to accepting them and trying to work them through.

The process of working them through is facilitated by two factors. Firstly, universities are basically egalitarian institutions with flat hierarchical structures; expertise rather than formal authority is the dominant basis of social power (French and Raven, 1959). Secondly, the groups are small, and this in itself tends to reduce the variety of disciplines and the values associated with them. Small size is well known to increase participation (French and Caplan, 1973) and participation reduces strain and conflict. These are, of course, statistical trends of moderate size—there is no guarantee that small size will lead to either of these desirable outcomes.

A minor, but sometimes important, factor which can inhibit intragroup processes in universities is that different disciplines are often located at different parts of the campus. Since teaching tends to take priority the system sometimes prevents individuals from different disciplines being physically close to each other. Solving this problem is not inherently difficult, but is administratively less often achieved than might be desirable. The researchers themselves are often willing accomplices in the sense that they are loath to give up their location and identity with the parent discipline. Out of sight can become out of consideration even if the bulk of cross-disciplinary research still gets published in discipline-based journals (Blauberg and Mirsky[1]).

Though some advantages have been identified for this sort of research group we might do well to heed the following comment about its suitability for solving cross-disciplinary problems:

> A university is well structured for small-scale basic research involving one or two members of the faculty working closely with a handful of graduate students. Such groups usually represent a single academic discipline. A university relates to large-scale, applied missions only with great difficulty.

Organized research sub-units such as centres, institutes and programs abound on practically every campus. Although many claim to be interdisciplinary most are closely tied to, or dominated by, one academic department (Lambright and Teich, 1981, p.313).

Large, University-based Groups

As implied in Table 1, these large groups are usually located in institutes and research centres attached to universities. As Lambright and Teich (1981) pointed out, such institutes are frequently involved in monodisciplinary or multidisciplinary projects rather than interdisciplinary ones. The recent establishment within the US National Science Foundation of an Office of Interdisciplinary Research is a recognition that science and universities in particular need to respond more vigorously to problems which ignore traditional discipline boundaries.

Handscombe's paper, already referred to in Chapter 3, describes an organization that falls into this category. It employs twenty-seven full-time staff, but also involves 100 to 150 members of the staff from the rest of the University of Salford. Many of its contracts are cross-disciplinary and the Centre itself provides the management expertise to ensure that the necessary coordination and cooperation takes place effectively.

The Institute of Research established at Gallaudet College and described by Trybus is another example of a large university-based group. In absolute terms it is not large, compared with Handscombe's group, but again it has the formal departments and hierarchical structure which make it a secondary group rather than a primary group. Trybus indicates that research actions are largely at the discretion of the researchers themselves but the functions of budget planning, expenditure of funds, equipment acquisition, and other administrative actions are centrally controlled. Since he also refers to a possible increasing involvement in research planning and objective setting by the Institute, it is likely that even this high level of research autonomy may be eroded in time as research teams become directed to solving problems defined relative to the Institute's general goals. All organizational designs are compromises, however, and the economies of scale, security of tenure, and resources which institutes provide allows the tackling of larger problems and the assembly of the variety of expertise needed to deal with them. These are obviously to be considered as reasonable trade-offs with the freedom of choice such as is enjoyed by smaller, more independent groups.

Organized research units

The establishment of an 'organized research unit', or ORU as Teich[1] described them, by a college or university is now a common event. Teich points out that many such ORUs have been established to meet the needs of specific clients such as government departments. Some of these have become so large and famous that they are *de facto* independent of the universities that first gave birth to them. Most remain part of the university but with different degrees of attachment and involvement in its affairs.

Teich's paper makes it clear that friction can develop between the university and the ORU. Administrative and financial control can become an issue as well as factors to do with the image of the two institutions. Many ORUs are much more problem/applied centred because of the nature of the contracts they undertake. Universities have traditionally favoured more fundamental research and promoted values of independent thought and action. The university environment is then a major constraint on those ORUs which have become large enough to develop power and influence in their own right. The institutes can offer financial and other inducements to the better graduate students so that they may compete directly with the host institution. Very large ORUs may even be able to offer careers and conditions that overcome the problems faced by those in small ORUs where researchers often have unfavourable terms and conditions when compared with the teaching faculty; to quote Teich[1], the researchers are 'in the university but not of the university'.

He is sufficiently impressed by the evidence indicating tension between universities and larger ORUs to suggest that universities may be well advised to resolve some of the difficulties by setting up what Brooks (1977) has called 'buffer institutions':

> These institutions are sufficiently distinct from their university bases that their staffs do not see themselves as second-class citizens in comparison to regular faculty members, yet they are close enough to contribute to the vitality of the university's research environment. Since part of these institutions may be considered government laboratories, their senior staffs may even have the job security of civil servants (Teich[1]).

In the United Kingdom the Medical Research Council has many units which have this sort of relationship with the university.

While this provides a structural answer to dealing with relationships between institutions good relationships still depend on having leaders who are skilled at and dedicated to maintaining good communications with other important organizations in their proximal environment.

Role of the sponsor

For many ORUs the most important organization in the environment is the sponsor. This relationship appears particularly delicate when the projects are genuinely interdisciplinary. Cutler[1] makes this point:

> IR is growing, but barely surviving at a majority of publicly funded universities, due largely to the tension between academic freedom and government intervention when Federal funding is involved.

Hattery[1] feels that this particular linkage is so crucial to the development of cross-disciplinary research that it should be the object of concerted research itself. He claims that the monitoring of cross-disciplinary projects by sponsors has led to much unhappiness, but the monitors who monitor least are not always the most successful monitors. The tension arises from the sponsor's need to assure they get quality and get it on time, and the desire of educated and articulate professional scientists to control their own destinies. Since little empirical knowledge exists about this relationship it is clear one cannot offer firm prescriptions as to how to solve it.

Both Cutler[1] and Hattery[1] point out that cross-disciplinary research requires more time and money in the earliest stages of the research process than does conventional research. This suggests that both researchers and sponsors may need to allocate both time and resources to negotiating the nature of their future relationships. Several models of how successful negotiations can be achieved exist and this experience may well be useful to the personnel who are involved in the management of this crucial boundary (Carlisle and Leary, 1981). Miles (1980) reviews the literature on boundary roles and suggests some of the qualities important for being successful in them. Both sponsors and large-scale ORUs might well need to train specialists for handling this interface, and Miles' review may help in the successful selection of candidates.

Internal structures

The strong desires for autonomy and independence expressed and expected by scientists cause problems not only at the interface between the ORU and its environment. These particular values are probably the main determinant of the internal structures that develop in larger cross-disciplinary research groups. In his seminal review of the literature on organizational structure Mintzberg (1979) argues that organizational structure arises from two main forces. One is concerned with achieving coordination among the major parts of organizations and the other is from the conflicts that arise between the parts of the organization itself. Mintzberg describes five organizational parts and five mechanisms for achieving coordination among the parts.

The five parts are the strategic apex (top management), the middle line (middle management), the operating core (the workers or in the case of research organizations the scientists), the support staff (personnel, secretaries, cooks, etc.), and the technostructure (corporate planning, O & M, etc.). The five coordinating mechanisms are direct supervision, standardization of work processes, standardization of work outputs, standardization of worker skills, and mutual adjustment. Mutual adjustment achieves coordination by the simple process of constant and continuing informal communications.

Mintzberg would claim that research scientists working on uncertain projects would prefer to achieve coordination through mutual adjustment. His assumption is that any particular structure has arisen from a resolution of conflicts among the five parts of the organization. Thus, if the strategic apex wins the conflict then it can probably use direct supervision to achieve good coordination. If the operating core wins then the dominant coordinating mechanism will be mutual adjustment. In ORUs the operating core are scientists and they tend to win the conflict.

Organizations with this latter pattern of relationships are described by Mintzberg as *adhocracies*. Adhocracies are characterized by much horizontal specialization, high levels of professional training, little formalization of procedure, and organic rather than mechanistic relationships. Typically, they are young organizations with highly technical and sophisticated technologies. A considerable amount of autonomy is given to lower levels in the organization but the autonomy is given selectively. The main control exercised from the top in adhocracies relates to project management. The other roles of those in the strategic apex are to do with external liaison and negotiation. Even policy formation is spread throughout the organization in the sense that what gets done *is* the policy. Innovation requires flexible and fast responses, and the lack of reliance on standardization combined with decentralization enables the adhocracy to achieve this response. Mintzberg illustrates this by quoting the fact that the Manned Space Flight Centre of NASA changed its structure seventeen times in the first eight years of its existence.

It is significant that in a book entitled *Managing Interdisciplinary Research* we have to emphasize the roles of managers in adhocracies: 'Managers abound in adhocracies-functional managers, integrating managers, project managers' (Mintzberg, 1979, p.435). They are not, however, engaged in the direct supervision so often identified with the management process. Their time is spent in liaison and negotiation with other teams, outside advisers, sponsors, etc. Even as managers they are part-time for they are themselves experts and are very likely to be involved in carrying out their own research—they are operators as well as members of the middle line.

The barriers to achieving successful cross-disciplinary research in large, university-based institutes may be diagnosed as ones which inhibit the workings of the adhocracy. People who have been socialized into university systems tend to have been socialized into particular disciplines and socialized out of the idea that management is a professional skill worthy of the same efforts as their science. To them their supervisory role is a matter of directing research, assisting their student assistants to solve day-to-day problems, and monitoring the quality of the output. The reward system encourages this narrow view of management. The main problem, then, is one of recruiting good scientists who enjoy the uncertainty and ambiguity of working in an adhocracy and who are committed to sustaining it as an organizational form. Professional scientists are pulled towards creating what Mintzberg calls a 'professional bureaucracy' (universities adopt this form of structure) and this tendency must be strongly resisted, particularly in cross-disciplinary research situations where such standardization based on skill or training is inimical to the interdisciplinary spirit so necessary to achieve successful integration among disciplines. It is perhaps clearer now why it is difficult to develop adhocracies within a university setting where the basic structure and values are inherently those of the professional bureaucracy.

Small, Industrial/Government Cross-disciplinary Groups

Governments rarely sponsor small, relatively independent groups solving complex cross-disciplinary problems. Such groups are much more likely to be funded from industrial sources where the industry wishes to set up its own research and technical advisory bodies, or by technical entrepreneurs who offer problem-solving skills through privately owned consultancies. In either case, they are small organizations that have highly trained, professional and technical personnel with secretaries as the main form of support staff. Being both small and highly professionalized means that they have a strong pull towards operating under mutual adjustment. Mintzberg (1979) distinguishes between operating and administrative adhocracies (see below), and these organizations have all the characteristics of the operating adhocracy. Small size, physical proximity to each other, and common professional values enable such organizations to effectively operate on mutually understood expectations and continual negotiations. At least, the conditions exist to facilitate this form of organization. As Mintzberg says, 'A key feature of the operating adhocracy is that its administrative and operating work tend to blend into a single effort.' No one in the operating adhocracy monopolizes the power to innovate or to act to meet the fluctuating demands of an enquiring environment.

It may be that the strength of such a system is the source of its ultimate weakness. The flexibility and innovativeness of these consultancy groups often go hand in hand with a reluctance to supply services that meet a customer's or sponsor's standard of reliability. They may not even know how to do it. At the conference Kirton presented a paper on recent research into personal characteristics which has a bearing on this possibility.

He identifies two extreme types, adaptors and innovators, one at each end of a continuum of problem-solving styles. Adaptors tend to find solutions within a framework of accepted theories, policies, and viewpoints while innovators tend to detach a problem from the conventional framework and restate it in a completely different form which may open up new ways to a solution. One would expect to find that innovators have less respect for administrative procedures than have adaptors. If innovators dominate a group, as they tend to do in the consultancy groups, then the use of standard procedures and formal systems will be discouraged. On the other hand, if one attempts to apply the remedy of bringing adaptors into the system then the organization is set on the road to becoming what Mintzberg calls a professional bureaucracy. Here standard, reliable, and efficient services are the preferred output.

When this happens the group may no longer be as effective in attacking the kinds of complex problems that interdisciplinary work involves. Thus, one of the barriers to effective performance in such groups is the 'rational' attraction of specializing roles and services. This can become particularly acute when the organization has successfully solved a particular kind of problem more than once and when the market for solving the problem is large. This situation offers a tempting niche to occupy, where income is increased and uncertainty decreased. Unfortunately the fun, excitement, and challenge that motivates such scientific entrepreneurs also disappears, and the skills and qualities that make for efficient professional bureaucracies are very different from those demanded by effective (they can not be efficient) operating adhocracies.

Another external constraint frequently encountered in these research teams is lack of financial resources. This may sometimes lead to lack of physical resources too: the right piece of equipment cannot be bought or even hired at a price that is affordable. Again, the dilemma is apparent — people who are creative and innovative risk-takers do not tend to make good accountants. Such organizations need to recognize the need for first-class services in the financial area. This financial vulnerability is almost inherent in organizations which are small, for they do not have the collateral, tangible or intangible, possessed by large organizations which may enable them to buy or borrow themselves out of trouble. On the face of it this problem is easily overcome by hiring a good finance man, but he too will need to have the commitment to interdisciplinary working and risk-taking if he is to successfully mesh with the dominant values of the operating adhocracy. His role will not only be financial control but will contain a strong element of liaison and persuasion with sponsors, banks, and scientific equipment suppliers.

Manpower may be another scarce resource. Small organizations need to keep down operating expenses and avoid long-term commitments such as pension rights. This often puts them into the situation of having to make do with the skills they have rather than to employ an expensive professional. The challenge to these high innovators who set up such an organization is perhaps too readily accepted, but the combination of novelty, difficulty, and pressure linked to attractive intrinsic as well as extrinsic rewards make them vulnerable to self-imposed role-overload.

Apart from the stress this may produce (Fineman and Payne, 1981) it can lead to exhaustion and expensive errors. The opportunities for increased intimacy that small size offers can often prevent such a breakdown, but high intimacy can also lead to 'groupthink' (Janis, 1972) where the members collaborate in their own self-deception. Willingness to listen to the comments of outsiders and themselves is a prerequisite if this sort of folly is to be avoided.

In systems where the existence of 'slack resources' is at a minimum it is vital that the right people are chosen. Scientific and professional expertise needs to be balanced by commitment to collaboration and the openness of mind that requires acceptance of the time that interpersonal relationships take up and the ability to tolerate ambiguity and frustration.

In sum, the success of the operating adhocracy created by small consultancies depends heavily on the scientific ability and interpersonal skills of the people who are in them. Mintzberg puts the situation more eloquently, 'No structure can be more Darwinian than the Adhocracy—more supportive of the fit, as long as they remain fit, and more destructive of the weak'.

Large, industry-based groups

Large, industry-based groups have two origins. Firstly, they come into being when governments invest in large research institutions, parts of which become involved in cross-disciplinary research which is carried out in an interdisciplinary form, although some of the research is also carried out in a multidisciplinary form. Secondly, they arise when industrial organizations or whole industrial consortia set up more or less autonomous research organizations. Again, only parts of these may operate in a genuinely interdisciplinary mode, but these parts may be quite large in themselves creating secondary rather than primary groups. Even if the groups are small their location in the larger organization affects their context and their form. Mintzberg calls these large and (normally) older organizations 'administrative adhocracies'.

Administrative adhocracies differ from operating adhocracies in that instead of serving the social environment they tend to serve themselves. They set up projects because they, or their parent organization, wishes to know the answer to a problem. The administrative adhocracy differs from the operating adhocracy in that it makes a sharp distinction between its administrative function (strategic apex and middle line) and the operating core. The operating core is separate from the administrative function. This is achieved in three main ways according to Mintzberg. A separate company is formed to actually carry out the work once the adhocracy has decided which basic direction the research should take. A second way is to contract out the development and production elements in a problem: again this is done once the basic research and strategy have been decided. This was how NASA tended to function (Sayles and Chandler, 1971). The third solution to separating the operating core from the administration is to automate the production process and thus leave the administrative adhocracy to concentrate on the problems of the day after tomorrow. Some chemical and pharmaceutical companies have adopted this sort of structure.

Interdependence and ideology

Whatever variation on these three forms the organization takes one of the essential problems of the administrative adhocracy is the management of interdependence. This may be within the main part of the organization itself where there are large numbers of line and support staff with no clear bureaucratic divisions to signal who is responsible for what, and few stable policies to guide decision-making. This uncertainty exacerbates the problems of distributing resources and rewards both to departments and to individuals. The dual-career ladder is a symptom of these difficulties, for it is in administrative adhocracies that technical and support staff can be seen to make as important a contribution as the so-called line personnel. These conventional separations into line and staff do not sit very well in this kind of organization in practice, but greater size almost inevitably leads to increased segmentation and variety in organizational roles and titles (Pugh *et al.*, 1968).

McCann and Galbraith (1981) describe some of the problems that face organizations which of necessity must handle high levels of interdependency, this being the main problem facing the administrative adhocracy:

> Differing perceptions of interdependence, lack of agreement about strategies, and conflict are promoted when:
> a. asymmetries in status and access to information exists
> b. different people and departments use different performance criteria and reward structures
> c. some people and departments are pursuing short-run objectives and others are pursuing long-term objectives
> d. job dissatisfaction and task ambiguities stimulate unilateral action to change roles and to reduce ambiguities
> e. some shared resources are scarce
> f. different training and knowledge bases create semantic barriers and perceptual diversity.

These authors also point out that whether interdependence proves beneficial to the organization depends on creating shared appreciations of the value and the necessity of making interdependence work. Administrative adhocracies clearly face most of the problems identified by McCann and Galbraith and the successful ones must, therefore, be effective in creating this shared appreciation or ideology.

Starbuck (1982) and others have recently raised the issue of organizations as ideological systems. Its appearance as a 'special issue' reflects a growing concern in organizational theory to move away from understanding how organizations work only by examining their context and their adaptability to that context (Gerwin, 1981). The 'special issue' does not contain detailed prescriptions about how to create corporate ideologies, and indeed there is some debate as to whether they can be rationally and deliberately created at all (Brunsson, 1982). The role of heroic myth in creating ideologies and of ritual in sustaining them is much discussed by these authors, but myth-making in modern work organizations is a little understood process. Several of the papers in the special issue stress, however, the effectiveness of ideologies in dealing with the irrationality that pervades organizational life in such a way that it facilitates the return of a new rationality. Brunsson (1982) puts it well:

> Organizational decision-making tends to be irrational, and organizational ideologies bias organizations' perceptions. Much effort has been spent on prescribing how organizations should achieve more rationality. However, rational decision-making affords a bad basis for action. Some irrationalities are necessary requirements for organizational actions. Choices are facilitated by narrow and clear organizational ideologies, and actions are

facilitated by irrational decision-making procedures which maximize motivation and commitment.

It would seem clear that the role of ideologies in the large administrative adhocracies is important in generating commitment and a dominant element of their ideology must encompass a belief in the virtue or value of the process of problem-solving itself, rather than in solving the problems of particular disciplines. Watzlawick, Weakland and Fisch (1974) make the point that the *liberté* and *égalité* demanded by the French Revolution can only be achieved by a higher order bridging process, *fraternité*. In the present context this line of thinking suggests that physicists, engineers, biologists, administrators, and so on, need to see themselves as part of a problem-solving community or clan (Ouchi, 1980), rather than as the hired hands their financial contracts imply. An ideology of 'pragmatic problem-solving' may be more conducive to this than an ideology concerned with being 'scientific'.

It must not be forgotten, however, that it is the good financial rewards and resources possessed by large organizations that attracts the best scientists and the most interesting problems in the first place. As we have tried to show, the challenge is to create the intellectual and emotional bonds that synthesize the talents of these gifted scientists within the constraints of instrumental relationships, difficult goals, and ambiguous roles. Apart from the need for liaison roles, gatekeepers, and frequent multidirectional communication we have noted in connection with other organizational forms, we are suggesting that in large adhocracies in particular, ideology may supply a powerful lever for generating and sustaining motivation and commitment. Managers may do well to put more effort into creating an ideology suited to the dynamics of the adhocracy.

Large size brings both benefits and constraints as we have already seen. The administrative adhocracy is particularly susceptible to the pressures to standardize and centralize control, yet its existence was generated to innovate for itself and its industry so it must fight this pressure if it is to remain viable. This may mean the creation of new organizations or the continual change of key persons so as to provide renewal.'Change for change's sake' may not be a bad slogan for ambitious adhocracy.

This high rate of change and interpersonal communication is highly inefficient and produces very uneven workloads, but individuals must be selected and socialized so that they can tolerate such inequities and then work furiously when they need to. As Mintzberg says, in adhocracies 'the games are played without rules'.

Interinstitutional Groups

In the section on organizational forms we distinguished between large and small systems and between primary and secondary groups. Size takes on a different meaning for interinstitutional groups, however, for they are not really large in the sense that some other types of organization are large. Their members are often representatives of very large constituencies such as the general public or the government, but the interinstitutional systems themselves are unlikely to grow really big. Since they involve people from a range of organizations or institutions, however, they may well have the characteristics of secondary rather than primary groups for a majority of the members of the network. The effect of increasing size of these groups is therefore different from that in large organizations where its main effect is to produce very different structures and relationships. In the case of interinstitutional groups, increasing size is just as likely to increase the problems of coordination and communication, but the problems will surface as differences of degree rather than kind. We shall not, therefore, make the size distinction in this section.

Interinstitutional groups are the least researched in the literature of interdisciplinary research. Both the First Conference and the present Conference received papers about them: Bents and Horsmann[1] in the former and Sharp and Etzold in the latter. All three examples are about problems in the public domain. Summaries of the content of these papers have already been provided in Chapter 3. The spread of disciplines they involve is much wider than many of the interdisciplinary scientific projects represented in the other papers (e.g. the biomedical teams described by Moser and Levy-Leboyer). Another distinctive feature is that they start out as temporary groups. In the terminology of Aldrich and Whetten (1981) they are *action sets*—'groups or organizations that have formed a temporary alliance for a limited purpose'. They may last for several years, as appears to be the case in the Etzold example related in this volume, but when the problem is solved their dissolution should occur.

Cooperation requires communication which is a major problem for interinstitutional groups. Not only is there the problem of physical separation across towns and even countries but there is also a wider than average professional gap between the scientists and technologists on the one hand and the politicians and administrators on the other. Sharp's group relied heavily on computers to handle the vast amounts of data and yet provide timely access to summaries of it that could be used as guides by non-specialists. Bents and Horsmann[1] designed a structure where a small, permanent group collected, collated, and summarized the data requested by the policy group. This permanent group organized and then transmitted the information from the experts to the policy group. Both experts and the permanent group were satisfied since the experts dealt with knowledgeable colleagues directly, and the cross-disciplinary syntheses were achieved by the small, highly motivated permanent group.

The problem of motivation and commitment is considerable in such groups, for there may be little reward for some of the members of the action set. Bents and Horsmann makes some useful comments about how the system they developed encouraged motivation:

1. It furthered motivation if the study work was also acknowledged in the home institution of the participant, and if the person or group was made fully responsible for its work output.

2. Motivation and flexibility were enhanced because some of the work was budgeted and paid for as private, additional work, not belonging to the home institution.
3. The time/money budget should contain some unassigned reserves. These can be used as 'creativity packages' and/or as a buffer against additional or unanticipated work packages.
4. The project should not be fully allocated to persons at the beginning. Their interest in follow-up packages also motivates an efficient preparation of the already assigned ones.

Despite their success in managing this project Bents and Horsmann still acknowledge the 'delicate balance between organizational activities and the internal motivation of study workers. Even internally highly motivated workers need some amount of organizational "coercion" to reach the study objectives.'

It is possible that 'coercion' is a little strong here, but other studies of work motivation have shown it is important for people to know what they are supposed to be doing and how it fits into the general scheme of things so that they can develop some personal identification with the task (Campbell and Pritchard, 1976). These conditions are obviously not easy to achieve when the 'team' may include people who never meet each other. In such cases the carrots need to be particularly attractive since in such action sets there are often no 'big sticks'; interinstitutional groups are not usually organized hierarchically. They are loosely coupled with each part, having no obvious power over other members of the action set. In many cases it does not matter to particular individuals if they leave the action set halfway through the project. Many individuals or groups may be giving their services voluntarily anyway. As Cutler[1] observed at the First Conference, cross-disciplinary problem-solving costs a lot more than the mere sum of the parts, and sponsors have to budget for that.

Keeping the action set to a manageable size in very complex problem-solving systems may well involve making use of experts but directing their attention strictly to matters inside the confines of their own expertise, i.e. building a relationship of the kind Gold and Gold define as contractual. This avoids the possibility of being drawn into the main network permanently—where too much variety might overload the communication system and lead to chaos. Jönssen (1982) describes a failure in a municipal authority (a clear example of a cross-disciplinary group of the kind under consideration) which arose because a sub-committee's lay members had not been given the time to absorb the information provided by the authority's officials. This prevented them from undergoing the 'cognitive tuning' necessary to them before they could be committed to action flowing from the information. Nothing was therefore done. Cognitive tuning takes time, especially when non-experts are exposed to the disagreements which so often occur between experts. It will be recalled that a similar possibility was discussed in connection with the project described in Sharp's paper in this volume. Reduction of complexity must be a major concern in dealing with transactions between lay persons and experts.

Conclusion

Although the need to communicate, coordinate, and motivate arises in all the problem-solving groups that we have considered in this chapter the measure to deal with them and the lessons about success and failure differ markedly from one setting to another. The problem of obtaining the high levels of cooperation needed in cross-disciplinary research is neither universal nor homogeneous.

CHAPTER 5

The Implications for Management

It has been suggested (Lane, Beddows, and Laurence, 1982) that in the case of large-scale research programmes it is useful to distinguish between the technical, political, and organizational logic of the situation. Using such a framework it can be argued that the manager can operate within the organizational logic to direct the technical logic, but can only influence the political logic. The Manager's individual ability to solve problems or to make use of opportunities is then limited by the freedom available to manipulate the variables of the organizational logic which are under his or her control. This apparent acceptance that some of the variables are defined by the environment and outside the control of the manager's decision-making framework does not, however, make it any less important to use every possible means to try to influence the political logic. For example, every effort must be made to convince the sections of the environment from which support might be gained of the competence of the group and of the scientific feasibility and technological value of the task to be undertaken.

To gain the commitment of external influence groups, e.g. sponsors, funding agencies, pressure groups, lay public, etc., may require that they be actively involved in key tasks such as formulating objectives and assisting in the implementation of the results. It may be expedient to set up formal groups including such persons as full members and to accept their ideas and suggestions in areas which would previously have been seen as the sole responsibility of the discipline or technical group. For some institutions this would be a change from the past, and could be seen as a possible threat to their own internal power system based on previously well-accepted norms and customs. Some support for the view that this is worthwhile comes from the innovation literature, which reports that major changes in direction frequently come from people outside the established fields. The contribution of outsiders in identifying potential problems has previously been noted and reinforces the value of encouraging an environment in which more people are invited to participate in a constructive way.

Redefining Disciplines

In this respect it is also important that we use the widest possible definition of 'discipline'. This must be extended to include all groups of people with common interests and affiliations whose opinions, expertise, and cooperation are required at a particular stage of the project. For example, at the stage of project identification and formulation, we would envisage inclusion of politicians, environmentalists, industrial representatives, and so on, if ultimately the implementation of the project's findings depended on their commitment to its aims.

For many readers this widening of interest groups which should be involved will remind them of earlier discussions in areas such as technology assessment. As pointed out in Chapter 3, some of the papers at the Conference fit quite comfortably under this heading, with the distinction being that we are concerned not just with the involvement of political disciplines in the assessment but also with the actual management of the research process.

Complementarity of Inter- and Multidisciplinary Forms

We make a distinction between the multidisciplinary and interdisciplinary form of organization. From a management point of view they both imply a team operation focused on a task. They therefore both require attention to the process of team management, i.e. to the What, Who, and How of team-building, but a major difference will be in the area of How — in particular in the procedures which are likely to be necessary to resolve conflicts and obtain agreement on controversial issues. The frequency with which such procedures are likely to be called upon will also be higher in the case of the interdisciplinary form of organization. Management will want to consider the implications of this for the choice of project leader and possibly also for the choice of key members of the project team.

A corollary of this is that management should choose carefully the organizational form for a project in the light of its likely characteristics, i.e. after the problem has been clearly identified. This is in agreement with the research which suggests that a more interdisciplinary form is likely to be more appropriate in the early stages of project identification and formulation but may not necessarily be correct at later stages. Without claiming that we have adequate evidence, we suggest that it would appear sensible to encourage a flexible approach in larger and longer term projects — adopting where possible a multidisciplinary approach for much of the work but an interdisciplinary one at key points, such as evaluations, revaluations, and reviews.

This strategy would call for considerable management ability on the part of key people and might be helped by the use of some structured aids such as, for example, potential problem analysis.

Coming to Terms with External Sponsorship

The political logic can impose barriers to this wider definition of interdisciplinary working in the form of institutional structures, administrative procedures, norms, and values. This would, for example, seem to be a problem for universities, which may wish to maintain their resources of know-how and facilities by attracting external sponsorship but at the same time may have to accept many of the norms of commercial practice. This must lead to some rethinking in such areas as career structure, advancement and reward, recruitment and staff turnover, and the management of multiple sponsors. There will also be the need to consider the use of external resources, implying a knowledge and acceptance of qualities outside the institution and an ability to collaborate with such resources. When new problems arise they may suggest the need for the development of new disciplines but their creation in the short term with the risk of abandonment later does not fit easily into institutional structures with well-established and relatively narrowly defined boundaries. The need for taking risks and for encouraging longer term funding for such activities is suggested from the experience to date.

In some institutions a movement to cross-disciplinary work also implies a movement to multisponsorship. It has been argued that this adds another dimension and frequently causes problems which require much effort to solve. The need for getting agreement between the various clients and the research organization is stressed, as is the adequate provision of time and resources to plan, monitor, and review the work programme. In most cases these are areas which are not well done and it is argued that more attention must be paid to management in areas of cross-disciplinary research which involve multiclients and possibly multi-institutional contributions. This has long been recognized by the reputable contract research organizations but many of the recent entrants into the field have underestimated the effort required.

Using the Problem to Produce Group Cohesion

As stated earlier, it may be useful to examine the problem before deciding upon the organizational form. Considering the group of potential contributions and their future as well as present needs will be very fruitful. Some of the papers suggest that the 'problem' helped the group to work together. If this is so then the form of working may modify people's abilities to collaborate and change attitudes.

This will pay dividends in future time periods for the possibility of using cross-disciplinary projects as a means of encouraging different working relationships could be a powerful tool of management. The practical value of this suggestion would be supported by much of the literature on communication patterns in R & D as well as the literature on personal and team development.

An additional point worth noting is that certain 'new technologies', e.g. the computer, have considerable potential for encouraging integration and communication between different disciplines. The longer term benefits of establishing good working relationships in cross-disciplinary activities is brought out in a number of papers. In most establishments where this has happened a major driving force has been external pressure, e.g. on funds. An implication which might be drawn from this is that means can be taken by management to encourage more cross-disciplinary activity if this is thought to be a desirable movement from a research point of view.

Research Team Composition

One appreciates the force of Birnbaum's[1] remark in his paper to the 1979 Conference that 'research team composition is a highly complex phenomenon'. Not only does there not appear to be one 'best way' to assemble and lead research teams but different 'best ways' appear over time.

Clearly this is a matter deserving of much more investigation. Not only may the nature of the project outcome be important but other factors such as the institutional organization (functional, project, matrix) and the nature of the task in terms of its urgency and predictability should be considered (see the paper by Pearson, Payne, and Gunz[1] presented to the First Conference and already referred to). A useful insight into the special qualities required of a project manager in a university context is provided in the paper in this volume by Saxberg and Newell.

At the 1981 Conference participants were invited to complete the Kirton Adaption–Innovation Inventory (1980). This is designed to measure certain behaviour characteristics of individuals which infuence the way in which they tackle problems. Research to date using this instrument has shown that people can exhibit very different problem-solving behaviour and that those at either extreme of the spectrum do not always understand and appreciate the way in which those at the other end behave. This can have considerable implications when collaboration is required and although no specific data were available for interdisciplinary situations the implications are that such personal characteristics could play an important part in determining the likelihood that effective collaboration would be possible.

The findings presented were only of a preliminary nature but suggest that attention must be paid to the personality characteristics of individuals in teams if they are to be effective. Previous work by researchers such as Belbin (1981) have also indicated the importance of this dimension. If this is accepted it means that extra effort must be expended in matching personal as well as technical attributes in research teams, which can be rather difficult in some institutional settings.

Implications for the Education Process

The notion of the 'bridge-scientist' is also suggested from various pieces of research which have shown the important part played in innovation by people occupying various roles with names such as 'technological gatekeeper', 'key communicator', and even 'product or project champion'. In almost all cases these people already have an established reputation and are recognized as such, as indeed are people we have referred to as 'interdisciplinary individuals'. This requirement is a challenge to management. Younger and less established people may have a lot to contribute to cross-disciplinary work but need to look to research in systems which tend to have career paths following single discipline lines. This is clearly a more important consideration in universities than in most parts of industry—hence the different attitudes shown in discussions on the subject of managing interdisciplinary research by people from different institutional backgrounds. This Conference did not resolve these differences but it did indicate the urgency of thinking about changes which may be necessary —indeed will probably be forced upon certain institutions in the near future. The implications for education, recruitment, and manpower development are obvious. The question must be raised as to whether some of the existing institutions will be innovators in this process or whether the changes will come from outside, as has so often been the case in the past.

A point to consider with regard to the creation of new disciplines and the working together of people from existing ones is the important role played by teaching in the university sector. Although teaching is not the *raison d'être* of a university it is this activity which currently appears to be receiving most attention. In the past this has been supported at such a level that a good deal of slack existed for research and other activities of the academic's own choosing. Research interests could be changed and new fields opened up without necessarily affecting teaching programmes. Again, because of the slack in the system, many research projects could be initiated which were subsequently disbanded—not necessarily because the problems were unimportant but because the work did not develop in line with the individual's interest or in some cases was proving too difficult to obtain the required output, e.g. published papers in the time demanded by career progression needs. The current pressure on university resources and the increasing importance being attached to relevance is going to have a significant effect on the management of resources and hence on those responsible for guiding future directions.

There is some evidence that interdisciplinary research can be a good lead into teaching, but it was suggested at the Conference that it might not be desirable to encourage full-time appointments in new areas but to operate a joint appointments system wherever possible. The setting up of new and separate teaching programmes may well cause antagonism from existing groups and reduce the potential impact upon the institution.

Reward Structures

Generally speaking work carried on within a single discipline will be evaluated on scientific and technical quality. Work of a cross-disciplinary nature, and particularly if carried out in an interdisciplinary way, must be evaluated along more dimensions. Management and process variables must be given added weight and, as mentioned on a number of occasions, reward structures may need to be modified to take this into account. A difficulty inevitably arises as to how to allocate weights to the different factors, indeed what factors to include. This is an important aspect of management and the obvious suggestion is that careful attention should be paid to past experience and the contribution which different factors have made to the success or otherwise of research projects assessed against the organization's objectives.

Universities as problem-solving communities

It has been argued that size is an important factor to consider, with the very small establishment being unable to draw upon sufficient quality resources and the large likely to become too structured and inflexible and hence less innovative than is desirable. The concept of a small group of dedicated 'pragmatic problem-solvers' providing the focus of activity and drawing upon other resources as and when required is suggested by some of the papers. This would appear to be a useful design in a university setting although a number of problems can be seen. For example, career progression for the core group does not look attractive and must be given serious consideration by management if they are not to look to increase their own size in an attempt to provide stability or to have a high turnover rate and reduce their effectiveness due to the lack of experienced researchers.

Core groups could end up recruiting directly if they do not get satisfaction from 'university tenured' faculty, e.g. priorities, urgency. In this sense they would become comparable to project managers in industry who might be allowed to buy outside if they cannot get satisfaction inside. This would raise issues of who controls resources—an issue not necessarily resolved by industry. This could also lead to development of a two-tier system of payments in, for example, universities. Staff would be paid a basic salary—low but 'tenured'—with extra cash being earned from research contracts to which they would be encouraged to make a contribution. There can be advantages in such a system but there are also dangers.

The need for certain institutions to see themselves as part of a 'problem-solving community' and to be rewarded as such is suggested. The implications for organization structure, reward systems, and recruitment, etc., are clearly considerable and much thought will need to be given by management to the many alternatives.

Is interdisciplinary always the best way?

Several reasons have been given in the preceding sections for using an interdisciplinary approach to problem-solving. Viewed objectively one might conclude that the reasons, though plausible, are not self-evident and need testing. If the statements are taken as completely true the implication is that the only way to carry out research of any kind is via interdisciplinary teams. Admittedly, several authors make the qualification that from an educational point of view a discipline can be acquired only by a deep and specialized study of the subject matter of that discipline. Nevertheless, the conclusion could still be drawn that, given enough monodisciplinary research to train the teachers and their pupils, serious research ought always to be interdisciplinary. Is this truly the case? Birnbaum's paper reproduced in this volume provides some empirical evidence upon which some judgements can be made. He attempted to measure the degree of integration achieved in cross-disciplinary teams by asking each member of a team how much unity of effort had been achieved. An eight-point scale was used as a measure: full unity was rated as degree 1 on the scale and complete lack of interaction as degree 8. He then used a number of measures of output such as research article quality, quantity of papers, technical reports, patents, and so on.

Stated in the broadest terms, his conclusions are that integrating is most valuable when the desired output of the team is a technical report but is contraindicated when the output is to be a paper or a patent. If one assumes that a technical report contains the results of a problem-solving or mission-oriented project then his finding is in accordance with some of the reasons already suggested. The conclusion that interdisciplinary research is not productive of papers for learned journals is not surprising if one considers that most of the highest quality journals are monodisciplinary and editors are probably biased against cross-disciplinary papers. In fact, as will be discussed in detail later, it could be this factor that is the greatest barrier to undertaking interdisciplinary problem-solving in the universities. The conclusion that the interdisciplinary form is less effective for generating patents is something of a surprise and directly contradicts an important reason for carrying out interdisciplinary research. In fact it seems to contradict the conventional wisdom of idea generation in which, in general, collective sessions are widely believed to foster the development of new ideas.

Conclusion

Our analysis suggests that there is an increasing demand for cross-disciplinary activity and that this is being reflected in many ways, not all of which are necessarily going to produce benefits to many institutions. There is therefore a need to consider carefully the actions which might be taken now rather than to wait until reaction to pressure is the only available alternative. Our view is that the research available, coupled with the experience to date of many research establishments, is a good starting point for analysis. However, there is not much evidence that management in general is aware of this research and experience or of its implications in their own situation.

In this chapter we have therefore tried to pick at some of the most important implications as we see them. We trust that the reader will be encouraged to delve deeper into the papers included in this volume as well as into some of the references and to draw out those parts which they feel are most relevant to their own situation. If this does happen then we will feel that the First and Second International Conferences on the Management of Interdisciplinary Research have been of great value and we look forward to adding to our knowledge in this area through continuing research and future conferences.

Papers Presented at the Second International Conference on the Management of Interdisciplinary Research

LEADERSHIP BY OBJECTIVES IN R & D

S. A. BERGEN
R & D Research Unit, Manchester Business School, Manchester, England

Abstract

A key idea in Hersey and Blanchard's concept of leadership style is that it should be matched to the maturity of the group being led. The author puts the case that the process of transactional analysis provides a useful psychological framework for using Hersey and Blanchard's concept.

The aim of carrying out a transactional analysis is to ascertain during any transaction (typically that between a superior and a subordinate) what are the psychological states of each of the actors. According to transactional analysis these states can be of one of three kinds—that of parent, child, or adult, reflecting the role the actor is assuming at that time. The application to the leadership style situation can be exemplified as follows:

> If the working environment is that described in Hersey/Blanchard terms as structured (the least mature situation) then it would be expected that the superior/subordinate transactions would be that characterized as parent/child; if the environment were that described as delegating (the most mature) then the appropriate style would be adult/adult. To the extent that the styles conform with these norms the transactions will be more or less productive.

The author advocates the use of this form of analysis in the service of team development. For example, the manager can view objective setting as the opportunity for moving the superior/superior relationship from the parent/child to the adult/adult state on the assumption that the Hersey/Blanchard situation will then move away from that requiring the structured towards that requiring the delegating leadership style, so building a team more inclined to be self-motivating.

PREDICTORS OF LONG-TERM RESEARCH PERFORMANCE
P. H. BIRNBAUM
Graduate School of Business, Indiana University, USA

A recent review of the literature on research effectiveness has indicated that there are two major problems with existing treatments. The first problem relates to the number of variables used to measure research performance, many with unclear referrents. Secondly, most research has been cross-sectional rather than longitudinal and consequently has not been able to adequately represent the linkages between research activities, research outcomes, or the progress that may result from outcomes.

The past two decades have witnessed an explosive growth in the number of variables used to measure research performance. In the decade from 1956 to 1965, for example, only seven variables appeared in the English language literature as measures of research performance, while in the next ten years over thirty-five different performance measures appeared (Birnbaum, 1980). Part of this diversity has been due to the variety of samples studied since some indicators, such as articles, are more appropriate for academic than for industrial or governmental research. However, even when the variables are separated by samples, there is a wide variety within each group. The most diverse set of variables are associated with academic research where over twenty-seven variables have been used.

In addition to the number of separate variables used to measure performance, a second major problem has been the cross-sectional nature of these studies and the resulting lack of linkage between what Moravcsik (1977) has referred to as 'scientific activity, scientific production, and scientific progress'. Scientific activity refers to the short-term interpersonal interactions which transform resources such as money and personnel into outputs such as new knowledge discoveries or problem solutions. Scientific production refers to the outcomes of scientific activities such as articles or patents. Scientific progress is concerned with the long-term consequences of scientific production and the extent to which substantive contributions to knowledge or the solution of problems actually occur.

The present study is longitudinal and focuses on academic research attempting to relate scientific activity to scientific production. More specifically, this study uses indicators of scientific activity that have previously been separately identified as important for scientific production in a joint analysis to identify which of these are the most significant in predicting specific research products over time.

Background

Scientific products

There is general agreement in the literature that researchers contribute knowledge in exchange for recognition from their peers (Blau, 1974; Hagstrom, 1965, 1971) and that these individual outputs form the basis of evaluations of their organizations (Hagstrom, 1971). There is also evidence that researchers and research administrators are congruent in their preference for outputs as performance measures (Chau, 1978; Gross and Grambsch, 1968; Jauch and Glueck, 1975).

Among the most frequently used measures of academic products are the quality of articles and the quantity of articles, books, technical reports, published papers, and patents.

Scientific activity

Scientific activities involve the process of interactions between scientists within a structure of interpersonal relationships. Among the more important aspects of these activities are characteristics of the scientists, their division of labour, their integration of effort, member turnover, conflict resolution methods, and the relationship between leaders and members.

An important characteristic of the scientists themselves is their previously earned eminence or recognition which has been positively related to the quality of their products as measured by citations (Cole and Cole, 1967, 1968; Hagstrom, 1971; Jauch and Glueck, 1975).

Another important element in scientific activity is the extent to which the group's labour is divided or differentiated both horizontally among peers and vertically between superiors and subordinates. Differentiation between tasks has been positively related to scientific production as measured by the quantity of articles (Meltzer and Salter, 1962), technical reports, and patents (Farris, 1966). Related to the division of labour is the issue of integration of effort among those who perform separate tasks (Lawrence and Lorsch, 1967).

Integrated efforts have been negatively related to turnover (Price, 1977). Turnover, however, has been found to be positively related to perceptual measures of performance such as 'scientific contribution' and 'usefulness' (Wells and Pelz, 1966), as well as being associated with increased creativity (Ziller, Behringer, and Goodchilds, 1972). However, the relationship between integration, turnover, and products such as articles, technical reports, books, or patents has not yet been reported.

The method of conflict resolution is another important component of scientific activity. Open discussions of disagreement or confrontation as a mode of conflict resolution have not been significantly associated with scientific production when measured by article *quality* (Potchen *et al.*, 1967), but have been positively associated with article quantity (McClarrey and Edwards, 1973; Pelz, 1956), book quantity (McClarrey and Edwards, 1973; Pelz, 1956), and report quantity (Pelz, 1956).

Team research

As disciplines have become increasingly specialized and research problems have become increasingly complex, scientists have joined together into research teams. All teams vary in the extent to which the individual members represent different areas of expertise and possess different skills. This individual variation is increased for teams with members from different disciplines.

Interdisciplinary as opposed to multidisciplinary research refers to research teams in which the effort is integrated into a unified whole. Multidisciplinary research refers to research in which scholars from different disciplines work independently and are joined together externally through editorial linkages (Rossini *et al.*, 1979). The results of interdisciplinary research are more like a 'seamless garment' then a 'patchwork quilt' (Nilles, 1975).

Team research, particularly interdisciplinary research, is very difficult to evaluate. Interdisciplinary research articles may, for example, have publication difficulty in the more discipline-oriented journals (Hattery, 1979). There are also some research efforts which attempt to train students rather than produce research findings or in which the participants disagree over whether outputs should even be produced. Previous work on interdisciplinary research has used the level of integration in outputs produced (Rossini *et al.*, 1979) and a perceptual index (Birnbaum, 1977). However, both of these indicators of performance have been measured in cross-sectional as opposed to longitudinal designs.

Method

Sample

Random sampling was used to control for alternative explanations due to unmeasured or controlled variables in the study.

A stratified sample of eighty-four academic research projects was drawn in 1975 from: Harvard University; Massachusetts Institute of Technology; Stanford University; the University of California at Berkeley, Los Angeles, San Diego, and San Francisco; the University of Chicago; the University of Houston; the University of Illinois; the University of Ottawa; the University of Pennsylvania; the University of Southern California; the University of Washington; and the University of Wisconsin. The US institutions were among the top twenty-two in terms of federal research support and accounted for 45 per cent. of all federal research obligations to universities for the fiscal year 1973, the latest figures available at the time of selection.

The first stratum of forty-three projects was judgementally selected by interdisciplinary research managers familiar with where such research was under way in order to increase the representativeness of the sample. The second stratum of forty-one projects was drawn using proportional random sampling without replacement from a sampling frame of 103 projects constructed using the *Research Centers Directory* (Palmer, 1972) and its latest supplements. Potential bias in sampling due to drawing only those projects under the aegis of a centre or institute was partially solved by including projects in the judgemental stratum that were independent of centres or institutes. These two strata were combined in the analysis by weighting each by the inverse of its sampling ratio in order to adjust for over- and undersampling.

Data were gathered in 1975 by personal interviews, historical records, and questionnaires. Interviews were conducted and historical records gathered from principal investigators, project members, and institute directors. Questionnaires were left with each group and projects were considered to be usable data points when one principal investigator and at least one other project member had returned completed questionnaires. This size was necessary in order to include some two-person interdisciplinary research projects. An overall 94 per cent. response rate of questionnaires was obtained which was reduced to 80 per cent. when the usability criterion was applied. In the majority of instances when groups had to be rejected, it was due to insufficient responses from group members and not from principal investigators. Those groups rejected appeared to be similar enough in response pattern to the sixty-seven projects retained in the sample, based on principal investigator responses, to rule out the possibility of bias due to non-representativeness of respondents.

In 1977, data were gathered by questionnaires and historical records from projects which were retained in the 1975 sample. Responses were received from sixty-one of the original sixty-seven projects, of which fifty-nine were usable, for an 88 per cent. usable response rate. Of the six non-respondents, the principal investigators of three projects were unable to respond in time, due to being out of the country; the three others chose not to respond for unknown reasons.

The 1977 sample of fifty-nine projects were initially examined for leader–member agreement on the importance of output goals based on their responses to the 1975 questionnaire. These responses were to questions based on Gross and Grambsch (1968) which asked the relative importance (great—some—little—no) to the following goal types: (1) develop a specific product that with respect to scientific rigour is absolutely top quality, (2) develop a specific service that with respect to scientific rigour is absolutely top quality, (3) carry on 'applied' research—seek to apply knowledge to a specific problem, and (4) develop a useful project or service. Forty-one projects (69 per cent.) in the 1977 sample were identified in which leaders and members agreed that these output goals were of great or some importance. It is on this sub-set of projects, in which leader–member agreement existed on output goals, that the subsequent analysis was performed. As the comparison of characteristics between the total 1975, total 1977, and 1977 agreement samples in Table 1 indicates, the

Table 1. Characteristics of 1977 and 1975 samples

Characteristics	1977 Number	1977 Percentage	1975 Number	1975 Percentage
Geographic dispersion				
West US	37	63	42	63
Mid-West US	15	25	17	25
South US	1	2	1	1
East US	5	8	6	9
Canada	1	2	1	1
	59	100	67	100
Public–private universities				
Public	49	83	54	81
Private	10	17	13	19
	59	100	67	100
Affiliation				
Centre/institute/laboratory	47	80	54	81
Independent of centre/institute/laboratory	12	20	13	19
	59	100	67	100
Subject area of research				
Biological science	21	36	26	39
Engineering	13	22	14	21
Physical science	8	14	9	13
Social science	17	29	18	27
	59	100	67	100

demographic differences are slight. List-wise deletion of missing values was used in the analyses to insure that the 1977 agreement sample and 1975 sample were matched for all computations.

The researchers represented over fifty separate disciplines and worked on projects which included research on electrical properties of bone, epilepsy, deep-sea drilling, arms control, urban transportation, mental retardation, pollution control, social indicators, and space exploration. Projects ranged in size from two to as many as seventy with the median size between five and six people and ranged in age from three to twenty-two years. Eighty-five per cent. of the projects were in the implementation or concluding stages of their research with 15 per cent. completing the project between 1975 and 1977. Of those completed, only three projects were unable to obtain continued funding when it was sought.

The projects in the sample drawn varied in their degree of interdisciplinary characteristics from a low of 50 per cent. to a high of 88 per cent. (Birnbaum, 1977, 1978). While the sampling procedures were intended to allow inferences to be drawn to the population of interdisciplinary projects, the lower characteristic groups drawn are probably not unlike many non-interdisciplinary research teams.

Independent variables

The following eight variables were measured in 1975 and were used as predictors of research performance in 1977: (1) horizontal differentiation; (2) vertical differentiation; (3) integration; (4) turnover or organizational stability; (5) leader–member relations or group atmosphere; (6) open discussion of disagreements; (7) prior scientific recognition; and (8) an in-process performance index.

1. *Horizontal differentiation* or division of labour was measured by counting the number of different functions performed within each group.
2. *Vertical differentiation* or the number of hierarchical levels was measured by the number of people involved in setting the project's policy.
3. *Integration* was measured consistent with Lawrence and Lorsch (1967) by asking team members whether the relationship between each position was (a) sound, with full unity of effort achieved, (b) almost full unity of effort, (c) somewhat better than average relations, (d) average, sound enough to get by even though there were many problems in achieving joint effort, (e) somewhat of a breakdown in relations, (f) almost a complete breakdown in relations, (g) such that it could not be worse—bad relations—with serious problems existing which could not be solved, and (h) where relations were not involved.
4. *Turnover* or organizational stability was measured as the ratio of the average number of personnel joining and leaving the project to the total group size per year.
5. *Leader–member relations* were measured by leader responses to the group atmosphere scale (Fiedler, 1967). This measure consisted of ten eight-point bipolar items: pleasant—unpleasant; friendly—unfriendly; bad—good; worthless—valuable; distant—close; cold—warm; quarrelsome—harmonious; self-assured—hesitant; efficient—inefficient; and gloomy—cheerful.
6. *Open discussion of disagreements* was measured by team members' disagreement to a six-point scaled statement that disagreements were never openly discussed.
7. *Prior scientific recognition* was measured as a factor score composed of the standardized average for each project of the number of books published, the number of articles published, the number of national committee memberships, and the number of professional organizational memberships.
8. *In-process performance index* was measured as a factor scale from three indicators of performance: self-evaluated effectiveness (Georgopoulos and Tannenbaum, 1955), goal achievement (Gross and Grambsch, 1968), and the group process measure devised by Mahoney and Weitzel (1969). The rationale and construction of the in-process performance index has been described previously (Birnbaum, 1978).

Dependent variables

The following criterion variables were measured in 1977 and were used as measures of long-term research performance: (1) research article quality (Durand, 1974); Jauch and Glueck, 1975); (2) the quantity of published articles (Cole and Cole, 1967, 1968; Cox and Catt, 1977; Drew and Karpf, 1975; Hagstrom, 1971; Henry and Burch, 1974; Jaurch and Glueck, 1975; Lightfield, 1971); (3) the quantity of books published (Glaser and Taylor, 1973); Lightfield, 1971; McClarrey and Edwards, 1973); (4) the quantity of technical reports (Chau, 1978; Farris, 1966; Glaser and Taylor, 1973; Pelz and Andrews, 1966; Shaw, 1967); (5) the quantity of presented papers (Chau, 1978; Glaser and Taylor, 1973; Jauch and Glueck, 1975); and (6) the quantity of patents (Blau, 1974; Chau, 1978; Farris, 196; Smith, 1971).

Research article quality was measured through the use of average project influence weight per year assigned to the journals in which project articles published through 1977 appeared. These influence weights were developed as size-independent measures of the weighted number of citations a journal receives from other journals, normalized by the number of references the journal gives to other journals (Narin, 1976). The mean of the average influence weight per author for each group was 0.60 with a standard deviation of 0.32, indicating an influence within science for cross-disciplinary research approximately equal to that of clinical medicine (0.59), greater than biology (0.47), and considerably less than physics (2.10) or mathematics (2.97).

The quantity per year of articles, books, technical reports, papers, and patents were linearized by logarithmic transformations. Data on these variables were obtained through 1977 from averaging questionnaire responses substantiated, where possible, from documents such as team member résumés, project bibliographies, and copies of articles. The median for the number of published articles in each group per year was 3.08. The median for the number of published books, technical reports, papers, and patents in each group per year was less than one.

Methodology

An analysis was conducted which used step-wise multiple regression procedures to determine the optimum set of predictor variables for each of the six criterion variables consistent with the regression assumptions. Appropriate transformations were performed on variables identified as non-linear and only predictor variables which correlated higher with the criterion variable than with each other were entered into the regression to reduce the likelihood of multicollinearity.

Results

Results of the multiple regression analysis are presented in Table 2. The intercorrelation matrix, means, and standard deviations are presented in

Table 2. Beta weights and multiple correlation coefficients for each criterion variable ($N = 45$)

	Quality of articles (Y_1)	Log of quantity of articles (Y_2)	Log of quantity of books (Y_3)	Log of quantity of technical reports (Y_4)	Log of quantity of published papers (Y_5)	Log of quantity of patents (Y_6)
Horizontal differentiation (X_1)	0.48#	0.28#		−0.49#		
Vertical differentiation (X_2)				0.65#		
Integration (X_3)	−0.46#	−0.58#				
Turnover (X_4)						0.38#
Leader–member relations (X_5)			0.56#			
Open discussion of disagreements (X_6)				0.27#		−0.26*
Scientific recognition (X_7)						0.28#
In-process performance index (X_8)		0.24*		0.21#	0.20	−0.32#
R_2	0.57	0.73	0.56	0.91	0.20	0.64
R	0.32	0.53	0.31	0.83	0.04	0.41

$Y_1 = -0.36 \;\; -0.60\ (X_4) \;\; +0.51\ (X_1)$
$ (0.15) (0.17) (0.14)$

$Y_2 = -0.12 \;\; +0.26\ (X_8) \;\; +0.24\ (X_3) \;\; -0.53\ (X_3)$
$ (0.11) (0.12) (0.10) (0.11)$

$Y_3 = -0.34 \;\; +0.17\ (X_5)$
$ (0.03) (0.04)$

$Y_4 = -0.24 \;\; -0.97\ (X_1) \;\; +0.10\ (X_2) \;\; +0.39\ (X_8)$
$ (0.01) (0.01) (0.02) (0.04)$

$Y_5 = -0.46 \;\; +0.56\ (X_8)$
$ (0.04) (0.04)$

$Y_6 = -0.18 \;\; -0.34\ (X_6) \;\; +0.23\ (X_7) \;\; -0.46\ (X_8) \;\; +0.51\ (X_4)$
$ (0.17) (0.16) (0.10) (0.17) (0.17)$

* $p < 0.05$; # $p < 0.001$ F-test; ( ): Standard error of B

Table 3. Intercorrelation matrix, means, and standard deviation ($N = 45$)

	Y_1	Y_2	Y_3	Y_4	Y_5	Y_6	X_1	X_2	X_3	X_4	X_5	X_6	X_7	X_8
Article quality (Y_1)	1.00													
Article quantity (Y_2)	-0.02	1.00												
Book quantity (Y_3)	0.21	0.09	1.00											
Technical report quantity (Y_4)	-0.31	-0.38	0.08	1.00										
Paper quantity (Y_5)	-0.13	0.17	-0.02	0.05	1.00									
Patent quantity (Y_6)	0.03	0.01	0.05	-0.06	0.01	1.00								
Horizontal differentiation (X_1)	0.36	0.47	0.04	-0.72	0.13	0.21	1.00							
Vertical differentiation (X_2)	-0.24	-0.31	0.10	0.59	0.01	0.38	0.22	1.00						
Integration (X_3)	0.01	-0.62	0.32	0.23	-0.05	-0.26	-0.32	0.09	1.00					
Turnover (X_4)	-0.33	0.21	0.15	-0.01	0.15	0.39	0.26	0.45	-0.16	1.00				
Leader–member relations (X_5)	-0.05	-0.12	0.56	-0.15	-0.12	0.08	0.19	0.04	0.30	0.07	1.00			
Open discussion (X_6)	0.05	0.03	-0.03	0.20	0.10	-0.30	-0.15	-0.24	0.03	0.01	-0.21	1.00		
Scientific recognition (X_7)	0.21	0.21	0.08	-0.34	0.07	0.33	0.37	-0.06	-0.15	0.14	0.18	-0.03	1.00	
In-process performance (X_8)	-0.14	0.15	0.17	0.13	0.20	-0.28	0.04	-0.09	0.17	0.10	0.39	0.08	0.09	1.00
Mean	-0.04	-0.01	-0.36	-0.29	-0.43	-0.08	0.38	-0.36	0.18	-0.20	-0.14	0.24	0.53	0.43
Standard deviation	1.03	0.82	0.22	0.15	0.21	1.06	0.96	0.68	0.89	0.78	0.75	0.81	1.28	0.75

Table 3. The results in Table 2 indicate that two variables, horizontal differentiation and turnover, yielded significant regression weights for predicting the quality of research articles without being more highly correlated with each other than with the dependent variable. This optimum regression equation yielded a multiple correlation coefficient (R) of 0.57 which accounted for about 32 per cent. of the variance in the quality of articles.

Three variables, integration, horizontal differentiation, and the in-process performance index, yielded significant regression weights for predicting the log of the quantity of published research articles. These three variables were not as highly correlated with each other as they were with the dependent variable. As Table 2 indicates, the multiple correlation coefficient (R) was 0.73, which accounted for about 53 per cent. of the variance in the dependent variable.

The log of the quantity of books published was predicted by self-evaluated leader–members relations, as Table 2 indicates. This variable yields a significant regression weight and accounted for more variance than any combination of predictor variables that were less highly correlated with each other than with the dependent variable. The correlation coefficient (R) was 0.56, which accounted for about 31 per cent. of the variance in the dependent variable.

The results in Table 2 indicate that four variables, vertical differentiation, horizontal differentiation, open discussions of disagreements, and the in-process performance index, yielded significant regression weights for predicting the log of the quantity of technical reports without being more highly correlated with each other than the dependent variable. The regression equation yielded a multiple correlation coefficient (R) of 0.91 which accounted for 83 per cent. of the variance in the dependent variable.

One variable, the in-process performance index, accounted for more variance than any combination of predictor variables that were less highly correlated with each other than with the dependent variable for predicting the log of published papers. However, the correlation of 0.20 between the in-process index and the log of published papers is, as Table 2 indicates, not significant and explains only about 4 per cent. of the variance.

The results in Table 3 indicate that four variables, turnover, the in-process performance index, prior scientific recognition, and open discussion of disagreements, yielded significant regression weights for predicting the log of the quantity of patents. The regression equation yielded a multiple correlation coefficient (R) of 0.64 which accounted for about 41 per cent. of the variance in the dependent variable.

Conclusions

The present findings are consistent with previous research on the positive relationships between scientific recognition and leader–member relations and scientific production. However, the relationships between differentiation, the open discussion of disagreements, or turnover indicate that for some products the relationship is positive while for others it is negative. Thus, these results indicate that scientific activities tend to be product-specific. Clearly defined division of labour (horizontal differentiation) facilitates article quality and quantity. A loosely defined horizontal division of labour and participation by many people in decisions facilitates technical report production. Thus, attempting to achieve the tight integration of activities, usually associated with interdisciplinary research, is negatively related to article production. Turnover acts both to decrease article quality and improve patent activity. Good leader–member relations facilitates book production and inhibits patent activity. Previous scientific recognition facilitates patent activity. Members' perceptions of their intermediate performance is a significant predictor of article quantity, technical report quantity, and, inversely, patent activity. These data, however, do not allow for accurate paper prediction. Thus, research managers who sail blindly ahead on the assumption that clearly defined tasks, integrated effort, reduced turnover, open discussions of disagreements, and self-evaluations of successful performance are universally desirable are likely to experience problems. The appropriateness of various structures and processes depend upon the outputs desired.

Research managers concerned with production of articles and books are generally advised to clearly define the division of labour, to try not to achieve too tightly integrated efforts, to reduce turnover, to maintain good leader–member relations, and to take actions that improve the members' perceptions of performance. Managers of research projects primarily concerned with technical reports are advised not to clearly define the division of labour, to encourage participation by many people in decision-making, to encourage open discussion of disagreements, and to take actions to improve the members' perceptions of performance. If patent activities are the desired output of research team activity, research managers are advised to select personnel with prior scientific recognition, to try not to encourage open discussion of disagreements, to not take action to improve members' perception of research team performance, and to try not to reduce turnover.

In this study we have tried to refine the choice of intermediate performance criteria useful to research managers in achieving alternative long-term outcomes. These data clearly indicate that the sophisticated manager is well advised to determine the desired research output(s) prior to selecting appropriate structures and processes. The structure and processes appropriate to one outcome may be inappropriate and even counterproductive to another. These data were developed from a sample of academic research teams at the leading American research universities and the results, therefore, may only be appropriate to a similar population. The emphasis on research outputs in the form of articles, books, and papers tends to be high at such institutions, and the research tradition tends to be in favour of independent and only loosely coupled efforts. It is hoped that further study in a variety of research settings will provide additional insights into the appropriateness of these findings for other organizations.

References

Birnbaum, P. H. (November 1977). 'Assessment of alternative management forms in academic interdisciplinary research projects', *Management Science*, **24** (3), 272–284.

Birnbaum, P. H. (Spring 1978). 'Academic contexts of interdisciplinary research', *Educational Admin. Quart.*, **14** (2), 80–97.

Birnbaum, P. H. (June 1980). 'Research on research effectiveness: where do we stand in 1980?', Paper presented at the Manchester Business School Conference, *Industrial R & D Strategy and Management — A Challenge for the 1980s*, Manchester, England.

Blau, P. M. (1974). *On the Nature of Organization*, Wiley, New York.

Chau, J. L. (April 1978). 'Organizational consensus regarding the relative importance of research output indicators', *The Accounting Review*, **LIII**(2), 309–323.

Cole, S., and Cole, J. R. (June 1967). 'Scientific output and recognition', *American Sociological Review*, **32** (3), 377–390.

Cole, S., and Cole, J. R. (June 1968). 'Scientific visibility and the structural bases of awareness of scientific research', *American Sociological Review*, **33** (3), 397–413.

Cox, W. Miles, and Catt, V. (October 1977). 'Productivity ratings of graduate programs in psychology based on publication in the *Journal of the American Psychological Association*', *American Psychologist*, **32** (10), 293–813.

Drew, D. E., and Karpf, R. S. (October 1975). *Evaluating Science Departments: A New Index*, Paper Series, Rand Corp.

Durand, D. E. (September 1974). 'Citation count analysis of behavioral science journals in influential management literature', *Academy of Management Journal*, **17** (3), 598–683.

Farris, G. F. (1966). 'A causal analysis of scientific performance', *Twentieth Conference on Administration of Research*, October 26–28, pp.26–32.

Fiedler, F. E. (1967). *A Theory of Leadership Effectiveness*, McGraw-Hill, New York.

Georgopoulos, B. S. and Tannenbaum, A. S. (October 1955) 'A Study of Organizational Effectiveness', *American Sociological Review*, Vol. 22, No. 5, 534–540.

Glaser, E. M., and Taylor, S. H. (February 1973). 'Factors influencing the success of applied research', *American Psychologist*, **28** (2), 140–146.

Gross, E., and Grambsch, P. V. (1968). *University Goals and Academic Power*, American Council on Education, Washington, DC.

Hagstrom, W. O. (1965). *The Scientific Community*, Basic Books, New York.

Hagstrom, W. O. (Fall, 1971). 'Inputs, outputs, and the prestige of university science departments', *Sociology of Education*, **44** (2), 374–397.

Hattery, L. H. (1979). 'Interdisciplinary research management: research needs and opportunities', in *Interdisciplinary Research Groups: Their Management and Organization* (Eds R. T. Barth and R. Steck), Vancouver, BC.

Henry, W. R., and Burch, E. E. (January, 1974). 'Institutional contributions to scholarly journals of business', *The Journal of Business*, **47** (1), 56–66.

Jauch, L., and Glueck, W. F. (September 1975). 'Evaluation of university professors' research performance', *Management Science*, **22** (2), 66–75.

Lawrence, P. R., and Lorsch, J. W. (June 1967). 'Differentiation and integration in complex organizations', *Admin. Sc. Quart.*, **12** (1), 1–47.

Lightfield, T. E. (May 1971). 'Output and recognition of sociologists', *American Sociologist*, **6** (2), 128–133.

McClarrey, M. W., and Edwards, W. A. (June 1973). 'Organizational climate conditions for effective research scientists' role performance', *Organizational Behavior and Human Performance*, **9** (3), 439–459.

Mahoney, T. A., and Weitzel, W. (September 1969). 'Managerial models of organizational effectiveness', *Admin. Sc. Quart.*, **14** (3), 357–365.

Meltzer, L., and Salter, J. (June 1962). 'Organizational structure and the performance and job satisfaction of physiologists', *American Sociological Review*, **27**, 351–362.

Moravcsik, M. J. (1977). 'A progress report on the quantification of science', *Journal of Scientific and Industrial Research*, **36**, 195.
Narin, F. (1976). Evaluative Bibliometrics: The Use of Publication and Citation Analysis in the Evaluation of Scientific Activity, Final Report NSF Contract C627, March 31, PB-252-339.
Nilles, J. (1975). 'Interdisciplinary research management in the university environment, *Journal of the Society of Research Administrators*, **6**, 9-15.
Palmer, A. M. (Ed.) (1972). *Research Centers Directory*, 4th ed., Gale Research Company, Detroit, Michigan.
Pelz, D. C. (1956). 'Some social factors related to performance in research organizations', *Admin. Sc. Quart.*, **1**, 310-325.
Pelz, D. C., and Andrews, F. M. (1966). *Scientists in Organizations; Productive Climates in R & D*, Wiley, New York.
Potchen, E. J., Rashford, N., Harris, G. I., Schoenbein, W., Sontag, B., Lazen, A., and Auld, R. M. (1976). *The Management of Large Scale Interdisciplinary Activities in Medicine*, Final Report NSF Grant NM 44353, 109, PB 262 205.
Price, J. L. (1977). *The Study of Turnover*, The Iowa State University Press, Ames, Iowa.
Rossini, F. A., Porter, A. L., Kelly, P., and Chubin, D. E. (1979). 'On the integration of the disciplinary components of interdisciplinary research', in *Interdisciplinary Research Groups: Their Management and Organizations* (Eds R. J. Barth and R. Steck), IRGIP, Vancouver, BC.
Shaw, B. T. (January 1967). *The Use of Quality and Quantity of Publication As Criteria for Evaluating Scientists*, Miscellaneous Publication No. 1041, USDA, Washington, DC.
Smith, C. G. (1971). 'Scientific performance and the composition of research teams', *Admin. Sc. Quart.*, **16**(4), 486-495.
Wells, W. P., and Pelz, D. C. (1966). 'Groups', in *Scientists in Organizations* (Eds D. C. Pelz and F. Andrews), Wiley, New York.
Ziller, R. C., Behringer, R. D., and Goodchilds, J. D. (1972). 'Group creativity under conditions of success or failure and variation in group stability', *Journal of Applied Psychology*, **42**, 43-49.

NOISE CONTROL R & D IN THE UNITED KINGDOM
J. BUTLER
R & D Research Unit, Manchester Business School, Manchester, England

This paper makes the case that research into noise reduction must be interdisciplinary to be effective. The implementation of such research requires some form of institutional support at present lacking in the United Kingdom and an appeal is made for the setting up of a Noise Technology Support Unit to conduct the necessary strategic studies.

Noise, by definition, is sound of unpleasant quality and excessive intensity. It is both a nuisance and a health hazard. Traffic noise, for example, is a nuisance; occupational noise is often a health hazard. Most noise is technological in origin and needs technical or technological change to reduce its impact if the duration of exposure is not limited. What is regarded as an acceptable level of noise must be determined by considering social, economic, psychological, and physiological factors (the latter based on the results of extensive fundamental research); what can be achieved in practice depends on managerial, economic, ergonomic, and technological possibilities. Legal and industrial relation concerns may impose additional constraints. In short, an adequate understanding of noise generation and its effects requires interdisciplinary research. The ability to modify noise sources or design and develop quieter products and processes is also interdisciplinary.

The following considerations illustrate further this need for collaboration between disciplines. Noise levels (as distinct from sound intensity levels) have to be measured in ways that recognize that the human ear imposes a bias on the perceived level of sound and the instrumentation used must allow for this bias, as must also the interpretation of the results of the measurement. Furthermore, integrating procedures must be included to take into account varying exposure during the working day. How this is to be done is still an open question for we still do not know how much extra weighting, if any, should be given to short-duration, high-intensity as distinct from continuous, moderate-intensity noise.

Secondly, noise not only impairs hearing, which has been its most thoroughly researched effect (and its most serious), but it can also affect sleep patterns, have secondary nervous and psychological impacts, and at certain levels and frequencies can damage body tissue and organs. Research is under way in some institution on the effects of noise on the unborn child. 'Whitefinger' is a well-known symptom of the associated phenomenon of vibration. Noise may also affect concentration and hence productivity at work, especially in intense situations such as in aircraft control towers or when piloting an aircraft, and may also prevent the communication of a warning signal to individuals in a hazardous environment. Vibratory 'paging' systems are one commercial development that acknowledges this aspect of industrial noise, and it is interesting to note that a major contribution to the noise levels experienced by pilots is their radio headphone.

Noise is also a comfort or 'quality' factor in office equipment and consumer goods, especially domestic appliances, motor cars, typewriters, and teleprinters, but it has not yet widely reached this status in industrial goods. A few products (e.g. bearings, hydraulic pumps, chains, electric motors) are sometimes advertised as quieter models but this probably reflects on the specifications of the products into which the components will be assembled, and is not fully a quality determinant of the component itself. Other industrial goods that stress reduced noise levels are sometimes marked as 'quieter' in anticipation of occupational noise legislation or because reduced noise levels have been achieved incidentally. The ability to obtain noise-level reduction incidentally is another interdisciplinary aspect that will be expanded later.

Noise Control Technology

Even if the contribution of physiology and behavioural sciences are ignored there is a need for collaboration among the engineering sub-disciplines. To some extent, existing or 'textbook' knowledge can be used to solve a particular problem; sometimes only informed commonsense is required. However, these are exceptional cases and for the more difficult problems usually encountered a combination of knowledge of different engineering technologies is essential.

Even noise reduction by acoustic enclosure rather than 'at source' can be an interdisciplinary problem, since heating and ventilation, maintenance accessibility, and mechanical guarding can be involved. Research and development to improve enclosure design or absorption materials for enclosures requires collaboration between acoustic engineers and materials scientists.

Several projects have depended upon collaboration between organizations (e.g. the Drop Forging Research Association and two universities; the National Engineering Laboratory and the British Hydromechanics RA; Sound Research Laboratories and Wadkins Ltd; manufacturers of diesel engines, commercial vehicles, forklift trucks, fuel-injector pumps, etc.), some of which have been more successful than others. The more exciting developments described below involve a mix of technologies as well as organizations.

1. 'Anti-noise' is at the demonstration project stage in the United Kingdom, e.g. on a British Gas turbine exhaust stack. Development work has proceeded at Cambridge, Essex, and London Universities. Mathematics, electronics, and acoustics knowledge have been combined. At the first two universities a company, Topexpress, and a university–industry collaboration unit are involved.
2. Laser diagnostics techniques are under development in a number of application areas including car panel vibrations, e.g. at the Department of Automobile Engineering, Cranfield Institute of Technology.
3. In the heavy metal-working industries automation, remote sensing, remote manipulation of the workpiece or process equipment, and eventually robots, are desirable for several reasons, including thermal stress, noise, and mechanical efficiency. Recruitment difficulties in the industry have been as important as noise legislation expectations. In the steel industry some projects have been supported by the ECSC (e.g. the noise levels of electric-arc furnaces). In the forging industry the most immediate noise-reducing benefits derive from work on stillages and other mechanical handling devices, while longer term research has focused on computer modelling of forge and hammer structure vibrations.
4. The application of microprocessor speed-control to canning-line layouts increases and flexibility and efficiency of the line via debottlenecking and increased throughout as well as reducing noise levels below that regarded as hazardous. In addition, the improved reliability of such layouts facilitates the operation of the line from an acoustically isolated workstation or cabin,

using closed-circuit television. Elsewhere plastics have been used extensively on conveyor systems, and retrofit surrounds have been fitted. Many packaging innovations, especially plastic containers, have an obvious impact on the noise levels of packaging machinery, but the use of such innovations has been largely determined by unit price, throughput, aesthetics and marketing, sterilization procedures, etc. In the food industry noise problems often translate into hygiene problems; hygienic surfaces such as ceramic tiles and stainless steel are highly reverberant.

5. Some new manufacturing methods are inherently quieter than the processes they could replace. Sintered components can replace various forgings, castings, and machine processes. Adhesive bonding not only can replace certain noisy fabrication stages but can also result in a product that is itself quieter in operation. This has been demonstrated on machine-tool structure prototypes at Birmingham University. Microelectronics avoid the noisy manufacture of electromechanical components (e.g. the high-speed stamping of conventional watch mechanisms can be eliminated). Generally, technical progress has been towards higher speeds, higher capacity, and more volume throughout, and hence increased noise levels, albeit perhaps experienced by fewer and fewer workers. In texturizing processes several noise-reducing innovations have been effectively cancelled out by further speed increases. Investment casting (an ancient process) is a quieter form of foundry practice that also eliminates the need for some machining operations because of its precision, but has not been encouraged by noise considerations. Neither has the relatively recent V-process, or vacuum moulding. Welding as a replacement for rivetting is an exception to this trend but unfortunately the fumes produced by this process are possibly hazardous.

6. A particular design of pneumatic road-breaker, the Compair Zitec 20 (in 1981 a Design Council Award winner), demonstrates that noise levels can be reduced significantly at no extra cost, combined with good value engineering, manufacturing process efficiency, improved marketability, and lighter weight, resulting in less operator fatigue. The previous design was over thirty years old.

7. The Union Carbide Linde plasma-arc cutting process for steel plate was submerged under water to reduce glare, noise, and improve technical performance. Specialized acoustics knowledge was not an essential part of the development project.

8. Current research at the Department of Acoustics, University of Salford, into noise levels around quarries relies strongly on interaction with meteorological authorities since weather conditions have a significant, but poorly understood, effect upon noise 'contours'.

Progress in Noise Control and Noise Control Technology

The above examples illustrate what is possible in noise control R & D. Unfortunately the effort applied overall is far from adequate if the number of dangerously noisy work environments is to be significantly reduced. A major problem is that R & D is not often enough brought into the discussion between employers' and employees' representatives at national or firm level and the need to legislate at a high level of aggregation across industry sectors prevents many opportunities for noise reduction within sectors from being developed. Most importantly, it is not known to what extent either new solutions or cheaper solutions to noise problems can be found if an appropriate R & D effort were applied in certain areas. (No reliable quantified estimates appear to exist.) It is only known that many diverse problems exist and that there is a spectrum of problem difficulties.

The investigation of potential solutions is an interdisciplinary task, for which no one in the United Kingdom currently has responsibility. As far as the author is aware there is no organization in the world that fully assumes such responsibility. The Environmental Protection Agency in the United States approaches the task but still results in relatively superficial treatment.

It is believed that a continual scanning and monitoring of innovations and design trends is needed, cross-fertilization of ideas should be encouraged, and priorities should be established for R & D programmes based on factors such as the number of employees exposed to the noise problem, the likelihood of effective solution, technological obsolescence, industry obsolescence, etc. This scanning and monitoring should be related to the incentives (voluntary and compulsory) and constraints (organizational and technical) on different types of organization.

In addition to the anticipation of legislation, noise-reducing activities may be begun for a number of reasons, such as the installation of quieter new machinery because of operator objections to older machinery, an opportunity to combine noise control measures with expansion or reequipment programmes, loss of hearing compensation claims in an industry, or the cost of insurance premiums. Depending upon the structure of the industry noise reduction may be the responsibility of either the user or the manufacturer of equipment or both, but which is not always clear.

Firms can respond to noise problems in a number of ways that do not involve R & D. In fact this is probably the most likely situation. It is partly because curative rather than preventative treatments exist that R & D has been neglected, even though the use of personal ear defenders is a very poor substitute and machinery enclosure can be costly to maintain. Firms in the noise control equipment industry do not carry out adequate R & D; consultants that become involved in 'at source' solutions could be more active in collaborative R & D, devizing new solutions as well as applying known ones. Government support would probably be required unless the client company had a large number of installations with similar noise problems.

A few large firms now specify maximum noise levels in equipment purchasing specifications but the practice is not sufficiently widespread and does not readily induce a change of technology, apart from incremental modifications, even if alternative technologies are commercially available. Only a very few Health and

Safety Inspectors are noise specialists and few can have been machinery designers; they are unlikely therefore to understand the extent to which improvements in noise level can be brought about by such methods and guidance from their National Industry Group is limited. The full potential role of Section 6 of the UK Health and Safety at Work Act (that referring to research and development) is not exploited.

The Noise Technology Support Unit

The need for a Noise Technology Support Unit (NTSU) was identified during a study by the author of recent developments in noise control R & D. This study was supported by the Social Science Research Council and an attempt was made to relate any developments that were found to the social, legal, and economic influences that exist. In particular, noise legislation in the United Kingdom was expected to be formalized in 1980 (still not implemented in 1982) and it was thought that the amount of R & D and the rate of innovation before and after the formalization could be compared. Many questions about the patterns of R & D and interactions between industry sectors, institutions, and the legal and union forces had been prepared for the study, in order to examine the technical change processes as much as progress in noise control compliance, but it was not possible to make any practical recommendations on the latter except to suggest the formation of the NTSU or, alternatively, smaller studies aimed at similar but less ambitious and comprehensive objectives.

The idea for the NTSU came by way of analogy with the Energy Technology Support Unit, Harwell, England. This prepares reports on all forms of energy production and utilization and initiates and manages R & D projects. It also has an effort on energy conservation. Opportunities for energy conservation exist in a wide range of industries and situations, in a similar way to the opportunities for noise reduction, and can be incidental to efficiency and design improvements and materials conservation (e.g. the Pintie milk bottle). High noise levels are indicative of some mechanical inefficiency, although the actual energy needed to produce sound is relatively low. There is a need for more R & D and for more university–industry collaboration in energy conservation, just as in noise reduction. Further still: distinctions can be drawn between energy conservation 'at source' and by insulation; there is no one institution that has responsibility for energy conservation, since it transcends technology areas; and energy conservation opportunities like noise control problems can be identified and ranked by a 'top-down' strategy as well as by monitoring 'bottom-up' initiatives. Some of the Department of Energy Papers prepared by the ETSU indicate the size of potential energy savings in each sector that have been estimated by energy usage patterns and energy audits (top-down strategy); incentives for bottom-up initiatives are strong because of the cost of energy, but there is still need for coordination and catalysis in the initiation of ideas. The position of 'coordinator' was created within the UK Science and Engineering

Research Council (SERC) organization specifically for this task and was filled by an ETSU member.

Neither top-down strategy preparation nor monitoring of bottom-up initiatives are yet undertaken for noise reduction. The organizations involved in the overall situation (i.e. the Health and Safety Executive, Trades Union Council, Confederation of British Industry) do not have the resources and do not recognize the R & D issues explicitly. The organizations involved in R & D (i.e. research associations, universities, consultancies, acoustics enclosure manufacturers) do not have a perspective beyond their own industry or particular field, and therefore do not look systematically at the mechanisms facilitating technology transfer between sectors, or between universities and industry, or between ideas for solutions and implementation of solutions.

Until the legislation is formalized there will be insufficient incentive for companies to reduce noise levels and much less incentive to indulge in noise control and R & D. Despite the philosophy of self-regulation implicit in the UK Health and Safety at Work Act there will still be value in monitoring initiatives and fostering them wherever appropriate after the regulations have been introduced.

Summary

Noise effects research and noise control R & D are interdisciplinary in several ways: medical and instrumentation expertise need to be combined; product design engineering and acoustics skills need to be combined; social, economic, and legal factors impinge on the incentives and constraints for noise reduction; industry life-cycles and technology trends can have incidental influences for or against noise levels, and the implications of such changes need to be assessed and integrated with R & D aimed explicitly at noise reduction.

There is a need for greater coordination of effort, and for a strategy indicating where progress is most likely and would be most beneficial. Research and development could be considered more explicitly in cost–benefit equations associated with the implementation of legislation if such a strategy were prepared.

A Noise Technology Support Unit, or perhaps staff attached to a university noise control department, should be established to prepare such strategies and to monitor progress. This would facilitate interaction between universities, industry, and consultants, and between the Health and Safety Executive, the Trade Unions, and the Confederation of British Industry, specifically on the availability of technology. It would encourage the cross-fertilization of ideas and, because of the nature of noise control problems, probably increase the level of interdisciplinary R & D aimed at solutions. In the same way that the formation of teams for pollution control and health and safety legislation has had spin-off benefits for the company, there may be similar benefits from 'noise' teams in particular.

Acknowledgements

The SSRC funded a study of the factors influencing the reduction of industrial noise by R & D and design. Mr Alan Pearson recognized that the findings of this study were relevant to the theme of this Conference.

INDICATORS OF INTERDISCIPLINARY RESEARCH: A BLUEPRINT FOR ANALYSIS

D. E. CHUBIN, A. L. PORTER, T. CONNOLLY, and F. A. ROSSINI
Georgia Institute of Technology, Georgia, USA

Abstract

The authors present the plan of a project they are about to start with the aim of providing indicators for interdisciplinarity and strategies for their construction. In the paper they begin by attempting a clarification of the nomenclature used in the literature. They then propose a research strategy, building on existing databases and an earlier project of theirs in the field. The strategy consists in measuring product, process, and usage contained in interdisciplinary articles and reports. Finally, they outline a procedure for constructing indices of interdisciplinarity based on research area, institution, journals, and the kinds of authors who collaborate.

They aim by this means to answer many questions of interest in the assessment of interdisciplinary research, such as whether there is a tendency for some disciplines rather than others to feed their results to interdisciplinary audiences and whether interdisciplinary combinations reflect intellectual curiosity, problem urgency, pressure from sponsors, or the wishes of the employing organization.

THE TENDENCY OF FIELDS OF SCIENCE TO FORM INTERDISCIPLINARY RELATIONSHIPS

G. DARVAS and A. HARASZTHY
Hungarian Academy of Sciences, Budapest, Hungary

Introduction

The paper we presented at the First Conference (at Schloss Reisensburg, 1979) reported our work to relate the performance of research groups to their degree of interdisciplinarity. We used the data produced by the UNESCO study (Andrews, 1979) into the characteristics and performance of research groups in six European countries. We found that the measure of scientific reputation in the group and of its productivity in terms of publications correlated with its degree of interdisciplinarity.

Haraszthy established this relationship and drew the conclusion that interdisciplinarity may be a causal factor with respect to effectiveness. We have gone more deeply into the question of how to bring about the necessary collaboration in particular situations. We have started with the study of a particular factor, the identification of which fields of science are most inclined to form interdisciplinary relationships or conglomerations. The results of our study constitute the main content of this paper.

An answer to this question may play an important role in organizing future interdisciplinary research groups. For example, if the current existence of these conglomerations reflects spontaneous trends on the past development of science, the potential affinities of certain disciplines should be recognized when new interdisciplinary programmes are being organized.

Data Base

For our research we needed a set of data providing information on a great number of research groups by which disciplines or fields of science their activities could be characterized. For this purpose we carried out a secondary analysis relying on the questionnaires of the UNESCO programme (Andrews, 1979).

Secondary analysis had a great advantage to our study: in the original selection of the research teams to be surveyed the mono- or interdisciplinary character of their research activities had been disregarded. There was, therefore, a random access to interdisciplinary and non-interdisciplinary teams in the sample. Consequently, the sample was representative of the proportion of interdisciplinary research within all R & D activities. Naturally, this proportion differed with respect to various indices characterizing the degree of interdisciplinarity. (See our paper on these indices presented at the above-mentioned Conference; Barth and Steck, 1980.)

Our present study was based on the data describing the disciplinary character of the research activities of individual teams. In the original survey the heads of research teams were allowed to indicate up to six sub-disciplines characterizing—in their opinions—their activities. For specifying the sub-disciplines a standard nomenclature was used, made available by UNESCO. It guaranteed a unified terminology and we made use of it in coding and processing the data.

The structure of the nomenclature was such that insomuch as the team did not perform interdisciplinary research only the two last figures of the six-digit code numbers denoting their sub-disciplines differed; the first four figures of the codes were identical, indicating the same disciplines. If their research activities belonged to several varied disciplines but within the same field of science, the four last figures of the code numbers of the specified sub-disciplines differed from one another but their first two figures denoting the same field of science were identical.

Teams whose activity was characterized by sub-disciplines marked by code numbers differing in their first two figures were regarded as having the highest degree of interdisciplinarity, since their activity covered several fields of science.

The Method Used

The way of processing was as follows. We selected the data of the teams whose activities covered several fields of science. This could be easily achieved by computation, using the above-mentioned codes from among the responses to a given sheet of nil questionnaire (relating to a given team) in which the code numbers were examined to see whether they differed in their first two figures or not. To identify teams regarded as interdisciplinary one can rely above all on these.

Then the frequency matrix of the common occurrence of various fields of science was set up. The x_{ab} element of the matrix denoted the frequency of the common occurrence of *field a* and *field b* of science in the interdisciplinary activities of the individual teams. Naturally, most constituents of the matrix had a value of zero as not every field of science can be studied along with any other one within the framework of a piece of interdisciplinary research, but certain points of density can be shown even here.

However, the frequency matrix is inadequate for reaching any conclusion. It is highly dependent on the selection of the sample, since research teams in various fields of science were not proportionally represented in the sample. Moreover, representatives of some fields of science were completely absent. This latter shortage could not be overcome, our analysis being a secondary one. However, the former disproportion could be eliminated by a normalization. This resulted in losing the symmetry of the frequency matrix but additional information was gained, for in some cases we learned which field of science was approaching the other during their interlinking. The normalization was done by dividing each factor of the frequency matrix by the number of teams who denoted as their main field of activity the field specified in the given line of the matrix. The values obtained were less dependent on the absolute number of research units from the given field of science which had been included in the sample.

The Y_{ab} element obtained by this carries the information of how frequently the researches performed in *field a* of science are interlinked with those of *field b* of science, e.g. $Y_{ab} = 0.5$ indicates that interdisciplinary linkages may be established approximately in every second case. This is a very high value, the occurrence of which is very rare, but it is worth mentioning. If, simultaneously, Y_{ba} Y_{ab}, then researchers active in *field b* of science necessitate cooperation with their colleagues in *field a* more rarely than in the contrary.

Some fields of science were highly underrepresented in the survey as regards the number of research teams. Consequently, the information gained from them, especially concerning their interdisciplinary activities, is not reliable enough to use to reach conclusions. Therefore, we reduced the normalized frequency matrix of the common occurrence of the fields of science by omitting the columns and lines whose fields of science were represented by fewer than twelve research teams in the sample. The reduced, normalized frequency matrix obtained became a size of 11 × 11 compared to the one of 24 × 24 potentially available by the nomenclature used; this, in an overall, target-oriented survey, should have provided reliable information on all fields of science. Nevertheless, the block sized 11 × 11 indicates how significant interdisciplinary interconnections are among the fields which can be taken into consideration.

This method was used repeatedly not only for the various major fields of science but also the disciplines represented within them as well. However, the number of disciplines were so high (245) as compared with that of teams represented in the sample (1,222 research units from six countries) that their data were distributed over the whole of the matrix. The scarcity of data prevented us from producing results appropriate for reaching conclusions at the disciplinary level, but our experiment could be repeated in a survey with a wider data base, using the method described here. However, our investigations conducted in the same subject revealed that real interdisciplinary links should be identified not between narrow disciplines but broader fields of science. In the light of this our findings presented here can be regarded as satisfying.

Results

The results can be seen in the Y matrix presented in Table 1. It is obvious that, taking the reduction also into account, significant interdisciplinary links are concentrated in relatively few pairs of fields of science. Even within this boundary the distribution of values above 0.25 shows that there is a tendency on the part of the other sciences to establish interdisciplinary links *with* chemistry, life sciences, and engineering, i.e. the inclination for making contacts is not a special faculty of the field of science taking the initiative but rather density may be found in those fields towards which the others tend.

However, a more extensive study based on a wider scope of data should be conducted in the future in order to confirm our statements more precisely. Some other preliminary investigations were also made; we have compared the interdisciplinary fields of science in Hungary, Poland, and Finland. The method and results were demonstrated at the Fourth International Conference on Management of Research, Development, and Education in Wroclaw, 1980.

Table 1. The normalized distribution matrix Y of interconnection of research themes

Classification No.		Mathematics 12	Physics 22	Chemistry 23	Life sciences 24	Earth and space sciences 25	Agricultural sciences 31	Medical sciences 32	Technological sciences 33	Economic sciences 53	Juridical sciences and law 56	Sociology 63
12	Mathematics	1.00	0.33	0.25	0.19	0.16	0.11	0.09	0.40	0.05		
22	Physics	0.12	1.00	0.34	0.11	0.06	0.03	0.04	0.37	0.01		
23	Chemistry	0.05	0.19	1.00	0.25	0.05	0.11	0.17	0.27			
24	Life science	0.05	0.08	0.33	1.00	0.11	0.22	0.23	0.13			
25	Earth and space sciences	0.11	0.11	0.15	0.28	1.00	0.15	0.02	0.09	0.04		0.01
31	Agricultural sciences	0.04	0.03	0.19	0.31	0.08	1.00	0.06	0.21	0.01		
32	Medical sciences	0.04	0.06	0.43	0.45	0.01	0.08	1.00	0.23	0.04		0.01
33	Technological sciences	0.08	0.19	0.26	0.10	0.03	0.11	0.09	1.00	1.00	0.06	0.01
53	Economic sciences	0.08	0.02	0.04			0.18	0.02	0.31	0.20	1.00	0.08
56	Juridical sciences and law				0.07		0.06		0.07	0.17	0.13	0.20
63	Sociology				0.08		0.04	0.08	0.08			1.00

Table 2. Classification of fields of science used in the study

11.	Logic
12.	Mathematics
21.	Astronomy and Astrophysics
22.	Physics
23.	Chemistry
24.	Life sciences
25.	Earth and space sciences
31.	Agricultural sciences
32.	Medical sciences
33.	Technological sciences
51.	Anthropology
52.	Demography
53.	Economic sciences
54.	Geography
55.	History
56.	Juridical sciences and Law
57.	Linguistics
58.	Pedagogy
59.	Political science
61.	Psychology
62.	Science of Arts and Letters
63.	Sociology
71.	Ethics
72.	Philosophy

References

Andrews, F. M. (Ed.) (1979). Scientific Productivity. The Effectiveness of Research Groups in Six Countries, Cambridge University Press–UNESCO.
Barth, R. T., and Steck, R. (Eds) (1980). *Interdisciplinary Research Groups: Their Management and Organization*, IRGIP, Vancouver, BC.
Management of Research Development, and Education (1980). Wroclaw, p.229.
Mirski, E. M. (1980). *Mezhdisciplinarnie Issledovanija i Disciplinarnaja Organizacija Nauki*, Nauka, Moscow, p.303 Bibl., 339 items.

MANAGEMENT, PLANNING, AND ORGANIZATION IN INITIATING, SUPPORTING, AND COORDINATING AN ONGOING FRESHWATER DIVERSION PROJECT

D. J. Etzold
University of Southern Mississippi, USA

Introduction

In August 1973, a group in the seafood industry requested that the Mississippi Sea Grant Program and the University of Southern Mississippi assist them in solving some of their problems. One of the problems was the decline of seafood productivity, with one of the reasons for the decline being the lack of fresh water on a controlled basis into the several estuaries in the Mississippi and Louisiana areas. It was agreed by the group that this project was important enough to pursue and to seek possible ways and means of solving the problem.

Prior to the building of the levee system along the lower Mississippi River, periodic flooding would replenish the estuaries with fresh water. The fresh water carries nutrient salts that are utilized by marine life as a food source and deters salt water encroachment. The present levee system, while doing an excellent job for its intended purpose of preventing flooding, diverts the fresh water through the mouth of the Mississippi River and out into the Gulf of Mexico. This flow bypasses many of our marine estuaries.

Experience from fishery establishments on the Mississippi and Louisiana coasts, observations, and scientific studies indicate and support the conclusion that appropriate discharges of fresh water into estuarine areas, on a *controlled* basis, enhance fish and wildlife productivity. Fishery production, similar to land crops, is hindered by too much fresh water as well as the lack of it. Various projects have been undertaken to control flood waters and the adverse effects of droughts on land crops; however, very little effort has been expended to supply fresh water to our estuaries when needed.

A task-force was established by the group to explore ways and means of obtaining controlled fresh water into the estuaries east of the Mississippi River via the Bonnet Carré Spillway. Task leaders were established as Victor Mavar (Mavar Shrimp and Oyster Company, Biloxi) and David J. Etzold (Sea Grant Principal Investigator, University of Southern Mississippi).

It was determined that a study would need to be conducted to establish a document to be presented to Congress requesting that Congress direct the US Army Corps of Engineers in New Orleans to develop ways and means of solving the problem.

Methods

As a first step, a preliminary plan was made, which attempted to anticipate both the advantages and disadvantages of the proposed project. A listing was prepared of those who might be opposed to as well as those in favour of such an endeavour.

A summary of that planning session to assess the feasibility of the project included the need for the following factors to be considered and evaluated:

1. *Technical.* Will the course of action be a viable effort that does not approach or exceed the state of the art?
2. *Environmental.* Will the course of action change the environment in acceptable ways only, in both the short and long runs?
3. *Economic.* Will the course of action result in a benefit-to-cost ratio of 1.0 or greater? Have all costs, including social, been considered?

4. *Financial.* Will there be funds available to pay for implementing the course of action?
5. *Social.* Will those involved respond to the course of action in a manner commensurate with program goals and objectives?
6. *Political and legal.* Can the course of action acquire and maintain the political support required for successful implementation? Does it conform to applicable laws or must they be changed?

Before any 'best' alternative can be considered totally viable, efforts must be expended to determine the consequences of such action and summarized in a manner that decision-makers can use in selecting a best composite course of action for use in a specific situation for both short- and long-run implications. Thus, a total systems approach must be taken, which implies performing a complete effort involving much time by a number of people.

Using the above framework, some of the activities included the following:

1. Determine *what* needs to be done and *who* can best do it.
2. Set up a timetable of events so that progress (or lack of it) can be measured.
3. Be flexible in plans.
4. Solicit help from existing agencies that can contribute towards understanding and success of the project.

A summary of the level of detailed efforts expended in organizing and planning the initial stages of this project is outlined in a publication by Etzold and Williams (1974). Some of the efforts included a trip to New Orleans to discuss the project with the Executive Director of the Gulf States Marine Fisheries Commission and to solicit his guidance. All activities relative to the project were coordinated with the Mississippi Sea Grant Advisory Services. The project was discussed with the Mississippi Marine Conservation Commission and a meeting was held with the Executive Director of the Mississippi Marine Resources Council and his staff.

Discussions ensued with the National Marine Fisheries Service at Pascagoula, Mississippi, and discussions and guidance were obtained from members of the Gulf Coast Research Laboratory at Ocean Springs, Mississippi. Several discussions and visits were made to the New Orleans Army Corps of Engineers Planning Division, the Mississippi Director of the Office of Science and Technology in Jackson, and the NASA Earth Resources at the Mississippi Test Facility in Bay St Louis.

A presentation to the National Sea Grant site team in November 1973, at Biloxi, Mississippi, included this project, which was funded. Articles appeared in the Mississippi Gulf Coast newspapers a number of times and the project was discussed on WLOX-TV. The project was discussed with the Mayor and a City Commissioner of Biloxi, Mississippi. The Coastal Zone Management meeting at Baton Rouge was attended in February 1974 to discuss the project with Louisiana attendees.

A formal presentation was made to the Gulf States Marine Fisheries Commission Technical Coordinating Committee in New Orleans on March 20, 1974, to gain support for utilizing the Bonnet Carré Spillway as a freshwater source. In effect, the Technical Coordinating Committee would not endorse the project without a feasibility study being conducted first.

A meeting was next held in Vicksburg on April 10, 1974, with Major General Charles Noble, President of the Mississippi River Commission and Division Chief of the US Army Corps of Engineers, and members of his staff. General Noble expressed interest in the project and stated that he felt the best route to pursue would be a general feasibility study to determine *all* alternative potential sources for supplying supplemental fresh water on a controlled basis to enhance seafood productivity, sports fishing, and other wildlife activities in the estuarine areas. Upon our requests, General Noble assigned members of his staff to help in formulating a resolution for presentation to the appropriate legislative delegations for consideration and action.

As a result of comments from the Gulf States Marine Fisheries Commission Technical Coordinating Committee and General Noble, the approach was altered. Instead of focusing on utilizing the Bonnet Carré Spillway as *the* freshwater source, the plan was modified to request a general feasibility study to encourage all alternative source possibilities of freshwater diversion into the necessary estuaries.

The next step was to review a copy of House Document 308-88/2 (under the title of *Mississippi River and Tributaries Project*, in six volumes, 1964, US Army Corps of Engineers). This study supported the introduction of fresh water into estuaries to improve seafood productivity. However, it could not determined who should supply the necessary funds. Since that time, there has been a change in policy. Several other studies were reviewed for background information.

The Resolution written on our behalf by the Vicksburg Division of the US Army Corps of Engineers is reproduced in full:

> RESOLVED BY THE COMMITTEE ON PUBLIC WORKS OF THE U.S. SENATE (AND HOUSE) THAT THE CHIEF OF ENGINEERS OF THE U.S. ARMY BE, AND IS, HEREBY REQUESTED TO REVIEW THE REPORT ON THE MISSISSIPPI RIVER AND TRIBUTARIES, PUBLISHED AS HOUSE DOCUMENT 308, 88th CONGRESS, AND OTHER PERTINENT REPORTS, WITH A VIEW TO DETERMINING THE ADVISABILITY OF MODIFYING THE RECOMMENDATIONS CONTAINED THEREIN WITH PARTICULAR REFERENCE TO PROVIDING FRESH WATER INTO LAKES MAUREPAS, PONTCHARTRAIN, BORGNE, AND MISSISSIPPI SOUNDS AREAS IN THE INTEREST OF IMPROVING THE WILDLIFE AND FISHERIES RESOURCES OF THIS AREA.

With the receipt of this Resolution, the next planning efforts entailed the solicitation of widespread support for the project. The following endorsements were obtained during the next twelve months:

Mississippi Marine Conservation Commission	May 1974
Louisiana Oyster Dealers and Growers Association	August 1974
American Shrimp Canners Association	September 1974
Mississippi Marine Resources Council	September 1974
Gulf States Marine Fisheries Commission	October 1974
New Orleans Sportsmen's League Directors	November 1974
Gulf Coast Research Laboratory	February 1975
Louisiana Wildlife Federation, Inc.	March 1975
Louisiana Outdoor Writers Association	March 1975
Louisiana Wildlife Biologists Association	March 1975
Louisiana Wildlife and Fisheries Commission	March 1975
Mississippi Game and Fish Commission	April 1975

With the above endorsements supporting the project, it was determined that sufficient support on a broad basis had been established and the next step was taken. A document was put together for presentation to the US Army Corps of Engineers and appropriate members of Congress (House and Senate). The document (unpublished) was an industry request for the US Army Corps of Engineers to conduct a feasibility study with a view to determining potential sources of fresh water to Mississippi and Louisiana estuaries and their controlled diversion to these estuaries to enhance fish and wildlife production. The contents of this document included:

I. Conclusions and purpose
II. List of previous endorsements
III. Resolution draft written by the US Army Corps of Engineers
IV. Appendices
   A. Resolutions
   B. Participants to contact
   C. Extracts from previous studies

Through the efforts of many, a meeting was set up on March 4, 1976, in the Forrestal Building in Washington, DC, for presenting our request to the Chief of the US Army Corps of Engineers, Lieutenant General William C. Gribble, members of his staff, and the Mississippi, Louisiana, Alabama, and Texas representations of Congress. Our task-force included nine people, with Mississippi, Louisiana, and Alabama personnel in marine fisheries biology as well as seafood industry personnel. It is felt that the strong showing of interest plus a well-researched and documented plan greatly enhanced acceptance of our request.

The agenda presentation was as follows:

I. Introductory comments
II. Brief history of committee actions
III. Overview of supporting documents

IV. Biological and technical aspects of controlled freshwater flow
V. Questions and discussion

We were commended for our depth of preparation during the past two years and the documentation submitted for review and consideration. The outgrowth of the presentation was that Lieutenant General Gribble and his staff reviewed the Resolution to insure adequacy of its contents. The draft was then turned over to the appropriate members of Congress to be submitted to the Committee on Public Works of the US Senate and House. Our task-force agreed to assist both the US Army Corps of Engineers and our Congressional delegations in whatever manner necessary to enhance early initiation of the study.

The study, entitled 'Mississippi and Louisiana Estuarine Areas', was authorized by a Resolution adopted September 23, 1976, by the House of Representatives at the request of Congressman Trent Lott of Mississippi. Thus, with the prime responsibility of the project shifted to the New Orleans District US Army Corps of Engineers, the first phase of the task (which encompassed a time-frame of some three years) was completed. The major thrust of the task-force remains as one of monitoring and support, as may be required.

Continuing efforts have been keeping interested parties informed as to the status of the project. Periodic reports have continued to be made at the annual American Shrimp Canners Association conferences, as well as the semi-annual Gulf States Marine Fisheries Commission conferences. In addition, support to the US Congress remains an annual event, especially at budget input and hearings times. Review with the New Orleans District US Army Corps of Engineers remains on an 'as required' basis.

As of August 1979, the New Orleans District US Army Corps of Engineers issued a Mississippi and Louisiana Estuarine Areas Project Information Sheet, which summarized the current status of the project, as follows. Work on the study was initiated on October, 1977. Fiscal year 1978 funds were used to conduct a field reconnaissance of the area by the interdisciplinary team on November 7 and 11, 1977. Initial public meetings were held in Gulfport and New Orleans on Feburary 1 and 9, 1978, respectively. Coordination meetings were held with the US Fish and Wildlife Service and Corps of Engineers, Mobile District. Fiscal year 1979 funds were used to initiate preliminary planning and preparation of a reconnaissance (stage I) report. Currently underway are reconnaissance scope studies to determine the engineering feasibility, environmental acceptability, and economic justification of the freshwater diversion measures. The US Fish and Wildlife Service is currently preparing a report on environmental base conditions and future conditions, optimum environmental requirements, the relationship between freshwater inputs and increased productivity of the fish and wildlife resources, and the fish and wildlife benefits that could be expected.

The project was funded for the fiscal year 1980, with funding for the fiscal year 1981 expected to be approved, as requested. Efforts continue with the US Army Corps of Engineers, members of Congress, and other interested parties. For example, concerted efforts were made to insure proper turnout for the

1978 public hearings in Gulfport and New Orleans. Not only was it considered important to the continuation of the project to have a strong supportive group in the audience, but also a sufficient number of statements made (written and oral) were necessary.

On Feburary 22, 1980, a meeting was held in New Orleans with the US Army Corps of Engineers Project Staff to insure continuation of interest, pledge of support, and review of the status and planned future efforts. On April 23, 1980, the New Orleans District Corps of Engineers made a presentation in which it reviewed 'our' project with two other freshwater studies. The thrust of this is to tie together several programmes that have a common purpose, although the areas may differ somewhat. The Mississippi and Louisiana Estuarine Areas Study encompasses Hydrologic Unit I and the Mississippi Sound. The other studies are west of Hydrologic Unit I.

A planning aid report on the Mississippi and Louisiana Estuarine Area Study, Fruge and Fuelle (1980), prepared by the Fish and Wildlife Service for the New Orleans District Corps states that the introduction of supplemental fresh water from the Mississippi River is expected to provide monetary benefits to fish and wildlife totalling between $4.4 million and $5.2 million annually. In addition, it was stated that the diversion is also expected to substantially reduce the serious loss of marsh presently being experienced in the Louisiana portion of the study area as a result of saltwater intrusion, subsidence, and erosion.

Seven years of effort has been expended on this project by many people. It is estimated that before fresh water can flow into the estuarine areas, another eight to ten years of effort and time will elapse. Fifteen years is a long time to keep an informal group together, with no monetary remuneration, motivated for a single purpose. It takes dedication, organization, planning, persuasive leadership, and perseverence.

Conclusions

Although no conclusions can yet be drawn because the project has a long way to go before it is completed, some observations can be made. Success of the project can only be determined by the actual flow of fresh water into the estuaries, when and where needed, and with proper monitoring to assess the results of such actions.

Most of what remains to be done is in the hands of the US Army Corps of Engineers, the several local, state, and federal fish and wildlife agencies, and the US Congress. Our task-force will support and assist wherever possible. We will remain associated with the project until that 'sweet water' flows.

Although everything we did was not the optimum approach, we were able to modify our plans where necessary and to keep the project organized on a going basis. We believed that the methodology described in this paper is worthy of consideration by others who plan to undertake the management, planning, and organization of a large-scale project. The basic problem of the need for fresh water was alluded to back in 1904 and 1906 in the first (and second)

Annual Report(s) of the Oyster Commission of Louisiana. Compared to the year 1904, the seven years on the project with eight to ten more to go does not appear quite so long in duration.

References

Etzold, D. J., and Williams, D. C., Jr. (1974). Data relative to the introduction of supplemental fresh water under periodic controlled conditions for the purpose of enhancing seafood productivity in Mississippi and Louisiana Estuaries, Mississippi–Alabama Sea Grant Consortium, 41pp.

Fruge, D. W., and Fuelle, R. (1980). A planning-aid report submitted to the US Army Corps of Engineers, US Fish and Wildlife Service, Division of Ecological Services, 86pp.

Mississippi River and Tributaries Project (1964). 6 Vols, US Army Corps of Engineers (also printed as House Document 308-88/2).

THE MARINE TECHNOLOGY DIRECTORATE AND INTERDISCIPLINARY RESEARCH

G. FORD and M. GIBBONS

PREST,* University of Manchester, England

The work described here is an activity of which both the authors are part. One of the authors (Ford) is currently the Group Leader for those projects within the North Western Universities Consortium for Marine Technology (NWUCMT) that fall within the general rubric of 'economic appraisal and management studies', while the other (Gibbons) is the Chairman of the Steering Committee that manages the same Consortium. As such the perspective from which this is written is that of participants rather than observers. Equally, both of the authors have spent considerable time working in the area of 'science, technology, and society', and are aware of the literature on the mechanics of technical change and innovation. The enterprise of which this work is a part has two important dimensions: firstly, much of the work being done under the auspices of the NWUCMT and all the work within Group 4 is interdisciplinary research; secondly, an attempt is being made by the Marine Technology Directorate (MTD), who are funding this work, to change the orientation and purpose of academic research (Adye, 1980). In some ways the enterprise as a whole is an innovative approach to work-promoting and studying innovation. The authors thus bring to their work a self-awareness of their roles which can be disconcerting.

PREST, The University, Oxford Road, Manchester M13 9PL, England. Glyn Ford is Coordinator of the Marine Resources Project and Michael Gibbons is Head of the Department of Liberal Studies in Science.

This chapter attempts to look at the *process* and *objectives* rather than the *product* of this work in general, and more particularly that of the Marine Resources Project (MRP), where the research work led by the authors takes place. As said above, this work is funded in the main by the MTD through the NWUCMT. The scale of the operation is significant when viewed against academic research in Britain.

For the period June 1981 to July 1983 the MTD budget is £7 million. The NWUCMT is to receive £1.93 million of this. The NWUCMT consists of the five universities of Manchester, Salford, Manchester Institute of Science and Technology (UMIST), Bangor, and Liverpool. From these five there are fifty-four academic staff from twenty-three separate departments in receipt of Consortium funds with ninety-one staff employed by the Consortium. More details of the division between different topics and between universities can be seen in Tables 1 and 2. In order to explain how this came about one needs to go back a decade or more.

Table 1. NWUCMT projects within groups (1981–83)

Group Title		Number of projects
1	Wave and Environmental Loading Studies	10
2	Sediment Transfer and Coastal Problems	8
3	Materials and Structures	11
4	Economic Appraisal and Management Studies	6
5	Instrumentation for the Marine Environment	4
6	*Consortium Administration*	—
7	Seabed Studies	3
8	Marine Biology, Pollution, and Mariculture	1
	Total	43

These figures were supplied by the Centre Office of the North Western Universities Consortium for Marine Technology.

Table 2. Projects within the Consortium universities

Bangor	5
Liverpool	11
Manchester	14
Salford	7
UMIST	6

Some projects span more than one university; this table shows the location of the first-named investigator.

The Robbins' expansion of universities in Britain, with the massive increase in student numbers, brought in its trail a similar increase in Research Council funding. This was particularly true in science and technology, fired as it was by the 'Wilsonian' white heat of the technological revolution. The allocation of these funds remained with the 'peer review' system, whose criteria was academic merit. Two analyses of the 'peer review' system within the Science Research Council and its impact upon 'selectivity' and 'concentration' have been given by Farina and Gibbons (1979, 1981).

More recently, Britain's continued and accelerating economic decline has meant that the work of the Research Councils has come under fresh scrutiny. Money is less readily available. In fact, it has been so limited that the 'peers' have complained that there was insufficient to fund all the first-class proposals, let alone others, in certain areas. At the same time questions have been asked about the efficacy of this research in contributing its mite to helping resolve the national crisis.

As a result of these factors the Science and Engineering Research Council (SERC), then the Science Research Council, made a major policy shift and decided that it would select and concentrate most of its support to areas deemed to be of special national importance. This at one and the same time started to deal with both the problems of limited finance and usefulness of the products of the research (see Farina and Gibbons, 1979, 1981; Gummett, 1980; and Science Research Council, 1970). If this was the SERC strategy, it drew from this two tactical conclusions. Firstly, while it recognized that in some cases the mere provision of special funding might be sufficient to stimulate increased research activity, this would not always be the case. There would be a need to establish new organizational arrangements to encourage the take-up of funds in some areas. Secondly, if the products of this increased endeavour were to have a *relevance* and *timeliness* that would mean they contributed towards the solution to Britain's industrial decline it would be necessary to temper the views of the 'peers' with those of the consumers.

One of the subject areas the SERC selected for special support was marine technology, and as a result the MTD was established in 1977. The reasons for the selection of marine technology in the mid-seventies are too obvious to require lengthy presentation. The coming of North Sea oil and the Organization of Petroleum Exporting Countries (OPEC) both made its importance to the British economy indisputable. This was reinforced by publicly voiced concern that British companies were not capitalizing as fully as they might on the available opportunities, and this was due in part to a lack of technological competitiveness.

Stimulating research activity

The two objectives the MTD had to achieve were *growth* and *direction*, i.e. they wanted to increase the amount of research in marine technology in the universities and make it relevant to industrial needs. They tackled the first of these by encouraging departments within universities, and even universities themselves, to link together to submit packages of research proposals—the theory being that this cooperative approach would reinforce both capabilities and interest. A number of Consortia were established in London, the North East, the North West, and Scotland.

Prior to the mid-sixties academic research on marine technology was not a fashionable area. What was taking place was almost entirely confined to Departments of Shipbuilding and Naval Architecture. This began to change as each new discovery was made in the North Sea. Academics began to tailor their interests more towards the problems of the marine environment. The result was that by the mid-seventies, with few exceptions, research on marine technology was rather like a doughnut, with great activity on the periphery emerging from the shifts towards the area by academics in engineering, physics, oceanography, biology, and other departments. In contrast, almost nothing existed at the core, with groups of skills being applied in a coordinated way to particular problems of marine technology.

The consortium style of approach almost inevitably acted as a forcing house for such a unified approach. The bringing together of academics from a variety of disciplines in a self-managing group encouraged fruitful interaction between individuals. It also had other consequences. The act of working together produced an 'invisible college' of people interested in marine technology. Of course, they retained their previous web of informal contacts in their own disciplines as well. This community was reinforced as young research workers were brought in to work on the various projects. Many of these were particularly able with academic posts of any kind at a premium.

These research workers are a valuable part of this community. The result of 'throwing money' at marine technology was effective in sharply increasing the amount of research on marine technology and beginning the establishment of a new discipline—marine technology grew like Topsy.

Directing research activities

The MTD's second objective was to encourage research of national relevance. The question was how to set criteria to establish this. Initially it was viewed as sufficient that it fell within the remit of marine technology. It became, with later funding records, increasingly refined. Relevance came to be associated with the successful outcome of two parallel activities. The Steering Committees were asked to draw up strategic plans indicating the directions they wanted to see emphasized in their overall programmes. They were expected to make decisions accordingly. The MTD itself saw industrial interest and most specifically financial support as a simple and convenient indicator of relevance. Thus renewed support for ongoing projects required that they fitted with Consortium strategy and demonstrated that partial industrial funding was likely to be forthcoming.

After this look at developments at the MTD and Consortium level it is important to focus our attention down to the individual project level. The MRP is part of the programme of Policy Research in Engineering Science and Technology (PREST) at Manchester University (copies of the last PREST Annual Report being available from the Coordinator of PREST). This programme was established in 1977 to provide an independent source of analysis of those social economic and political problems which in some way depend upon, or are caused by, science and technology. Apart from work on marine technology, PREST has covered a wide spectrum of research topics. It has ranged from the impact of microelectronics on employment prospects in one Manchester Borough to a comparison of patterns of innovation in the Japanese, German, Italian, and British tractor industries, and from the control of carcinogens to a comparison of regulatory regimes in Britain and the United States for road traffic safety. Thus PREST's work ranges from empirically based analysis to long-term forecasting. Its services are available on a contract, consultancy, or advisory basis to government departments, industrial companies, and other independent agencies or groups.

PREST is the research wing of the Department of Liberal Studies in Science at Manchester University. This department, which was set up in 1966, is based on the philosophy that it is wrong to limit the notion of science education just to the sharply focused teaching of narrow specialisms. While there will always be a need for people with such a training, there is also a long-felt, but neglected, requirement for trained scientific generalists, i.e. people who combine with a knowledge of science a high degree of literacy and communication skills. For its undergraduates the department offers combined degrees in one of the sciences plus a package of courses that puts science in its social context. At the postgraduate level there is an MSc programme under the title 'The Structure and Organization of Science and Technology'.

The general departmental philosophy sees the relationship between science, technology, and society as one where each interacts with each, a philosophy which depends very much on the seminal work of Kuhn (1962). The approach of PREST reflects this belief; hence the work of the MRP attempts to use an approach that implicitly recognizes this, while dealing with the concerns of the NWUCMT. Certainly the MRP is multidisciplinary. Allowing for dual qualifications, it currently has on its full-time staff two geologists, one oceanographer, an engineer, two economists, an international lawyer, and two policy analysts. In the four years this project has been in existence it has studied a number of marine topics, including deep ocean mining, ocean thermal energy conversion (OTEC), Red Sea metalliferous mud mining, and phosphorite nodules (see, for example, Cameron *et al.*, 1980; Ford, Niblett, and Walker, 1981; Georghiou and Ford, 1981; and Guest and Ford, 1982). In progress, or due to commence shortly, are studies of uranium extraction from sea water, high-level nuclear waste disposal at sea, and a pre-feasibility study for a Mersey barrage.

In terms of work organization all staff are expected to involve themselves in each of the projects, although a leading role is taken by different individuals for each area. Intellectually the work is organized, as mentioned above, around the conviction that science, engineering, economics, politics, and law do not impinge on each other in a unidirectional manner, from science through to law, but rather each influences each. It may be worth explaining here what is meant by this.

The technical choices made in the United States with regard to OTEC were influenced by the fact that the US Department of Energy, schooled on large reliable sources of energy, distrusted renewable systems that were too small to be incorporated into the grid system and were dependent on the vagaries of the weather. The principle behind OTEC is extremely simple. It is to use the temperature difference between the warm surface waters of the ocean and the cold bottom waters as a source of energy. The required temperature difference (Δt) is 20 C°. This is normally found close to the tropics. In this area OTEC has the potential to supply *baseload* power. America lies close to areas of ocean with good OTEC resources, in particular the Gulf of Mexico. The 1973 OPEC-fired oil crisis, in both its financial and political dimensions, spurred the search for *new* and *independent* sources of energy. OTEC was ideally suited to mesh in with the tenor of thinking of the US Department of Energy, coupled with that of the large, high-technology companies like Lockheed, TRW, and Global Marine. The result was a US R & D programme, actively supported at Congressional level, aimed at an OTEC capacity of 10,000 MWe by the end of the century based around floating units with an individual output of 400 MWe.

The result is that almost a decade on, OTEC development in the United States is almost dead. Elsewhere Japanese, French, and Swedish companies are pursuing contracts for OTEC plants that are: small, around 10 MWe; land-based, or at least close to shore; in conjunction with mariculture or possibly desalination plants. These are all for small tropical islands devoid of indigenous fuel resources. Instead of the United States being a part of this the politics of the American energy scene took a promising technology down a developmental cul-de-sac. This case has been dealt with fully by Ford and Georghiou (1982).

Other similar examples exist. The proposed international regulations for controlling deep-ocean mining, being drawn up by the United Nations Conference on the Law of the Sea, have influenced technical choices, while the proposals for mine site allocation have been a factor in the evaluation of resources availability.

To create and sustain industrial interest in all these areas the MRP has to translate such insights into forecasts for future developments and indicate 'opportunities' available to (British?) companies who are either directly involved or able to service such industries. For an academic group the 'product' of the work is much more closely tied to industrial concerns than is usual. To do this effectively it is necessary to be closely in touch with scientific and technical developments.

To ensure this is the case the MRP has been increasingly working jointly with other research groups in universities. For example, the ongoing work on uranium extraction from sea water is being undertaken with the Department of Chemistry at Salford University. They are developing chelating ion-exchange resins that will 'strip' the uranium out of solution. Similarly current proposals envisage: collaboration with the Institute of Oceanographic Sciences and the Marine Sciences Laboratory at Menai Bridge, a part of Bangor University, in the analysis of the prospects of disposing of high-level nuclear waste on or below the deep-sea floor; collaboration with the Department of Ocean Engineering at Newcastle and the Department of Geology at Imperial College (London) on a preliminary assessment of 'minerals from the sea'; and a joint programme spanning four universities and five academic departments to look at the feasibility of a Mersey tidal barrage.

Such links have advantages for all those involved. For the MRP it allows appraisals to be closely based on the latest developments in the thinking of the scientific 'invisible colleges' in these areas, far in advance of them appearing in the pages of the relevant journals. From their point of view it enables economic targets to be estimated for commercialization and identifies extra-scientific factors that should be taken into account in directing R & D. As an example, the disposal of high-level nuclear waste at sea will be strongly influenced in its technical development by political considerations. Monitoring will be an issue raised by many pressure groups. This may be conceded for political rather than technical reasons. The result would be a much narrower range of technical options available. Similarly the task of site-selection cannot cut across the terms of international legal conventions and treaties.

Nevertheless, links with other academics, albeit scientists and engineers, is only a partial answer. If the work of the MRP—and the NWUCMT and MTD—is to serve industry as it is intended, then an *active* involvement of industrialists is necessary, i.e. an involvement other than contracting for the occasional piece of research. At the level of the MRP this is being attempted through the medium of a 'Users Group' of companies.* In exchange for an annual fee they will obtain: access to the ongoing work of the project; regular information bulletins; membership of a steering committee. This steering committee will largely *determine* the work programme of the MRP in future. When confidence has been built up, it is hoped that this collaboration will mean access to new sources of information.

What are the Outstanding Problems?

Academically interdisciplinary research in itself can be unsettling enough to those who are used to the shared assumptions of a single discipline. This is compounded when 'academic merit' is tempered by 'industrial relevance'. A balance has to be maintained between the Scylla of becoming merely a cheap 'marketing organization' for a group of companies and the Charybdis of producing definitive appraisals of 'futures' already past. This limbo position and its consequent 'time scales' creates tensions. When a 'steering committee' determines the work programmes another academic article of faith—the right to freedom of research—will be under attack. This for some will be a cause

---

*Details of the 'Users Group' can be obtained from Roger Venables, Manager, UEG, 6 Storey's Gate, London SW1P 3AU, England. The UEG are assisting with the establishment of the 'Users Group' and see it as an activity which should be of interest to their own members.

for alarm. Yet this style of operation, although fairly new to Britain, is one that has been found in the United States, and elsewhere, for decades. If the universities in Britain are to maintain their important research function it is clear they will have to begin to adapt to such a role. Those who now control the finances and those likely to control them in the future seem united in the view that this is the direction that must be travelled. At the moment, apart from those few who have been initiated into research in this style, efforts to change often seem more cosmetic than real. The barriers are not all on one side. If the university finds 'industrial relevance' a difficult pill to swallow, industry finds the same with interdisciplinary research.

British industry is quite familiar with the use of university staff and facilities for particular 'technical' problems. Yet this is not true of seeking academic views on future industrial and technical developments where what is on offer are informed views and opinions, rather than a piece of equipment. The industrial view is that this is something industry does best for itself and should continue to do. The post-war track record of British industry seems to belie the first part of this. The case against the universities is 'proved' by sifting through the analysis to winnow out the gaps and errors in the technical information compared to that available to the companies. Certainly these are found, but the conclusion does not necessarily follow.

Such work can have a value to industry for two reasons. For companies on the edge of a field, although they can do the appropriate work themselves, it is cheaper and quicker to have someone else perform the long-range 'pathfinder' function of establishing likely important future developments on the more distant margin of the company's time horizon. Equally for those companies more directly involved, such an independent interdisciplinary group can provide a valuable second opinion. When new developments can require levels of investment in the £1,000 million range, it is not necessary to save a very large percentage to make a second opinion worthwhile. Obviously, the more companies are prepared to take such groups into their confidence the better the appraisal that will result.

Whether academics and industrialists can both come to appreciate the value and merit of such work is an important question. If they do not, interdisciplinary research may well face a bleak future in the new university research environment of the next decades.

Acknowledgements

The authors would like to thank the following for their assistance: Hugh Cameron, Luke Georghiou, Philip Guest, John Simnett, Daniel Spagni, and Michele Stone of the Marine Resources Project for discussing over a period of time many of the ideas contained here; Alan Corkhill and Avril Mee of the North Western Universities Consortium for Marine Technology Centre Office for supplying information about the current programme; and the Marine

Technology Directorate of the Science and Engineering Research Council for their financial support.

References

Adye, A. M. (1980). 'The SRC Marine Technology Programme—an overview', Paper given at the Society for Underwater Technology Conference, *Developments in the Science Research Council's Marine Technology Programme*, March 25, London.

Cameron, H., Ford, G., Garner, A., Gibbons, M., and Marjoram, T. (1980). *Manganese Nodule Mining: Issues and Perspectives*, PREST, Manchester.

Farina, C., and Gibbons, M. (1979). 'A quantitative analysis of the Science Research Council's policy of *selectivity and concentration*', *Research Policy*, **8**, 306–338.

Farina, C., and Gibbons, M.(1981). 'The concentration of research funds: the case of the Science Research Council', *R & D Management*, **11**, 63–67.

Ford, G., and Georghiou, L. (1982). 'Marine technologies for the 1990s', *Physics in Technology*, **13**, 11–17.

Ford, G., Niblett, C., and Walker, L. (1981). *Ocean Thermal Energy: Prospects and Opportunities*, PREST, Manchester.

Georghiou, L., and Ford, G. (1981). 'Arab silver from Red Sea mud', *New Scientist*, **89**, 470–472.

Guest, P., and Ford, G. (1982). 'Deep sea nodules help the farmer', *New Scientist*, **95**, 25.

SOME ELEMENTS OF A MODEL TO IMPROVE PRODUCTIVITY OF INTERDISCIPLINARY GROUPS
S. E. GOLD and H. J. GOLD
North Carolina State University, USA

This report is part of a study to develop methodology for guiding the functioning of interdisciplinary research and problem-solving groups. In this paper we formulate a model which is designed to serve as a basis for the development and identification of methods to improve individual and group productivity. The model focuses on the individual interpersonal transactions within the group and on the special problems that hinder the transactions when participants are drawn from different disciplines. The work of the group takes place through a network of these individual transactions. Examples of the group product might be: a report; a plan for action; a symbolic or mathematical model; a computer program; a design for a structure or machine; an actual structure or machine, usually regarded as a prototype.

In this paper, we will use the term, *research and problem-solving* (RPS) group, which we feel more appropriate than the more narrow R & D term.

In the first section, we discuss the concept of an RPS group as a network of coordinated and interdependent individuals. In the section, we present a model which describes the interpersonal transactions in terms of the degree to which certain key responsibilities are shared. The next two sections treat the disciplinary factors that hinder the individual transactions. Some methods for dealing with these factors are identified. The final section summarizes the main points of the paper and discusses how these ideas might be extended to more complex forms of interaction.

The Research and Problem-solving Network

Problems which demand an interdisciplinary approach are generally complex. That point was abundantly made at this Conference two years ago. Such complexity can often be made more tractable by partitioning the system into simpler parts. These parts are system components, which accept inputs and produce outputs (Figure 1a). These inputs may come from outside the system or from other components of the system. In the latter case, the output of one component becomes the input to another. In this way the system under study is described as a network of interdependent components.

Such a description is applicable to the RPS group as well as to the system which the group is investigating.

In general, the components of the RPS group may vary in size from a single individual to a research team, or even a collection of coordinated research teams. In this paper, however, the elementary component of the network is taken to be the individual research worker. The output-to-input relationships represent the interdependencies of individuals within the group. An individual accepts inputs from others and integrates them with his or her own creative processes to produce an output.

Figure 1 illustrates two basic interaction patterns, from which others may be built (such as those considered by Rossini *et al.*, 1979):

1. Sequential pattern. The individual accepts an input from one or more others and integrates these to produce an output.
2. Feedback loop. In this pattern, the individual produces an output which someone else uses to create another output, which is then fed back. The feedback may be either direct or through some intervening sequence. As indicated in Figure 1(f) and (g), an individual may participate in more than one such loop, thus serving as a link between sub-groups of investigators.

The interdisciplinary integrative burden on the individual arises from the disciplinary differences of the inputs from each other and from his or her own discipline. The magnitude of the burden depends upon the number of different disciplines, the type and degree of their differences, and upon the depth of integration required. When this burden is especially great, the network (i.e. the group) may benefit from including individuals whose primary function is integration and whose specialized training deals with integrative methodologies (e.g. system science).

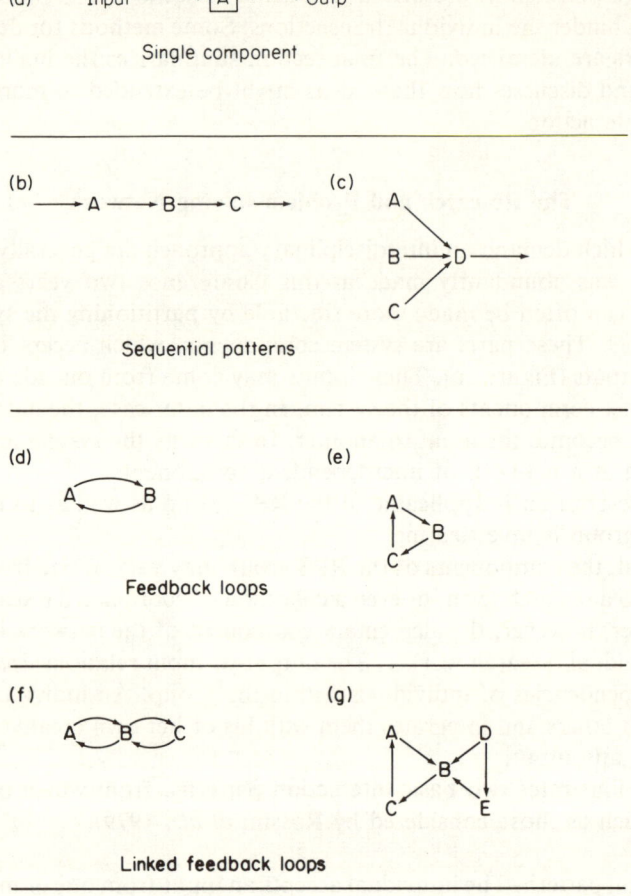

Figure 1. Basic interaction patterns, from which others may be built

The next three sections will primarily focus on the nature of the input–output interactions, as might be represented by any one of the arrows of Figure 1. These interactions cover a range of interpersonal transactions, which vary from close partnership to relatively impersonal contract arrangements. Between these extremes, which are rarely encountered in pure form, the process may be described as one of *consultation*.

Model of the Individual Transaction in the RPS Network

Description of the model

In this section we formulate a model of the interpersonal transactions which form the basis of the network. The relevant elements of an individual transaction, as depicted in Figure 2, are:

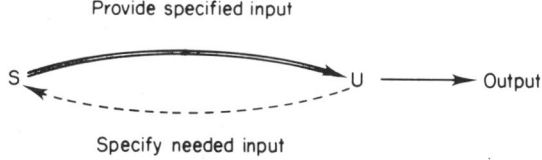

Figure 2. Elements of the Individual Transaction. S = Supplier of Input; U = User of the Input

1. Specification of the needed input;
2. Production of the specified input;
3. Use of the input to produce an output.

The individual transactions are described as being in one of a variety of *modes*, which are distinguished from each other on the basis of the division of responsibility borne by each party to the transaction can be assigned a value which varies from zero, indicating no responsibility, to one, indicating full responsibility. The mode of the transaction is characterized by the degree to which these three responsibilities are shared.

Table 1. Relative division of responsibility in the pure modes

Responsibilities	Contracting		Partnership	
	User	Supplier	User	Supplier
Specification	1	0	1/2	1/2
Supply	0	1	1/2	1/2
Use	1	0	1/2	1/2

Two 'pure' modes of interaction can be described, as shown in Table 1. They are characterized by clear assignment of responsibility. The assignment varies from complete separation of responsibilities in the contracting case to full sharing in the partnership case. Between these extremes is the broad range of mixed modes, in which the parties share some degree of responsibility for one or more of these elements. Consultation, as described, for example, by Bell and Nadler (1979), may be characterized by this range of mixed modes. For our purposes, consultation can best be understood in terms of its relation to the extremes.

Partnership

Fully shared responsibility, characteristic of partnership, is rarely encountered in practice and is certainly not typical of interdisciplinary groups. It implies that the partners have equivalent abilities and in fact carry out all responsibilities jointly. It requires a mutually held world-view and cognitive framework which is unlikely when participants come from different disciplines.

Contracting

In contracting, the person who needs an input (U in Figure 2) has complete responsibility for specifying what is needed. The specifications are given to a contractor (S in Figure 2) who has responsibility for supplying the needed input in accordance with the specifications. The contractor (or supplier) has no responsibility for insuring that what is specified is really needed or usable. The user takes full responsibility for building usefulness into the specifications.

For this form of interaction to be successful, the user must be sufficiently familiar with the special information, language, and cognitive framework of the supplier's discipline to be able to specify the need precisely and accurately. Such a requirement makes contracting difficult. It is rendered virtually impossible in situations of low predictability, which characterize many research and problem-solving activities (Pearson, Payne, and Gunz, 1979).

Consulting

The difficulties associated with specifying, producing, and using the products of other disciplines force the majority of interdisciplinary interactions into a consultative mode. In this type of transaction, the one who needs an input, the potential user, plays the role of client; the supplier plays the role of consultant. They share responsibility for specifying the needed input. The client usually has *lead* responsibility for using the input, while the consultant usually has *lead* responsibility for producing the needed input, but both of these responsibilities may be shared. The sharing of responsibility for making the input useful is especially important in activities of 'low predictability', because it may not be possible to specify in advance what the actual product will 'look' like.

As the consultant assumes more responsibility for using the input to produce the output, increased ownership is developed and the interaction moves closer to the partnership mode. As less responsibility is assumed, especially for specifying the needed input, the consultant moves towards becoming a contractor.

The depth of understanding that the client and consultant need from each other's discipline will vary according to the way that responsibilities are shared.

Consultation in general, but more especially in the case of interdisciplinary interactions, involves a heavy component of mutual education. Parties must develop the facility for utilizing each other and *being* utilized as learning resources. Guidelines for self-directed learning, developed by Knowles (1975), are extremely relevant.

The consulting mode is dynamic and continually shifting; as the personal relations between the individuals shift, their cognitive frameworks are expanded and the interaction barriers are reduced. By contrast, the pure modes tend to be relatively stationary. The contracting mode does not provide opportunity for the mutual learning activity that makes the consulting mode dynamic. On the other hand, in pure partnership, all such learning needs have been addressed.

Determining the 'appropriate' interaction mode

The following set of questions may help to determine the relative appropriateness of the contracting versus consulting mode.

The person needing an input, i.e. the potential client, must ask:

1. Can the input be precisely and predictably specified?
2. Can the client precisely and accurately specify the needed input in terms of the other discipline?
3. Does the client want to let someone else produce the input without his or her help?
4. Will the client be able to use the input without help from its supplier?

If the client answers 'yes' to each of these questions, a contractor is probably wanted, but if any one of the answers is 'no', a consultant is needed.

A person who is being asked to produce an input for another member of the group, i.e. the potential contractor, should consider:

1. Has the potential client precisely specified the desired input?
2. Is the specified input likely to accomplish what the client thinks it will?
3. Can the specified input be produced satisfactorily and predictably without the client's help?
4. Is the client likely to be able to use the input without help?

If the client answers 'yes' to all these questions, the individual may be satisfied to act as a contractor. If any of the answers is 'no' a consulting relation is likely to be more satisfactory.

The distinction between contracting and consulting modes parallels, at an operational level, the distinction often made between multidisciplinary and interdisciplinary work. The contracting mode is more characteristic of multidisciplinary work; the consulting mode is more characteristic of interdisciplinary work. Unfortunately, the array of differences between disciplines that gives interdisciplinarity its synergistic potential also prevents many consulting interactions from developing successfully. Even when consulting is called for, the contracting mode will often be used. Consulting, with its shared responsibilities and high levels of interaction, may seem too difficult to be worth the effort.

The following section discusses the way in which the disciplinary differences become barriers. We then proceed to examine how these barriers affect interdisciplinary consulting interactions.

Disciplinary Differences and Barriers

The most obvious differences between disciplines are those of specialized information, of specialized language for expressing that information, and of specialized methods for manipulating and adding to that information. The mutual learning activity, whose importance to the consulting process was stressed in the previous section, involves the sharing of this body of information, language, and methods. It is especially important, therefore, to understand the way in which the disciplinary structure of science creates barriers to that mutual learning process.

An individual receives and interprets information in terms of his or her disciplinary 'world-view', or cognitive framework, and within the social context of the disciplinary community. We divide the potential barriers to interdisciplinary collaboration into several categories: differences in individual cognitive frameworks; differences in subject matter characteristics; normative differences; need for services of the disciplinary community; individual identification with the disciplinary community. The categories are heavily interdependent, but suggest different types of barriers to collaboration and impose different requirements on the mutual learning process.

Cognitive framework

As developed by Kuhn (1970, 1977), there are three separate components to the disciplinary cognitive framework. They are: the underlying theory, or generalizations; idealized models and analogies; exemplars. In our interpretation, the underlying theory contains the statements of general principle which are assumed to apply in specific instances. The exemplars, on the other hand, *are* specific instances. They are chosen for the clarity with which they illustrate the operation of some group of principles; i.e. for their exemplary nature and paradigmatic value. Disciplines differ in the way generalizations are made, in the set of exemplars used for illustrating the generalizations, and in the way the two are related. Idealized analogies and models stand between theory and exemplars. They are make-believe examples, in the sense that they do not accurately or completely describe any real case. Rather, they abstract from a group or set of real cases what are felt to be essential characteristics. Such models are used on the one hand to aid the understanding of the principles and their application; and on the other hand to test, and thereby extend and modify, the theory itself (Gold, 1977). In the mutual learning process, the bridge between disciplines most often takes place through construction of shared models.

Subject matter factors

In this category, we include general characteristics of the system under study, which limit our ability to interact with, manipulate, and understand the system. Such factors are observability, controllability, uniqueness, and predictability. These characteristics influence the nature of the cognitive framework and provide a basis for some of the normative factors discussed in the next sub-section.

Differing concepts of what is observable may cause particular problems in communication. For example, although both the chemist and the physiologist may use the term 'temperature', and both may agree that they have reference to the reading on a particular type of meter, the reading is interpreted in widely different ways relative to the system under study. Problems in communication may arise because they think they are discussing the same concept.

An important subject matter difference between disciplines which is related to the level of complexity is the degree of control that can be exercised over the 'experimental conditions'. Most generally, the simpler the system in terms of the number of relevant variables and their interactions, the more rigorous the degree of control possible. The molecular physicist may demand temperature control to six decimal places, whereas the psychologist may be happy with an interview chamber regulated to within three degrees. Scientists working at one level will often view the efforts of those working at a more complex level with disdain, as not conforming to their own criteria with respect to requisite control.

Closely related to controllability but not identical to it, is the degree of uniqueness and repeatability, and therefore of predictability of the phenomena being studied (Elsasser, 1966, discusses this at a theoretical level while Holling, 1978, deals with it at a more operational level). We have, for example, countless numbers of hydrogen atoms, each of which has the same pattern of behaviour. At another extreme, we have only one solar system in which to observe the motion of the planets. The motion, however, has been seen to be sufficiently repeatable to enable us to generalize observations made within a specific time-frame as a basis for prediction. Yet another extreme is presented by the earth's biosphere or by a particular ecological system. It is not only unique, but within the time-frame of our observations it is to a large degree non-repeatable. The degree of uniqueness and of repeatability strongly influences the nature of the possible generalizations. A result is that often the kinds of generalizations made within one discipline fail to meet the criteria of another discipline.

Normative factors

The disciplinary world-view includes a variety of value judgements as to types of questions which are valid and appropriate subjects for investigation and worth the expenditure of one's time and intellectual energy. Also included are judgements as to what constitute valid answers to given questions and what are valid explanations and proofs of propositions (see, for example, Beckner, 1968, and Hempel, 1965). Questions which cannot be answered within the cognitive framework of a given discipline may be characterized as 'unallowed' or as 'unscientific'.

As a result of cognitive, subject matter, and normative differences, scientists of different disciplines may have difficulty agreeing upon appropriate sets of goals, an appropriate framework for pursuing those goals, and an appropriate evaluative framework.

Community services

The disciplinary community performs certain functions which are essential to the creative and professional life of the individual (Hagstrom, 1966). To the extent that the individual steps outside the community, as he does when participating in an interdisciplinary group, the community may be unable or unwilling to perform these services. In such cases, the interdisciplinary group must find ways of providing the needed services. Some of them are:

1. Exchange of information, ideas, and critical feedback.
2. Exchange of recognition. As pointed out in different contexts by Pelz and Andrews (1966) and by Hagstrom (1966), the desire for recognition may provide a needed constructive tension, which is an important contributor to the creative process.
3. Providing tangible reward and recognition by superiors. This, of course, is provided by the administrative structure, but is often heavily based on peer recognition and evaluation.
4. Review and critical evaluation as the basis for allocation of research resources. Within a given discipline, such review and evaluation is primarily with regard to what is needed to strengthen and develop the discipline itself. Interdisciplinary problems, however, originate outside the context of recognized disciplinary communities, making review and optimal allocation of research effort especially difficult.

Identification with the community

The training and socialization that the student in a discipline undergoes lead to an identification with the disciplinary community which comes prior to, and is generally regarded as more persistent than, identification with a specific employer or particular task. In combination with normative differences these feelings of identification and loyalty to the disciplinary community can, and often do, develop to the point of professional chauvinism, providing barriers severe enough to defeat interdisciplinary collaboration at the earliest phases.

A milder manifestation of community identification is that individuals from different disciplines tend at first to regard each other as exchangeable representative specimens of their respective disciplines. Such attitudes are very much in evidence in writings about how to structure and work with interdisciplinary groups (e.g. Holling, 1978; Wymore, 1976). This becomes more exaggerated the more divergent the cognitive frameworks of the disciplines become.

Often, indeed, the individual tends to consider himself to be participating as the agent of his own discipline. He may ask himself initially, 'What can I, as a chemist, contribute to this work?' He may seek within the group to gain recognition not only for himself, but for the value of the field he represents. Indeed, he may hope for reward within the disciplinary community for having extended the recognized value and applicability of the discipline.

A somewhat more subtle effect is the individual's association with a specialty or sub-community within the larger community. This association gives him a recognizable identity within the community. The need to maintain the integrity of this identity may make him unwilling to work on problems unrelated to his specialty, even though he may be competent to do so. That is, the scientist will try to pick problems that are in some sense contiguous with each other and with his chosen specialty. We refer to this as a need for professional contiguity.

Summary of disciplinary differences

1. *Cognitive framework*, which structures the way in which an individual receives and interprets information;
2. *Subject matter factors*, such as observability, controllability, uniqueness, and predictability;
3. *Normative factors*, by which the members of the community are disciplined;
4. *Community services*, which provide necessary incentives and supports;
5. *Personal identification* with the community, from which the individual draws his identity in the larger social and work-related community.

Effect of Disciplinary Differences on Intra-group Interactions

In this section, we discuss the way in which the disciplinary differences, as elaborated the last section, interfere with intragroup transactions. We then make some recommendations for minimizing their negative effects.

In the context of the model developed in the first two sections, most interpersonal transactions within the RPS group probably fall within the mixed, or consultation, range—between the extremes of partnership and contracting.

Lippitt and Lippitt (1978) describe consultation as 'a two way interaction—a process of seeking, giving and receiving help'. It is initiated when one person (the client) seeks help from another (the consultant). The overall process takes place in several stages, which have been described in related ways (as shown in Table 2) by Bell and Nadler (1979) and by Lippitt and Lippitt (1978).

In reality, consulting is never the orderly sequential process implied by these idealized descriptions. Within an RPS group, many consultations will be very informal, and may simply involve one group member helping another to 'muddle through' (Golde, 1976). Even in more formal consultations, *diagnosis* takes place during *entry*, and the agreement or 'contract' may be renegotiated any time during the process. In this section we use the phases shown in Table 2 as a framework for examining where the disciplinary differences become barriers, and how these barriers are related to changes in the three responsibility factors discussed in the second section.

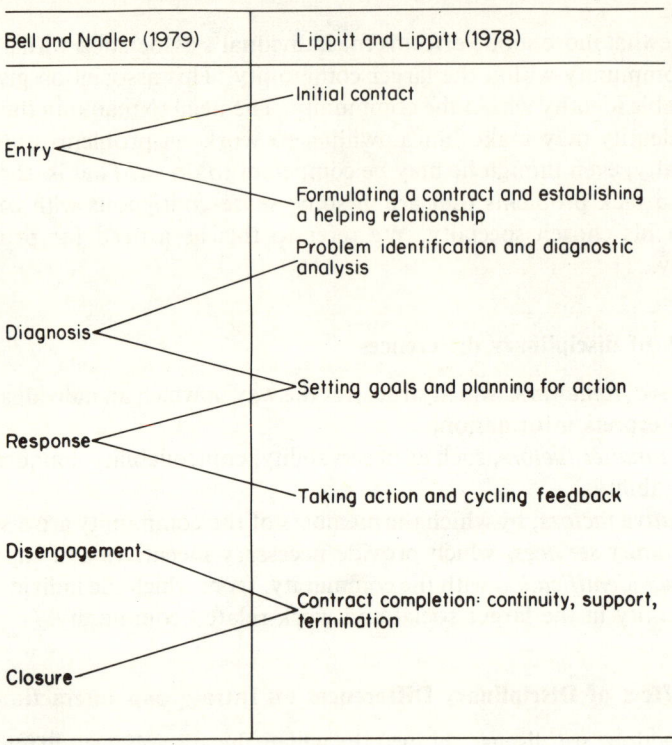

Table 2. Phases of consulting process

Entry

The entry phase begins as soon as U contacts S (Figure 2) about the needed input. This contact may take place between the two individuals or within the group setting. The work to be accomplished during this phase is mainly concerned with the client and consultant exploring the potential for working together. Hagstrom (1966) likens this to the first meeting between a boy and a girl exploring the potential for 'romantic collaboration'. The primary goal is to find sufficient clues to predict whether the interaction will be mutually profitable. A tentative agreement about the benefits of working together will conclude the work of entry and allow the interaction to proceed to diagnosis.

Community loyalties in the form of professional chauvinism may present barriers to effective entry. This is especially true if the potential client and consultant do not know each other and regard each other as undifferentiated representatives of their respective disciplines. Professional chauvinism, the belief that the cognitive framework of one's own discipline is superior to that of another, is clearly related to normative differences, such as those involving rigour of proof and judgements as to what are worthwhile questions for study. Activities which give members of the group an opportunity to know and respect each other as people rather than as disciplinary representatives can help minimize such effects. Research is needed to develop techniques that are specifically designed to help members of interdisciplinary groups recognize and address these problems.

Normative and community factors affect the way in which the potential consultant views his part in the transaction. Is such work considered worth while within his discipline? Will it gain him access to community recognition and reward? Planned involvement of group members in goal-setting and project-planning activities may be of help here. If the potential consultant feels ownership in the overall outcome of the group, either as an individual or as an agent of his discipline, he may be willing to forego some measure of reward within his own field—especially if he has faith in the internal recognition and reward structure of the group. Moreover, the goal structure may need to be expanded so that group members have their opportunity to get some measure of satisfaction of their professional goals in the process of satisfying the group goals. This point is developed within the theory of organizational hierarchies (Mesarovic, Macko, and Takahara, 1970).

Cognitive factors begin to operate as barriers during the *entry* phase. When U tries to explain to S (Figure 2) an input is needed, it is done so in terms of his or her own cognitive framework. At this early stage, before mutual learning can occur, S must make preliminary judgements about how closely the suggested work fits with other work he or she is doing or would like to be doing. U can facilitate the transaction by sharing the responsibility for exploring the potential consultant's need in this regard.

In contracting interactions, similar questions must be answered but here the situation is much less ambiguous. This is primarily because the needed input is specified by the client *before* entry so that the potential contractor can more easily make the necessary decisions.

Diagnosis (specifying the needed input)

If a tentative agreement is reached that there is the potential for working together, then *diagnosis* begins. The early stages of this phase are more productive if the client concentrates on describing to the consultant what he or she wants to accomplish, and not what the client wants the consultant to produce. Jay (1977) advises the client to 'express the consultant's job in terms of the end result you want to achieve'. He points out that the heart of the relationship is the distinction between ends and means—the client is the expert on ends; the consultant is the expert on means.

Such an approach has two beneficial effects. Firstly, it permits the consultant to identify options of which the client may be unaware. Secondly, it allows the consultant to develop ownership in the work. Shared ownership implies a sharing of responsibility and of potential reward.

During this phase, professional chauvinism has another opportunity to exert its influence. If the client regards the consultant's discipline as soft or unscientific, he or she may solicit the needed input grudgingly and be unwilling to share responsibility for its specification. Alternatively, if the project requires the use of input from the consultant, he or she may totally abdicate responsibility for its specification and turn it over completely to the consultant. This might result from the feeling that all inputs that come from the consultant's discipline are likely to be equally untrustworthy, so why bother.

If the consultant believes that the potential client's discipline does not deal with important matters, there may be an unwillingness to be involved in a consulting relation. In such a case a contracting role may be accepted, even though there is a suspicion that the client has not accurately specified the needed input. If the input is to be used for trivial purposes, it does not matter.

Cognitive and subject matter factors become major barriers during diagnosis and lead to the long start-up times often associated with interdisciplinary groups. The early stage of diagnosis is a mutual learning process. The consultant has to learn what the client is trying to accomplish so that an evaluation can be made of the discipline in general, and he or she in particular, can be of help. The client has to learn enough about the consultant's discipline to make a decision about the value of the proposed help. During this mutual learning process, the distinction between client and consultant is blurred. The learning process is facilitated if the client concentrates initially on what he or she wishes to accomplish, rather than on what is wanted from the consultant. This allows a partial time separation of their learning processes. Firstly, the consultant can concentrate on learning material from the client's field. Then, as he or she begins to explore possible useful inputs, the learner–teacher roles are reversed and the client begins to learn enough to evaluate the proposed help.

It is particularly helpful if each party takes a pro-active or self-directed learning role, as opposed to the passive role assigned to the learner in the usual pedagogic method. In the 'androgogic' approach advocated by Knowles (1975), the learner assumes control and responsibility for the learning process and for identifying what is needed, while the teacher assumes a helping, i.e. consulting, role.

The difficulties likely to be encountered at this stage will of course depend upon the degree of disparity between the disciplines; i.e. on the degree to which the theories, models, and exemplars are shared or at least overlap. If the mutual learning process is to be a basis for integrative collaboration, it is important to construct a set of agreed-upon models which can serve to bridge between the theory and exemplars of the two fields. Mathematical models are often found to be convenient pan-disciplinary tools, whose use reduces the time needed to find, explain, and interpret appropriate analogies (see Gold and Raper, 1981; Holling, 1978; Walker *et al.*, 1978).

As the cognitive frameworks of the participants expand and overlap, and greater understanding of the needed input is achieved, the process moves into specific goal-setting and planning for action, which bridges between the *diagnosis* and the *response* phases shown in Table 2.

Response (producing and evaluating the needed input)

If the specified input falls neatly into one discipline, the work becomes monodisciplinary; interdisciplinary factors no longer interfere. When responsibility for producing the specified input must be shared by the client and consultant, interdisciplinary barriers will continue to present problems. These problems will be eased if adequate attention has been paid to the mutual learning process during *diagnosis*.

During this phase, normative and subject matter factors combine to make intragroup evaluation one of the most serious challenges to interdisciplinary work. On the one hand, for reasons already discussed, members of one discipline may be unfair and overcritical in their evaluation of work in another discipline. On the other hand, the awareness of this danger, together with the difficulty of providing fair and accurate evaluation, may lead group members to abdicate their responsibility to do so.

Here, the group leadership can have considerable impact by establishing a climate in which rigorous evaluation of all work is the expected norm. This should include the early development of an agreed-upon evaluation plan, including the setting aside of resources for that purpose. It should include assisting group members to identify appropriate outside sources of evaluation, especially when the work is not professionally contiguous with their previous work.

Of greatest importance to a productive evaluation climate is the requirement that formal and informal evaluation be rigorous, but delivered in a non-judgemental manner (Gibb, 1961). The generally found low level of skill in giving rigorous, helpful feedback suggests the need to develop methods for training interdisciplinary group members in such techniques.

Disengagement/closure (using the input)

Once the needed input has been produced, it must be transferred to the client for use. The transfer may involve yet another teaching–learning phase, which depends upon the degree of flexibility and autonomy which the client wishes ultimately to use with the input. In a consulting relation, the consultant will usually assume some responsibilty for insuring that the input will be properly interpreted and correctly used. This may involve providing support to the client over an extended period of time (disengagement). Such support may be regarded by some consultants as a totally unrewarding burden. The RPS group leadership should try to find appropriate ways to recognize and reward group members who carry out this essential service.

If the client assumes most of the responsibility for integrating the input with his own work, the transaction moves towards the contracting mode. If the consultant becomes more involved with the client in the actual use of the input, the interaction moves more towards the partnership end of the scale.

An important consideration that must be faced at this point is the decision about allocation of credits and recognition and the location of an appropriate disciplinary or interdisciplinary community in which the work can 'claim kin'.

Any degree of dissatisfaction at this point will adversely affect the next round of consultation activities.

Concluding Remarks

In the second and fourth sections, we have focused on a model of the individual transaction within the RPS group. This can be extended to the build-up of the network described in the first section in a fairly straightforward way, as individuals within the group—in need of each other's inputs—trade consulting services. As the group proceeds through its sequence of tasks and separate activities, the network of these coconsulting relations will repeatedly need to be renegotiated, restructured, and realigned.

Hagstrom and Kuhn both stress, within the contexts of their separate discussions, that cognitive framework, disciplinary socialization, and community identification are unconsciously internalized and unconsciously used. This may be perfectly satisfactory when collaborating individuals are operating within a commonly held cognitive framework and set of norms, and identify with the same community. When they differ in any of these, it is grossly inefficient to rely, as is most often done, on unconscious processes for the development of the necessary common ground. The process must be brought to the conscious level before it can be explicitly addressed and plans drawn for anticipating and dealing with difficulties.

Consciousness of the process would, of course, be of value in any research and problem-solving group. Some of the needs which are magnified by interdisciplinarity and which must be addressed by the individual parties to an intragroup transaction are:

1. Need to determine if contracting, consulting, or partnership mode is desired, and to negotiate the appropriate sharing of responsibilty elements.
2. Need for each to assume control of own learning within the consulting relation, as it applies to information content and cognitive framework; need for 'self-directed' learning approaches.
3. Need for each to be sensitive to the other's requirements relative to professional contiguity and disciplinary identification.

Training efforts would be especially valuable in the evaluative feedback technique and in strategies of building idealized models as tools for bridging between theory and exemplars of separate disciplines.

Group leadership should be aware of the particular importance of a climate in which rigorous but non-judgemental evaluation is the norm; of the need for the group to supplement services normally provided by the disciplinary communities, such as reward, recognition, information exchange, evaluative feedback; and of the importance of opportunities for group members to know each other well enough professionally to overcome disciplinary prejudices and to regard each other as more than representatives from each other's disciplines.

References

Beckner, M. (1968). *The Biological Way of Thought*, University of California Press, Berkeley.
Bell, C. R., and Nadler, L. (Eds) (1979). *The Client–Consultant Handbook*, Gulf Publishing Company, Houston, Texas.
Elsasser, W. (1966). *Atom and Organism*, Princeton University Press, Princeton, New Jersey.
Gibb, J. R. (1961). 'Defensive communication', *J. of Communication*, **11**, 141–148.
Gold, H. J. (1977). *Mathematical Modeling of Biological Systems: An Introductory Guidebook*, Wiley, New York.
Gold, H. J., and Raper, C. D., Jr. (1981). 'Systems analysis and modeling in extrapolation of controlled environment studies to field conditions', in *Crop Reaction to Water and Temperature Stresses* (Ed P. J. Kramer and C. D. Raper, Jr.), Westview Press, Boulder, Colorado.
Golde, R. A. (1976). *Muddling Through*, Amacom, New York.
Hagstrom, W. O. (1966). *The Scientific Community*, Basic Books, New York.
Hempel, G. C. (1965). *Aspects of Scientific Explanation*, Free Press, New York.
Herzberg, F. (1964). 'The Motivation–hygiene concept and problems of manpower, *Personnel Administration*, **1964**, January–February, 178–182.
Holling, C. S. (Ed.) (1978). *Adaptive Environmental Assessment and Management*, Wiley, New York.
Jay, A. (1977). 'Rate yourself as a client', *Harvard Business Review*, July–August.
Knowles, M. (1975). *Self-Directed Learning*, Follett Publishing, Chicago.
Kuhn, T. S. (1970). *The Structure of Scientific Revolutions*, 2nd ed., University of Chicago Press, Chicago.
Kuhn, T. S. (1977). *The Essential Tension*, University of Chicago Press, Chicago, Illinois, Chap. 9:225, Chap. 12:293.
Lippitt, G., and Lippitt, R. (1978). *The Consulting Process in Action*, University Associates, LaJolla, California.
Mesarovic, M. D., Macko, D., and Takahara, Y. (1970). *Theory of Hierarchical, Multilevel Systems*, Academic Press, New York.
Morris, W. C., and Sashkin, M. (1976). *Organizational Behavior in Action*, West Publishing Company, New York.
Pearson, A. W., Payne, R. L., and Gunz, H. P. (1979). 'Communication, coordination and leadership in interdisciplinary research', in *Interdisciplinary Research Groups: Their Management and Organization* (Eds R. T. Barth and R. Steck), Interstudy, Seattle, Washington, p.112.
Pelz, D. C., and Andrews, F. M. (1966). *Scientists in Organizations*, Wiley, New York.
Rossini, F. A., Porter, A. L., Kelly, P., and Chubin, D. E. (1979). 'Frameworks and factors affecting integration within technology assessments', in *Interdisciplinary Research Groups: Their Management and Organization* (Eds R. T. Barth and R. Steck), Interstudy, Seattle, Washington, p.136.
Walker, B. H., Norton, G. A., Conway, G. R., Comins, H. N., and Birley, M. (1978). 'A procedure for multidisciplinary ecosystem research: with reference to the South African savannah ecosystem project', *J. of Applied Ecology*, **15**, 481–502.
Wiley, G. E. (1973). 'Win/lose situations', in *Annual Handbook for Group Facilitators* (Eds J. E. Jones and J. W. Pfeiffer), University Associates Publishers, LaJolla, California.
Wymore, A. W. (1976). *Systems Engineering Methodology for Interdisciplinary Teams*, Wiley, New York.

UNIVERSITY-BASED TECHNOLOGY TRANSFER
R. D. HANDSCOMBE
Salford University Industrial Centre, England

Universities in their main-stream activities communicate with industry and are involved in technology transfer. The main examples are obviously that universities are sources of graduates and postgraduates, that they provide short courses for mature education, and that they are there for contract research and development either direct with industry through sponsorship or through the Science and Engineering Research Council and other government bodies. Also, they provide academic staff who can and do involve themselves in industrial consultancies. Thus, it can be argued that because they exist and do what they are set up to do, they are already involved in technology transfer.

However, by technology transfer in our sense we mean a specific service to some part of industry — a specific service for product and process development and innovation. We are talking of some additional feature to the university that is not its main stream activity — of a communication with industry which is relevant only if there is a package to offer that industry needs and which is clearly additional to what is available by the existing routes.

If we look at universities in the United Kingdom at the present time there are a number of ways in which the universities respond to this separate and special challenge. Generally speaking, the choice is liaison bureaux, departmental units, university units, or university companies. The university company shows itself to be an attractive option and has proved itself at a number of universities in the United Kingdom, including Salford. A review of these alternatives gives some explanation of why I see the university company as the best option.

The liaison bureau serves a useful purpose but it is limited. We are talking only of the interest that the academics and departmental groups have in the time they have available to respond to enquiries that are channelled through some central office where the key person and his or her secretary try to deal with the enquiries they receive. This is perhaps more efficient than the old-fashioned arrangement of letting the client phone up the university to try to get some assistance. However, it goes little further than making the system more efficient. The academic is not backed up with engineers and a full service is not provided to the enquirer. If it needs a programme of work the academic arguably will not be able to respond in the required timescale.

Departmental units in which the academics are supported by technicians and scientific officers are able to offer a more rounded service. The problems that arise are that the enquirer is talking to a single department which has limited facilities and nothing has been done to reduce the difficulty an enquirer has in reaching the right department. There is likely to be resistance of one department to pass the enquiry on to a more appropriate one, because it would mean loss of income. Finally, there is a conflict between the consultancy work and the existing responsibilities of the members of staff, technicians, and scientific officers in their main-stream departmental duties.

The university unit overcomes some of the problems of a departmental unit in that to some extent it breaks down the barriers between the departments. Because it is a university-based department it still has the problems of being involved in university activities and lacks the freedom of operation which is needed in dealing with industrial and commercial companies. The enquirers expect the unit to respond on the same basis that they do, which leads us to university companies. These are much the same as university units but now we have quite a distinct operation with no responsibilities at all for main-stream university activities. They are true companies with profit motivation and with desires to grow and develop as a company while interfacing with the academic departments of the university. The university company will receive the contract and then provide the service to the customer using in-house resources and subcontracting services from the university.

Before we move on to looking at the areas of technology to be offered it is worth summarizing the key aspects of the type of organization and its structure. The argument for a university company is that it provides the correct single-minded framework for operation. The company is audited annually, quite separately from the university, and therefore has the responsiblity of establishing and maintaining solvency. This is an excellent pressure discipline and concentrates the mind wonderfully upon the objectives of survival and the strategy and tactics of how to ensure this. For a university company to grow from a university unit, as has happened at Salford, a number of procedural and administrative changes need to take place such that the company becomes managed by a board, separate from the main management board of the university, to ensure the required freedom of activity. Yet at the same time, it needs to remain closely linked by university representation to ensure that the university company operates in a manner consistent with the university's image and capabilities. At Salford, as is the case with other university companies, the board is made up of university staff (Vice-Chancellor, Registrar, selected Professors), external representatives (local industrialists, selected representatives of the legal, banking, and accounting professions), and working directors.

Further down the organizational structure, there are the technology group leaders. These people, invariably qualified engineers and scientists, have supervisory responsibility for the engineers and technicians in their group as well as the responsibility to keep abreast of their technologies and be able to assist the sales effort. Academics play a very valuable part in developing and sustaining technology areas but our experience at Salford is that a full-time technology leader is:

1. Always available for company business because it is his full-time job;
2. More aware of the need to give prompt service and careful attention to clients' desires because his job depends on it;

3. Single-minded as to the reason he is talking to a customer or potential customer.

I have no desire or intention to denigrate academics, quite the reverse, but we have many examples of academics feeling satisfied with a sales visit if the outcome has been related to student placement or sponsorship, to stimulating discussions, or to the witnessing of new equipment in action. I can understand their satisfaction but from the viewpoint of the company's growth and survival, I cannot share it.

A final comment with regard to in-house leaders is that such people are likely to be highly marketable and thus the company has to be structured to offer them career growth and also to accommodate their department.

If we turn our attention now to the areas of technology which should be offered, to what markets they should be offered, and how those areas are identified, one can list the main principles as follows:

1. Identify a market need.
2. Identify the path to reach it.
3. Identify a service, product, or package to meet that need.
4. Assess the resource capacity to provide the service, the product, or the package.
5. Compare the size and growth prospects of both the market need and the resource capability.
6. Make a business decision to commit or to reinvestigate the market place.

The result of this is clearly that a company offers selective services for identified market needs based on those areas of technology where it has potential particular strengths. In practice a good mixture of luck and serendipity aid that process and one must be aware of a number of dangers. The danger of a technological push rather than a market pull is very real in a university environment. Secondly, there is the danger of engineering virtue taking precedence over market research. Dons are very apt to sit back and expound upon what should be done rather than carry out the vigorous market research that often proves the case one way or the other. There is also the danger of a university's technical excellence leading to overdiversification in an attempt to be all things to everybody.

Fourthly, there is the danger of ill-defined corporate policy. This, of course, comes back to the type of operation you are going to have and to the definition of its objective, the resource requirements, and the potential of self-financing. For example, if we consider the objective to be a stimulate product and process development and innovation then we are talking about a service to industry provided by the university that will require some kind of funding. This may be by the university itself because it is pushing its own prestige and ability and therefore enhancing its reputation; it may be the national government because the national government sees the need for industry to receive the technology that exists in a university. On the other hand, if the objective is to be in the business of product and process development and of innovation then this clearly can be profit-making. This, of course, implies that what is offered is that which is required and not what is felt by the university to be needed. I think it can be seen from this that a university company could end up developing some items and supplying them to a growth market, thus largely ignoring the existing problems in the main-stream of the industrial work in the neighbourhood of the university which would socially be in need of all the technology that the university can give. However, if that industry is having bad times it will be unable to pay the rates necessary for the company to sustain its growth and profitability. Clearly there is a conflict between running a successful company and providing technology transfer on a broad basis with national significance.

In this broader context it is perhaps worth considering collaboration between universities or even competition between universities. There is clearly a value in competition because a customer may well get a better service, a better package, when there is competition for his business.

With regard to collaboration we can give examples. The first is an integrated computer-aided manufacture project where we worked with UMIST for the US Air Force. The Air Force had carried out their market research thoroughly and had rated institutions, universities, and companies in order of interest. Both Salford and UMIST came out very high on the list and this coupled with the very close geographical siting led the USAF to demand a single contract. It proved an interesting arrangement, with Salford University Industrial Centre Limited (SUIC) being the contracting party and providing programme management and technical input and the two academic groups, one at Salford and one at UMIST, sharing the remaining technical workloads. With three separate groups working concurrently, the main problems were ones of scheduling work packages, different styles of presentation, communication of requirements, and subtle changes of these during the project, and ensuring a convergence of work to the client's objectives rather than a divergence as each group developed in its own direction. I mention these problems in the context of interuniversity work but they also exist in interdepartment work at a single university, and our ability to manage such projects has developed with experience and is now a significant feature of our expertise.

The second example is a research and development project from the Greater Manchester Council where the initial technical expertise resided in UMIST and SUIC provided programme management and coordination. The first-year investigation was concluded satisfactorily and a much larger second-year effort was mounted, involving equipment supply and complementary investigations at Salford University. From a small project with a team of three chemists, the project has been developed to a large chemical and chemical engineering investigation involving around twelve people at the two universities. SUIC's main role continues to be programme management but now with some technical input, and this programme management permits the specialists at UMIST and Salford to concentrate on technical developments within SUIC's controlled framework of client liaison, patent application, tendering for complementary and follow-on work, timescale control, and project coordination.

I have mentioned the value of competition in that it forces the companies offering the service to be smarter and it offers the customer a choice. Competition can arise accidentally, the two universities working in isolation receiving similar enquiries and building up their own teams of experts. On the other hand, collaboration (and this is the crux of interdisciplinary research) requires effort, coordination, a common purpose, and a driving force. With the US Air Force the driving force was quite simply that neither Salford nor UMIST would have got the job had they not worked together. In terms of the desirability of collaboration, clearly the example just quoted is one where the customer desired it. In other cases the university, local government, local enterprise, national government, or some international force (e.g. the EEC) may require collaboration, and if the requirement is a sufficient driving force then collaboration will occur. The practicality is that collaboration is more difficult than competition. It is less easy to coordinate people at two campuses (or in two departments) and there are political problems with two institutions. There is also the additional cost of the administration required. What I am really saying is that there has to be some strong and good reason for collaboration—it will not just happen.

Returning our attention to the specific operation at Salford, there are twenty-seven full-time employees and an involvement of 100 to 150 members of the academic staff. The technologies stretch across the engineering and science disciplines, where Salford University has particular strength. Many projects do not fall easily into subject classification and it is on these projects that cross several disciplines and draw on a variety of staff with the relevant skills and experience that the company has established a national reputation.

Not all projects are of an interdisciplinary nature and the management style differs from project to project. A common feature of all projects is the identification of a project leader whose responsibility it is to liaise with the customer and carry out or have carried out the required work in the required time. For single-discipline projects the group leaders or key engineers in their teams or the academics undertaking the work prove to be acceptable project leaders. The extra responsibility (over a project engineer) is expected of the group leaders, and project leadership is generally the route for engineers to progress up the salary scales.

For the academics consultancy payments are made; these vary in size not only with the technical work done but also the responsibility taken. Some academics and some group leaders (those with broad training and experience) are capable of handling multidiscipline projects and taking the lead in interdiscipline ones. However, only a few academics have the time for the larger interdisciplinary jobs, and the programme manager (a higher title) is usually a part-time task of one of the SUIC managers. Programme meetings, led by the programme manager and involving the key academics and engineers, are regular and essential features of the job and parallels with an industrial research manager are evident.

Because the manager is in effect the 'paymaster' a quasi-line discipline relationship builds up with the academics involved. It must, however, be recognized that their input can only be part-time—they have their academic duties—and that they respond to other 'paymasters'; it is a question of balance and leadership as well as crude incentive schemes.

An appreciation of why companies use SUIC is instructive. Size is clearly an important factor. Very small companies often have limited resources to use external services and very large companies often have sufficient in-house facilities not to need to look outside. Somewhere in the middle lies those companies who have a degree of in-house technology and the realization that the most effective method of ensuring correct product and process development is to supplement them with external resources.

The level of technology in a company is another factor. Low-technology manufacturers have little need of high-technology consultancy and the high-technology specialist manufacturers are often better equipped themselves to solve their own specific problems.

The third factor, and perhaps the most important, is the attitude of the executive in the company who is responsible for innovation and product and process development. Technology transfer is very much a two-way transfer and unless a company is willing to look out to us and to describe its problems, its constraints, its opportunities, and its horizons then we are unable to look in and try to provide the technology to enable that company to move on, to develop, and to prosper.

MOTIVATION: A DIAGNOSTIC APPROACH
J. HOLMAN
ICI Pharmaceuticals, Cheshire, England

Abstract

The paper advocates the use of the expectancy theory of behaviour as an approach to improving motivation in complex organizations. The basic tenet of this theory is that people make choices among the behaviour plans open to them based on their expectancy of the degree that a plan could lead to outcomes of value to themselves, taking into account the effort needed to carry them out. That is, every choice is perceived as having an outcome expectancy, a valency, and a performance expectancy.

A manager must therefore ascertain the outcomes that an employee values, define the kinds of output that are valued by the organization, ensure that the employee is capable of achieving that output, define the changes to the employee and the desired outcomes that will minimize the conflicts between the employee's aims and those of the company, and check the final plan for its all-round equity.

Although expectancy theory needs further testing and validation the author believes that enough is known to be able to conclude that it represents the most comprehensive, valid, and useful approach to motivation at present available.

PEER ASSESSMENTS IN INDUSTRIAL R & D DEPARTMENTS: SOME CONSIDERATIONS AND IMPLICATIONS FOR FUTURE RESEARCH BASED ON A REVIEW OF RECENT LITERATURE

E. JOCHUM, M. DOMSCH, and T. GERPOTT
Hochschule der Bundeswehr, Hamburg, W. Germany

Introduction

Various empirical investigations (Gaugler *et al.*, 1978; Holley, Field, and Barnett, 1976; Liebel and Walter, 1978) exemplify that the standardized performance appraisal of the individual employee represents a general accepted instrument of personnel management, especially in large-scale enterprises. Although there are collated exploratory hints on the dissemination of performance appraisals for scientific personnel in industrial R & D, it seems reasonable to assume that the appraisal of scientific personnel is primarily conducted by the supervisor.

Since it is difficult to appraise the performance of scientific personnel because of the complexity and novelty of scientific tasks, one has to raise the question of whether a single supervisor is actually able to appraise the *complete* performance of a scientist. Whereas the supervisor may be capable of appraising the performance of a scientist with regard to professional aspects of presented individual working results—assuming that the supervisor possesses an appropriate professional education—he or she is generally not able to observe the cooperating and supporting behaviour of scientists in R & D teams and, therefore cannot consider information about that type of behaviour in giving an appraisal. These intensive communicative and cooperative relations based on mutual trust are of vital importance for the performance and efficiency of an R & D unit (Farris, 1972; Kegan and Rubenstein, 1973; Mittermeir, Aichholzer and Wallach, 1977; Pelz and Andrews, 1976). A potential enlargement of the basis of information might be reached by incorporating peers in the rating process.

To ensure an adequate consideration of the applicability of peer assessment for the personnel appraisal of scientists the *peer rating technique* will be analysed in detail while other techniques of peer assessment will be mentioned only briefly. This restriction is justified by the fact that 'traditional' appraisals conducted by supervisors are mainly 'ratings'. Other techniques (e.g. ranking, nomination) are not widely spread so it seems reasonable to conclude that the rating technique has proved its practical work in numerous corporations.

Different Techniques (Methods) and Purposes of Peer Assessment

Up to now peer assessments have not been widely used in management practice. Nevertheless, there are several research findings — especially obtained in the United States — which make it possible to make some recommendations about the suitability of peer assessment for the appraisal of scientists. Firstly, it is necessary to define the term 'peer'.

In sociological literature the termination 'peer' is not used with a uniform meaning. While, for example, Mittermeir (1978) or Schultz (1964) include all scientists working in a specific professional discipline under the term 'peer' (independent of their organizational affiliation), Connor (1972) regards as 'peers' only '. . . a scientist's immediate colleagues . . . in the same laboratory or department'. The description of peer assessment made by Kane and Lawler (1978), which is accepted for the purpose of this paper, is based on the second type of interpretation of the term 'peer' (as given by Connor); herein peer assessments are considered as methods in which all members of a small group (e.g. a project team) pass mutual judgements on:

1. All members or a part of the members of the group;
2. Where all group members belong to the same hierarchical level of the organization; and
3. Where the judgements relate to certain personality characteristics, behaviour, or work achievements of colleagues.

The following techniques of appraisal are summed up under the term 'peer assessment':

1. *Peer nomination* implies that the raters determine '. . . a specified number of group members as being highest in the group on a particular characteristic or dimension of performance' (Kane and Lawler, 1978). The studies of Mayfield (1972) and Amir, Kovarsky, and Sharan (1970) indicate that this technique seems to be especially appropriate for predicting future success. Up to now the assumption of high prognostic validity of peer nominations has been primarily confirmed for the prediction of military leadership abilities and therefore it requires further investigations to examine the transferability of these results, especially with regard to appraisals in R & D units.
2. *Peer ranking* implies that the appraisal includes a ranking procedure (Kane and Lawler, 1978). Peer rankings involve discriminations among all persons rated. However, they do not include any information about:
   (a) Absolute standards of performance (performance independent from certain reference groups, measured by a given standard) and/or
   (b) The behaviour of the persons to be rated and
   (c) The differences in performance between the single members of a team.
3. *Peer rating* implies that individual performance and/or individual behaviour has to be rated by peers with the help of rating scales and with respect to

fixed criteria. In most cases personal average scores of the ratings conducted independently by the respective peers are computed on every criteria. A practical and frequent application of peer ratings can be observed in so-called assessment centres, e.g. that practised by the AGFA-Gaevert Company, Leverkusen, and by BAT, Hamburg.

After considering the three different techniques (methods) of peer assessment we will now take into account the purposes which are pursued by personnel appraisals, thus gaining a purpose method matrix with $n \times 3$ cells. The figure n which represents the number of purposes to be pursued by personnel appraisals ranges from three to four main purposes. The following three main purposes of an appraisal system are emphasized in the literature (Liebel and Walter, 1978; McMillan and Doyel, 1980; Neuberger, 1980):

1. Determination of remuneration;
2. Personnel management (especially the support of leadership functions and improvement of superior–subordinate relations);
3. Personnel decisions (e.g. personnel selection for transfers, promotions).

Proceeding from these main purposes of personnel appraisal the following matrix results:

Methods of peer assessment Purposes of appraisal	Peer nomination	Peer ranking	Peer rating
Determination of remuneration			
Personnel management			
Personnel decisions			

As stated above, only peer ratings will be discussed.

Peer Ratings for Appraising Scientific Personnel

The peers' possibilities of perceiving the performance and/or the behaviour of a scientist/engineer to be rated depend primarily on the manner and intensity of contacts between the participants.

Because of the increasing number of interdisciplinary, complex projects, the rising costs of technical equipment, and the continuing tendency towards scientific specialization, one must take into account that successful R & D organizations require a network of durable cooperative relations among their scientific employees (scientists and engineers (Mittermeir, Aichholzer, and Wallach, 1977). It is obvious that in team-based R & D peers possess numerous opportunities for perception of each other's performance and working behaviour. In most cases this precondition for the application of peer ratings is complied with.

Stahl and Steger (1977) conclude that '. . . colleagues, due to their technical expertise and familiarity with work are in the best position to evaluate the originality and usefulness of scientific/engineering output' but this claim is less valid for teams composed of scientists belonging to different functional disciplines (if, for example, a mathematician has to appraise the quality of performance of a biologist).

A way out of the above dilemma could be that appraisals of scientists in multidisciplinary or interdisciplinary teams are conducted only by those peers who belong to the same functional discipline, or ratings of all team members could be restricted to 'social' dimensions which concern the individual's behaviour within the respective team. This behaviour can be perceived by all peers to a similar extent and—at the same time—has to be regarded as a vital determinant of the performance of interdisciplinary research teams (Kegan and Rubenstein, 1973; Thom, 1980).

The ability for peers to discriminate the social (working) behaviour of a scientist from the professional dimensions of performance is one pre-condition for the applicability of peer ratings in industrial R & D units. References concerning the existence of that ability can be found in a study carried out by Tucker, Cline, and Schmitt (1967). In a peer rating of scientists the authors found that the criteria 'skill with people'—which is a social criteria of performance—correlated less with the remaining professional performance criteria (i.e. 'quantity of work', 'creativity', and 'overall work performance') than these professional criteria correlated with each other. It must be noted, however, that the correlation between the criteria 'skill with people' and the professional criteria which were used in the study in both samples was between 0.59 and 0.71 and between 0.71 and 0.85. According to these findings peers are able to discriminate the working behaviour of a scientist from professional dimensions of performance more easily than to discriminate the professional dimensions with one another. This interpretation of the study is affirmed by the results of McCarrey and Edwards (1973) which were obtained from studies in four Canadian government research laboratories. McCarrey and Edwards used a peer ranking technique for the measurement of individual performance; with that peer ranking technique the authors found that the communicative–performance–behaviour ranking correlated less with the 'productivity rank' and the 'creativity rank' (0.42 and 0.40 respectively) than both professional criteria correlated with each other (0.75).

In view of the lack of empirical research material one cannot decide definitely how far the reported findings may be generalized for the appraisal of scientists by peers in industrial laboratories. Further investigations carried out with other categories of persons (e.g. nurses) proved that:

1. Peer ratings are less affected by an overall impression of performance ('overall effectiveness rating') than supervisory ratings (Holzbach, 1978).
2. Peer ratings are more able to discriminate between professional competence and other criteria of appraisal (e.g. 'willingness to perform', 'skill in communication') than supervisory ratings (Klimoski and London, 1974).
3. Peer ratings show no more 'leniency' than supervisory ratings (Holzbach, 1978; Klimoski and London, 1974).
4. In cases of participation of the raters in the selection of rating criteria and the construction of rating scales, peer ratings are more able to discriminate different aspects of performance than in cases where a set of criteria is merely imposed (Borman, 1974; Holzbach, 1978; Klimoski and London, 1974).

Summing up the present state of empirical investigation it can be concluded that it is possible to comprehend social (performance) behaviours of scientists who are going to be rated by peer ratings and to discriminate this behavioural aspect from professional dimensions of scientific performance.

If the study of Tucker, Cline, and Schmitt (1967) is considered, the frequently expressed assumption that peer ratings could be contaminated by friendship bias (see for example v. Eckard-Stein and Schnellinger, 1978) cannot be held up; while supervisory ratings of scientists showed significant positive correlations to a 'likability rating', peer ratings were not significantly correlated with this rating. Furthermore, these (potential) contaminations have a less unfavourable effect when computing an average judgement score of several raters, compared to the consideration of single judgements alone. Therefore, under certain conditions which will be explained below, peer ratings seem to be appropriate to gain information about the social behaviour of scientists in teams even if the effects of friendship/sympathy are taken into account. Peer ratings provide valuable knowledge for personnel-assignment decisions, e.g. for the composition of research teams. Nevertheless, the question remains open as to whether sufficient personnel resources are available to allow selection according to requirements of this technique (Boerger, 1979; Forster, 1978).

In addition to the study of Tucker, Cline, and Schmitt (1967) an investigation by Stahl and Steger (1977) which was carried out in a US Air Force R & D laboratory examined the peer rating of professional performance components of scientists. Stahl and Steger used two criteria of performance—'productivity' and 'innovation'. These criteria were explained to the scientists who were asked to rate their work-group colleagues using a nine-point rating scale. The results showed an average interrater agreement (designated by a correlation coefficient) of 0.72 for the productivity criteria and of 0.66 for the innovation criteria. In this study colleagues obviously agree to a large extent upon the degree of *professional performance* of their respective peers.

As far as we know, further studies about interrater agreement in peer ratings of scientists are not existent. Kane and Lawler (1978), however, computed an average interrater agreement of 0.45 after reviewing the results of fourteen empirical investigations concerning peer ratings. A comparison of this figure with those reported by Stahl and Steger (1977) indicates that in R & D peers are possibly more in agreement with regard to the performance appraisal of peers than employees in other fields of activity. These results lead to the conclusion that the peer ratings in R & D are tenable, or at least are worth further investigation.

Even though scientists may be able to make these kinds of judgements successfully such a rating technique depends essentially on the peers' willingness to contribute to the rating system as a rater or as a ratee: the rating procedure has to be accepted by every single scientist. Kane and Lawler (1978) substantiate this necessity as follows: 'These methods are not unique in requiring the co-operation of their users in order to be effective but they seem more prone to failing to obtain such co-operation than most other methods. This is because they implicitly request that people consider privileged information about their peers in making their assessments.' Only if the rating procedure is accepted will the peers be ready to pass on the unique information which is accessible to them. Although there are no studies concerning the willingness of scientists in industrial R & D to participate in a peer rating procedure hints on the scientist's willingness to cooperate in peer ratings as well as hints on their acceptance of the method can be derived from other investigations.

The acceptance of peer ratings by the participating scientists can be proved by a 'functional norm' of science which is summed up under the label of 'organized scepticism' and includes the demand that the performance of a scientist '. . . should be subject to independent validation . . . by one's peers' (Parker, 1977). Whether peer assessment and acknowledgement of the performance of a scientist actually function as a strong incentive, and whether their ratings are accepted, could depend essentially on how far the standards of success used by the raters are felt as 'appropriate' by the scientists being rated. It cannot be generally assumed that in industrial R & D scientists mainly orientate themselves to general scientific standards of performance rather than to the relevance of that performance for the company. A study by Connor (1972) bears on this point.

Peer ratings were conducted in a university research laboratory and in an 'independent' laboratory (a laboratory which solicited external research orders). Only one dimension of performance was used—'scientific competence'. At the same time for every scientist it was recorded how often his publications were cited among the experts using the science citation index. For the scientists occupied in the university laboratory the number of citations showed a significant positive correlation with the peer rating scores (0.71). In the university laboratory the raters obviously orientated themselves more according to scientific norms. In the independent research laboratory, however, no association between these variables was discovered: the correlation was -0.03 (Connor, 1972). Those scientists who showed a high number of citations tended to be rated rather negatively by their peers (within this sub-sample the correlation of the two variables was -0.53). The results draw attention to the fact that non-university R & D scientists do not necessarily orientate their judgement about the performance of their peers towards scientific norms to the neglect of specific organizational performance criteria. Different scientists clearly base their judgement on different value orientations (Munson and Posner, 1979).

Even if the value orientations of peers are congruent the acceptance of the method by the participants is not secured. As a further condition for the efficient use of peer ratings Cummings and Schwab (1973) mention that '. . . a high level of interpersonal trust and sharing among peers, coupled with a non-competitive reward system' has to exist to avoid destructive competition and a lack of cooperation between peers.

During a peer rating the rater occupies a conflicting role if the results of the peer ratings are directly used for the allocation of promotional opportunities or for decisions concerning individual remuneration (Boerger, 1979; Neuberger, 1976). An almost objective rating of a colleague can result for the respective rater in a decrease of his or her own promotional opportunities and in a reduction of a raise in pay; therefore, the rater contaminates—consciously or unconsciously—the appraisal to improve his or her own opportunities for receiving the incentives offered by the company. The mutual trust of the scientists which is necessary for accepted and uncontaminated peer ratings implies that peer ratings cannot be imposed from above without participation of the affected scientists (no authoritarian introduction). Complete information about the purposes and the conduct of peer ratings for all members of an affected work group/department is of vital importance to ensure that scientists decide for themselves the new type of rating. If a voluntary decision in favour of this method is made then it seems to be possible to initiate with the aid of a peer rating an open discussion between the group members about mutual behavioural expectations as well as about communicative and coordinative problems, thereby increasing mutual trust within the work group.

This kind of application of peer ratings differs from the 'classic' purposes of personnel appraisal (which are primarily directed towards individual employees); in the method described above behavioural ratings of single scientists are made for achieving the purpose of increasing the efficiency of cooperation within a work group. Furthermore, peer ratings can be used as a basis for team development.

We are not aware of any empirical studies concerning the question as to how far an increase of mutual trust in industrial R & D teams can be reached with the help of peer ratings. But the studies of Argyris (1966) and of Kegan and Rubenstein (1973) indicate that in R & D teams 'trust' can be increased by organizational development measures which change personal interrelations and that at the same time that raising trust results in an increase of team performance. If a minimum level of trust exists in a work group, a peer rating method ought to be suitable for the achievement of personnel management purposes.

To gain applicable/empirical findings about the utility of peer ratings it is necessary to test this peer rating method in a practical pilot project in an industrial R & D unit.

That a total rejection of peer assessments must not be expected—even if you widen the considered circle of employees from scientists to all kinds of employees—can be concluded from the investigations cited and also from the results of an employee survey which took place in an enterprise in the German chemical industry; in that survey about 40 per cent of the respondents generally agreed to a peer rating and only 29 per cent. of the respondents rejected that kind of appraisal in principle (Gaugler, Lay, and Schilling, 1979).

Conclusion

To recapitulate the preceding arguments:
1. Because of working structures which to a large extent are team-oriented, scientists in R & D departments possess numerous opportunities for the mutual perception of their (working) output as well as, especially, of their (working) behaviour (input).
2. In functional homogeneous working teams the scientists also have a comprehensive competence for an appraisal of the scientific performance of their peers.
3. In functional heterogeneous working teams the team members are able at least to gain a close insight of the social (working) behaviour of their peers (dependent on the length and the intensity of cooperation).
4. Peers are capable of differentiating the professional dimension of performance from a social dimension of performance more easily than supervisors.
5. A comparison of peer ratings (assessments) and supervisory ratings at least induces the supervisor to check his or her own rating.
6. Peer ratings can be used as a basis for team development.
7. The results obtained about peer assessment approaches prove that these approaches are worth examining thoroughly in their theoretical as well as in their empirical aspects: e.g. what method of peer assessment (nomination, ranking, or rating) is suitable for what purposes of appraisal/personnel policy?

There still remains much research to be done.

References

Amir, Y., Kovarsky, Y., and Sharan, S. (1970). 'Peer nominations as a predictor of multistage promotions in a ramified organization', *Journal of Applied Psychology*, **54**, 462–469.

Argyris, C. (1966). 'Interpersonal competence, organizational milieu, and innovation', *Research Management*, **9** (2), 71–99.

Boerger, M. (1979). 'Die Beurteilung von Teamleistungen, Anmerkungen zu Möglichkeiten und Problemen von Teambeurteilungsverfahren', *Zeitschrift für Arbeitswissenschaften*, 33, 82–88.

Borman, W. (1974). 'The rating of individuals in organizations/an alternate approach', *Organizational Behavior and Human Performance*, 12, 105–124.

Connor, P. (1972). 'Scientific research competence, two forms of collegial judgement', *Pacific Sociological Review*, 15, 355–366.

Cummings, L., and Schwab, D. (1973). *Performance in Organizations, Determinants and Appraisal*, Glenview, Illinois.

Eckardstein, D., and von Schnellinger, F. (1978). *Betriebliche Personalpolitik*, Vol. 3, *Uberarbeitete und Ergänzte Auflage*, Munich.

Farris, G. (1972). 'The effect of individual roles on performance in innovative groups', *R & D Management*, 3 (1), 23-28.

Forster, J (1978). *Teams und Teamarbeit in der Unternehinüng*, Bern, Stuttgart.

Gaugler, E., Kolvenbach, H., Lay, G., Ripke, M., and Schilling, W. (1978). *Leistungsbeurteilung in der Wirtschaft, Verfahren und Anwendung in der Praxis*, Baden-Baden.

Guagler, E., Lay, G., and Schilling, W. (1979). *Einführung und Auswertung von Leistungsbeurteilungssystemen, Betriebliche Ansätze und Erfahrungen*, Baden-Baden.

Holley, W., Feild, H., and Barnett, N. (1979). 'Analyzing performance appraisal systems/an empirical study', *Personnel Journal*, 55, 457–459, 463.

Holzbach, R. (1978). 'Rater bias in performance ratings: superior, self- and peer-ratings', *Journal of Applied Psychology*, 63, 579–588.

Kane, J., and Lawler, E. (1978). 'Methods of peer assessment', *Psychological Bulletin*, 85, 555–586.

Kegan, D., and Rubenstein, A. (1973). 'Trust, effectiveness and organizational development: a field study in R & D', *The Journal of Applied Behavioral Science*, 9, 498–513.

Klimoski, R., and London, M. (1974). 'Role of the rater in performance appraisal', *Journal of Applied Psychology*, 59, 445–451.

Liebel, H., and Walter, R. (1978). 'Personalbeurteilung als Führungsmittel, Eine Umfrage in Wirtschaft und Öffentlicher Verwaltung', in Liebel, H. (Ed.): *Führungspsychologie, Theoretische und empirische Beiträge* (Ed. H. Liebel), Göttingen, Toronto, Zürich, pp.155–188.

McCarrey, M., and Edwards, S. (1973). 'Organizational climate conditions for effective research scientist role performance', *Organizational Behavior and Human Performance*, 9, 439–459.

McMillan, J., and Doyel, H. (1980). 'Performance appraisal: match the tool to the task', *Personnel*, 57, 12–20.

Mayfield, E. (1972). 'Value of peer nominations in predicting life insurance sales performance', *Journal of Applied Psychology*, 56, 319–323.

Mittermeir, R. (1978). 'Leistungsdeterminanten von Forschungseinheiten', Dissertation, Wien.

Mittermeier, R., Aichholzer, G., and Wallach, G. (1977). 'Organisatorische Einflußgrößen und wissenschaftliche Industrieforschung im Internationalen Vergleich, Internationale Vergleichsstudie über die Organisation und Effektivität von Forschungseinheiten, Endbericht', Wien.

Munson, J., and Posner, B. (1979). 'The values of engineers and managing engineers', *IEEE Transactions on Engineering Management*, **EM-26**, 94–100.

Neuberger, O. (1976). *Führungsverhalten und Führungserfolg*, Berlin.

Neuberger, O. (1980). 'Rituelle (Selbst- Täuschung, Kritik der irrationalen Praxis der Persoanlbeurteilung', *Die Betriebswirtschaft*, 40, 27–43.

Parker, R. (1977). 'Human aspects of R & D Organization', *R & D Management*, 7 (3), 167–172.

Pelz, D., and Andrews, F. (1976). *Scientists in Organizations, Productive Climates for Research and Development*, Revised ed., Institute for Social Research, University of Michigan, Ann Arbor.
Schultz, D. (1964). 'R & D personnel: two basic types', *Personnel*, **41**(2), 62–67.
Stahl, M., and Steger, J. (1977). 'Measuring innovation and productivity in R & D—a peer rating approach', *Research Management*, **20**(1), 35–38.
Thom, N. (1980). *Grundlagen des Betrieblichen Innovationsmanagements*, Vol. 2: *Völlig neu Bearbeitete Auflage*, Königsstein.
Tucker, M., Cline, V., and Schmitt, J. (1967). 'Prediction of creativity and other performance measures from biographical information among pharmaceutical scientists', *Journal of Applied Psychology*, **51**, 131–138.

THE SHIRLEY INSTITUTE—AN INTERDISCIPLINARY CONTRACT RESEARCH ESTABLISHMENT
D. JONES
Shirley Institute, Didsbury, Manchester, England

Introduction

The origins of the Shirley Institute go back to 1919 when a research and development establishment was created with the expressed purpose of serving local industry and in particular those companies associated with the textile trade. It was supported both by the industry through a general levy as well as by a matching grant from the government—a form of support also enjoyed by other similar R & D establishments in the United Kingdom. Since its inception the Institute has built up a sound reputation in the scientific and technical areas relevant to the industry.

However, the nature of this industry has undergone significant change over this period and particularly in recent times due to the growth of overseas competition in basic commodities and through the introduction of new interests and different methods of manufacture. At the same time industry and government attitudes towards the support of research have changed. More attention has been focused on the need to get 'value for money'. This has almost inevitably led to a movement in sponsorship towards the more short-term and more immediately relevant type of work. This situation does not easily permit the continuity and development in depth of research strengths which the Institute considered to be one of its major attributes. It was this attribute that had enabled it to maintain a reputation and encourage recruitment of good entrants who required positive and stable career opportunities.

The management saw the need to continue to offer a high level of expertise in a variety of subject areas and recognized that the Institute had available to it many skills, not least of which was the ability to offer 'practical problem-solving' in projects with interdisciplinary characteristics. Further, the ability to work with outside bodies, including other research organizations, was also an asset which could be put to good use as the following case illustrates.

Case Study: Development of a High-performance Fabric for Use in Aircraft Windshields

Following discussions in 1972 with staff from the Research and Development Laboratories of Pilkington Brothers Limited a project was initiated concerning a new concept in windshield design for the Boeing 747 aircraft by the Triplex Safety Glass Co. Ltd, a member of the Pilkington Group.

The new design consisted essentially of two curved plies of Triplex 'ten-twenty' high-strength glass laminated together with a layer of polyvinyl butyral (PVB) with a third high-strength glass facing ply. A light alloy frame and capping ring completed the windshield assembly, the intervening space being filled with Thiokol polysulphide rubber.

When the Institute was first approached, an edge restraint system was being sought which would provide a tertiary load path capable of withstanding the loads of aircraft pressurization if both of the main glass plies were broken and would also allow the PVB interlayer material to act as a diaphragm for long enough to allow the aircraft to descend to an altitude where pressurization would no longer be necessary. When the windshield is broken, the tertiary structure is designed to balloon outwards and be retained like this until descent.

To conform with a demanding performance and material specification a woven structure was designed containing 'rubberized' glass cord yarn in one direction of the fabric and textured nylon yarn in the other. Short samples of fabric were produced using the Shirley Miniplus technique in which the textured nylon was made into a warp from two supply packages. Problems were encountered in weaving owing to the tackiness of the rubber covering of the glass cord weft yarn. A fabric sample was produced, however, about 6 metres long in which the weft had been inserted by hand.

The subsequent test results obtained by Triplex were very encouraging and further supplies of wider and longer fabric were immediately required.

In an attempt to overcome the unwinding problem associated with the tackiness of the rubber-covered glass cord, this material was made into a warp from unrolling packages and set up for weaving again in a conventional shuttle loom. Difficult problems were experienced in weaving because tacky rubber deposits formed on the healds, reed, raceboard, shuttle, and the shuttle boxes. In addition, the fabric contracted about 30 per cent. from the reed but, despite these problems, about 40 metres of fabric were woven. The Triplex test results with this fabric were excellent, leading to a requirement for several hundred metres. An existing specialized loom was modified to enable the rubberized glass cord to be woven as weft by withdrawing the yarn tangentially from the supply package at the loom. To cope with the large rotating mass of the supply package and the intermittent demand for weft during the weaving cycle, a special weft metering and storage system was devised. This had several novel features including a system which compensated automatically for changes in pick length occurring as a result of the irregular surface characteristics and tackiness of the rubber-covered glass cord. The modifications were highly successful, enabling the difficult rubberized glass cord to be woven efficiently, and the resulting fabric quality was exceptionally good.

In use, the pressurization loads on the windscreen under normal 'no failure' conditions are carried by the two main Triplex 'Ten–Twenty' glass plies and transmitted into the aircraft structure via the Thiokol polysulphide rubber and the capping metal. Under these conditions the tertiary load path edging fabric is in a 'slack' state and transmits no load either to or from the windshield. Under double-failure conditions, however, i.e. with both main glass plies broken, the PVB acts as a diaphragm and provides a tertiary load path deflecting outwards with the rubberized glass cord fabric edge reinforcement, in these circumstances, transmitting the load from the PVB to the frame. The statutory minimum duration of applied pressure after breaking all glass plies is 15 minutes under test conditions in the hottest likely, most critical, environment to be encountered at altitude, as specified by the Boeing Company. These conditions were maintained for almost exactly three hours, at which stage the interlayer edge attachment system eventually failed, having withstood many times the 15 minute statutory period.

A full programme of qualification testing was completed to the satisfaction of the Boeing Company, the American Federal Aviation Administration, and the British Civil Aviation Authority. Commercially the windshield has been very successful and although relatively small quantities of fabric are required for the edge restraints of the windshield, the loom has twice been set up in the intervening period to produce further quantities of the fabric. An important point has been the improvement to the rubber-covered glass cord, resulting in a considerable reduction in tackiness of the rubber. The fabric can now be woven without the side unwinding weft-metering system by weft withdrawal direct from the interior of hollow cheeses.

The fabric edge attachment is now being successfully used on other aircraft products, notably new windshields for Boeing's next generation of aircraft, the Boeing 757 and 767 models, and multimillion dollar orders have been received by Triplex.

This work not only demonstrates the capability of the Shirley Weaving Section in dealing with technical problems but exemplifies the spirit of collaboration which the weaving staff strives to engender with contractors and without which its high success rate could not possibly have been achieved.

Other Collaborative Efforts

Many other examples could be given of the different types of work which involve the working together of people from different disciplines and from different organizations. These would include products undertaken in fields such as:

1. Degradation of polyurethanes. This involves people from chemistry, biochemistry, polymer chemistry, and microbiology, and has international multisponsorship. An interesting point to note is that the need was identified from incoming technical service work.
2. Health and safety. This involves chemistry, engineering, textile technology, government manufacturing, and dermatology in a project related to problems in the use of formaldehyde and cotton growing, textile technology, biochemistry, and mechanical skills related to a problem in byssinosis.
3. Filtration. This involves marketing, applied physics, fibre and textile technology, engineering. This project started as a market survey and has moved through various practical stages and in different directions as needs have been identified and agreed. This has meant that progress has been in steps and over time the team composition has changed.
4. Arterial prosthesis. This involves fibre science, film science, textile technology, physiology, and surgery.

Organization

The Institute has always been organized on discipline lines and for the majority of its life 'individual' R & D management has been the dominant mode of operation. That is, projects have been initiated and progressed by an individual's initiative. The importance of maintaining such initiatives is still recognized but more emphasis is now placed on group R & D management with a strong commercial and marketing orientation. This change has been one of evolution rather than revolution over about a ten-year period. During this time a marketing group has been formed and diversification has been encouraged both into new discipline areas and also into new industry sectors.

This has led to a more 'extrovert' organization and although more demanding the challenge has been accepted. All work must now have clearly defined objectives and must be completed to cost and time to ensure customer satisfaction and budgeted cash flow. No money now comes to the Institute 'as of right'—all has to be sought and all has to be earned. Individual scientists and particularly project leaders have to:

1. Help to identify needs in their sectors;
2. Become involved at an early stage in selling, and prepare and become committed to proposals with clearly defined objectives which specify the cost of the work and when it will be completed;
3. Manage their projects efficiently in a commercial as well as a scientific sense.

It is important to note that the individuals involved have to form interdisciplinary teams among themselves and with staff from organizations outside the Institute, e.g. from industrial firms, government departments, and universities both within and outside the United Kingdom. In fact, 30 per cent.

of the total income comes from overseas, with projects having been undertaken now for fifty different customers.

As mentioned in the case study, the Institute now has a more flexible organization structure which allows, indeed encourages, a project team to grow to a dimension where long-term opportunities are foreseen. It must also be assumed that the reverse will take place when problem areas decline in importance. Such changes must, however, be carefully managed to prevent short-term fluctuations due to too rapid reactions to external events.

Concluding Remarks

The recent history of the Shirley Institute clearly shows how a more narrowly based research establishment can make use of its skills in many directions. The example given illustrates how the main background expertise area—textile technology—can be combined with many other disciplines to attack a wide range of industrial problems.

This has not been done without a good deal of effort, particularly in the areas of communication and control, with emphasis being placed on the importance of inventiveness, innovation, and on technology transfer. The net result is a new and challenging organization to work in with a pragmatic problem-solving attitude but dedicated to the upholding of those quality aspects which were the main features on which its earlier reputation was built and which must be maintained if its future is to remain secure.

ADAPTORS AND INNOVATORS: THE WAY PEOPLE APPROACH PROBLEMS
M. J. KIRTON
The Hatfield Polytechnic, St. Albans, Hertfordshire, England

Abstract

(A full version of this paper appeared in *Planned Innovation*, March/April 1980, pages 51 to 54.)

According to recent research into problem-solving styles in which the author has been involved people can be divided into two extreme types: those who solve problems by adapting and those who solve them by innovating. The first type, the adaptors, accept the general environment of viewpoints in which a problem appears to be embedded. The other type, the innovators, stand back from the problem's current environment and see it from a new perspective. Consequently the two types tend to produce two very different kinds of solution. Furthermore, they tend to have incompatible temperaments which can make integration into the same team rather difficult.

The paper expands on this description, provides a list of behavioural characteristics which tend to go along with each of the two types, and makes some observations on how each type could behave in innovatory situations such as R & D. A mention is also made of a quantitative method of discovering the style to which a particular person exhibits, known as the Kirton Adaptation–Innovation Inventory. Most people are found to be mixtures of types, perhaps one or the other predominating. The paper concludes with a brief review of how the system is being used in creativity training, in which the author sees its main role as inducing a better mutual understanding between these diverse types.

MANAGEMENT OF SCIENTIFIC STAFF AT THE HARWELL LABORATORY OF THE UK ATOMIC ENERGY AUTHORITY
G. G. E. LOW
AERE, Harwell, Oxfordshire, England

Abstract

(A full version of this paper appeared in *R & D Management*, 1982, 12(1), 1–6.)

Harwell's primary role is to serve as the main research laboratory supporting the UK nuclear power programme, but it also carries out R & D outside the nuclear field for UK government and industrial customers. There is therefore a need to manage a very large number of separate and disparate items of work and coordinate them efficiently with the nuclear programmes. This is done through the use of a form of matrix management. Many of the technical, commercial, and personnel management decisions are devolved within the matrix organization to teams formed by mutual agreement between representatives of the two axes of the matrix. Such smaller interdisciplinary groupings of staff are effective in providing the environment in which good staff management practices can be induced and a constructive team spirit can be built up.

THE INTERDISCIPLINARY IMPACT
A. R. MICHAELIS
Editor, Interdisciplinary Science Reviews, *London, England*

Abstract

Partly as a result of the success of scientific specialization in creating the scientific progress of the nineteenth and early twentieth centuries scientists and many others in the cultural field have experienced a deeply felt isolation from one another and from ordinary people. A counter movement towards interdisciplinary rapprochement started in the forties and fifties, spurred on no doubt by the success of such collaboration in the military field. The paper reviews the history of this movement, giving a number of examples. The author believes this movement is spreading rapidly and is convinced that only by the extension of the interdisciplinary concept to solving the complex techno-politico-economic problems of our day can the catastrophe threatening mankind be averted.

GENETIC ENGINEERING—IS THERE A NEED FOR MORE INTERDISCIPLINARITY?
D. MILLER, A. W. PEARSON, and D. F. BALL
R & D Research Unit, Manchester Business School, Manchester, England

Introduction

Genetic engineering, despite its name, is not a sub-discipline of traditional engineering. Use of this term is no more appropriate than calling chemistry molecular engineering. A better name would be genetic manipulation, for it is concerned with modifying those parts of the cell that contain genetic information, by addition or removal of DNA. In fact, the term can be positively misleading, in that, even when the 'engineering' in the above sense is achieved, unique and difficult problems of chemical engineering will have to be solved before commercial exploitation is possible. Nevertheless, because of its common usage the term genetic engineering will be used in this paper.

The reason for raising genetic engineering in the context of a discussion of interdisciplinary research is that we believe that the introduction of technologies based on it will raise interdisciplinary problems more acutely than have ever previously been experienced. Our belief is based on case studies we have previously conducted into single-cell protein, high fructose corn syrup, and new smoking materials (Baker et al., 1978; Miller, Pearson, and Ball, 1980). The opinions put forward in this paper and its conclusions draws on the information contained in these studies.

The Contemporary Context of Genetic Engineering

The use by man of microorganisms to make bread, cheese, and wine using yeast and bacteria has extended over hundreds of years. The general term for such processes is biotechnology, in which there has been a heightened interest during the past decade. This has been stimulated by our knowledge of the structure of DNA and ideas of genetic manipulation, and also by improvements in enzymology, leading to improved knowledge of the ways to stabilize and reuse these biological catalysts. Additionally, there has been increased realization that microorganisms can be grown on a wide variety of substrates ranging from oil and cellulose to metallic sulphides. These factors have led to the belief that the eventual impact of biotechnology and genetic engineering will be comparable to that of microprocessors.

The present widespread interest in genetic engineering derives from the diversity of its potential application. There are seven main areas. The first is in energy production, both replacing existing sources and creating new ones. An example of this is the production of alcohol as a motor fuel in Brazil, which is expected to replace 25 per cent. of Brazil's petroleum needs within a few years. The second is in the production of food; e.g. ICI have already used genetic engineering to produce a protein animal feed from a methanol substrate and elsewhere genetic engineering is being used to produce food directly for human consumption. The third area is that of pharmaceuticals, a field that is being very extensively researched because in pharmaceuticals there is a high added value for a relatively modest volume. Of course, this is to some extent offset by the fact that legislation is now requiring increasingly lengthy and rigorous testing. The fourth field is agriculture, which covers better methods of producing fertilizers as well as breeding plants which, for example, have the ability to fix nitrogen directly. The fifth application is in resource recovery. The use of bacteria to dissolve metallic sulphides is well known and the potential for genetically engineering bacteria to operate in other fields of metal extraction has been recognized by the US mining companies who have been among the first to invest in research in this field. Bacteria may also be used in the extraction of oil, particularly from oil shale where current technologies are uneconomic. The sixth area is in the treatment of both liquid and solid waste where the microorganisms could not only degrade unwanted materials but could also be useful in generating heat or energy. finally, genetic engineering could be used to adapt microorganisms to perform functions which will enable the chemical industry to use renewable raw materials as an alternative to oil-based feedstock. There are clear signs of widespread interest in this in that Fluor, the international process plant contractors, have invested in a specialized research company, and chemical companies themselves have started their own research with ICI already having had some measure of success.

Interdisciplinary Implications

The question arises as to what is so special about genetic engineering that it may cause interdisciplinary problems different from those associated with the earlier developments in physics and chemistry. There are clearly similar problems but there are important differences. The first relates to the heightened awareness of government and population to both the opportunities and threats arising from a rapidly developing technology. This is exacerbated by the often-felt need to move rapidly to large-scale production. The pressure arising from this means that single-discipline aspects are pursued rapidly and independently, leading to eventual difficulty or breakdown at the interfaces when commercial operation is commenced. Not only is there a need to integrate the various disciplines but there also needs to be cohesion with the existing base.

Genetic engineering, therefore, as well as providing new opportunities, brings with it new problems. One of the most pressing is that concerned with safety. This includes the escape of potentially dangerous mutant strains from laboratories, the occurrence of mutations within the fermentor and subsequently in the products, the airborne spread of organisms from the production site, the alteration of the environment with the discharge of nutrients, and, for the workers, the release of microorganisms into the working environment. There may be an additional problem with the release of biological materials as opposed to chemicals, i.e. their potential to multiply rather than being diluted, as is usually the fate of chemical waste.

Such considerations have resulted in the field of genetic engineering becoming highly emotive. It is also associated with germ warfare, unnatural mutations in animals and man, and science fiction, which often relies for its impact on the uncontrollable growth of some invading species with consequent impact on life on the planet. It may well be that this will give rise to social and political problems of a severity only matched by nuclear power generation.

As a further example of the complexities, we refer to the case of the development of the single-cell protein process. This is an example of how crude political and economic pressures can influence what is at first sight a purely technical matter. British Petroleum were the first company to exploit the process of growing microorganisms for animal feed using oil as the substrate. The research for this started in the fifties when oil was plentiful and cheap. This was followed in the sixties by a variety of other companies examining a number of alternatives involving various substrates. By the early seventies British Petroleum had sufficient expertise to build a commercial scale plant in Sardinia, but this did not commence operation despite investment in excess of £20 million. This was for two reasons: the first involved the large increase in the price of oil following the Middle East war and the second the eventual withdrawal of permission to operate the plant by the Italian Government as a response to various political pressures.

Consequent Institutional Developments

A number of institutional developments, particularly those concerned with R & D, are taking place to deal with the impact of this new field of technological opportunities. Research activity is at present conducted in four sectors. Three of these are traditional—the university, government-financed research institutes, and conventional chemical companies. The fourth sector consists of a new type of industrial company which is now beginning to emerge. These companies deal only with genetic engineering and exhibit a combination of academe and industry rarely seen in the past. Found mainly but not exclusively in the United States their function is to carry out basic research for subsequent commercial exploitation by other companies (Fox, 1980). The opportunity for such developments was identified by business school graduates who persuaded established bioscientists to join them and obtained venture capital from such companies as Standard Oil, Dow Chemicals, Eli Lilly, and Monsanto. Some of these specialized research companies have persuaded academics to join them on a full-time basis or to associate part-time, thus retaining their academic affiliations. The inducements are not only financial since the companies are able to provide extremely good facilities and support staff, which permits progress at a rate difficult to sustain in the traditional university setting where the time schedule is imposed by the requirements of postgraduate degrees. This has caused difficulty for university research in terms of retaining staff and also the scientists can take their discoveries with them.

In March 1980 a working party set up by the UK government and headed by Dr A. Spinks proposed a number of ways to exploit the new technology (MSO, 1980). Among their recommendations was the establishment of a Joint Committee for biotechnology; greater coordination between government, research establishments, universities, industry, and research associations; and the setting up of a professional body. They did not propose a new government research establishment for biotechnology but only the expansion of a limited number of centres of excellence backed by the UK University Grants Committee. It has been argued that the techniques of the chemical engineers are not adaptable to the large-scale operation of biotechnology and that a separate new discipline should emerge. It is noteworthy that in Japan there are some four thousand doctoral students studying biotechnology and its application and in France there are two hundred.

Concluding Remarks

This brief résumé has illustrated a few of the factors that need to be resolved and integrated if the development of genetic engineering is not to be impeded. The food and drug industries have experience in handling microorganisms but for mining and bulk chemicals this will be an essentially new venture. For these latter groups experience plus normal corporate considerations will determine their application. This raises the question of the industries most likely to apply genetic engineering since it is here that the traditional interdisciplinary problems such as transition from research to production will arise. It is also these industries which will need to consider their development in a wider context to include consideration of potential social and political problems. The seventies have seen the emergence of strong environmental lobbies whose activities have initiated legislation and influenced political decisions.

In conclusion, this paper has set out to show that if genetic engineering is to be applied successfully it will have to take account of special problems which accrue from its very novelty. These are likely to occur at the interface between genetic engineering and other disciplines—if insufficient attention is given to this interface unscheduled difficulties and delays are likely to occur. For prospects which have required massive investment in both R & D and hardware and which, in the first instance, are likely to be marginally economic, the consequences of delay could be catastrophic.

References

Ball, D. F., Miller, D., and Pearson, A. W. (September, 1978). 'Matching technological opportunities to market needs', in *Third International Conference on Research, Development and Education*, Wroclaw, Poland.
Financial Times, January 17, 1981, 'Fluor buys into Genetech', p.23.
Fox, J. L. (March 17, 1980). 'Genetic engineering industry arranges', *Chemical and Engineering News*, pp.15–22.
HMSO (1980). *Biotechnology—Report of a Joint Working Party* Her Majesty's Stationery Office, London.
Miller, D., Pearson, A. W., Ball, D. F. (1980). 'Environmental gatekeeper—product of hindsight or tool for the future', *R & D Management Tenth Anniversary Conference*, Manchester.
Rothman, H., Stanley, R., Thompson, S., and Towaski, Z. (1980). *Bio-technology: A Review and Annotated Bibliography*, Francis Pinter, London.

RELATIONS BETWEEN DECISION-MAKERS AND RESEARCH WORKERS ON ENVIRONMENTAL PROBLEMS: THE CASE OF FRENCH RESEARCH ON NOISE*

G. MOSER and C. LEVY-LEBOYER
Université René Descartes, Paris, France

Environmental research is relatively young in France: governmental structures aiming at piloting research in this field were set up in 1971, together with a certain number of scientific committees, among which was the Noise Committee. These committees were granted finance and designed to launch research into the different fields of the environment through contacts with research teams in universities, industry, and other institutions.

Government concern on environmental problems stemmed from the fact that it was necessary to associate, with the initiation of the research, the people concerned with the decisions to be taken on the environment. More precisely, regarding noise, the acousticians expressed this necessity by a question addressed to the social sciences and formulated as follows:

Who or what determines the annoyance due to noise?

In the present study, our purpose was to analyse the way this question was answered through research work in an interdisciplinary setting:

*Research supported by DGRST, contract no. 78-70725.

Who answers, who does not answer, and why?

In other words, our purpose was to analyse the way research committees on noise have been working and in particular to analyse the relation between the research workers and the people seeking results:

Which laboratories have undertaken environmental research? Why do others not work in this field or do not enter in this type of applied research which mostly requires interdisciplinarity?

How does innovation, which is the necessary condition for a profitable research, intervene in the different processes implemented and what are the mechanisms helping or, on the contrary, hampering the diversification of research and the setting up of new approaches?

For these purposes, we have analysed the functioning of the Noise and Vibration Committee since the first contracts were implemented and up to 1976. In order to be able to interpret the results thus obtained, we compared the functioning of this Committee with the Air Pollution Committee which was set up at the same time but whose aim was narrower—to help to develop the knowledge on the impact of various polluting agents.

The purpose of the Noise and Vibration Committee is to analyse the impact of noise on man; it is therefore a typical committee of environmental research. Its objectives need collaboration between engineers, physicists, and research workers from the social sciences (psychologists, sociologists, architects, economists, and so on). We can say that it is an interdisciplinary committee turned to applied research.

On the other hand, the aim of the Air Pollution Committee is to identify the atmospheric polluting agents and consequently to pilot essentially technological research employing research workers from disciplines very close to one another.

They have similar tasks: define research priorities and seek research proposals from public as well as private research organizations by means of calls for proposals. The Committee then selects a certain number of proposals from among those it finances according to various criteria such as: expected results, reputation of the research team, methodology, etc.

Furthermore, the two committees work practically in the same way: the organization chart gives a chronological statement of the different processes they carry out (see Figure 1). Based on this chart, different analyses were made as part of our study.

1. A content analysis of the memoranda of the meetings, more particularly according to the type of intervention (we called 'intervention' the fact of taking the floor and being listened to):
   (a) Scientific discussion,
   (b) Evaluation of submitted proposals,
   (c) Organizational interventions.

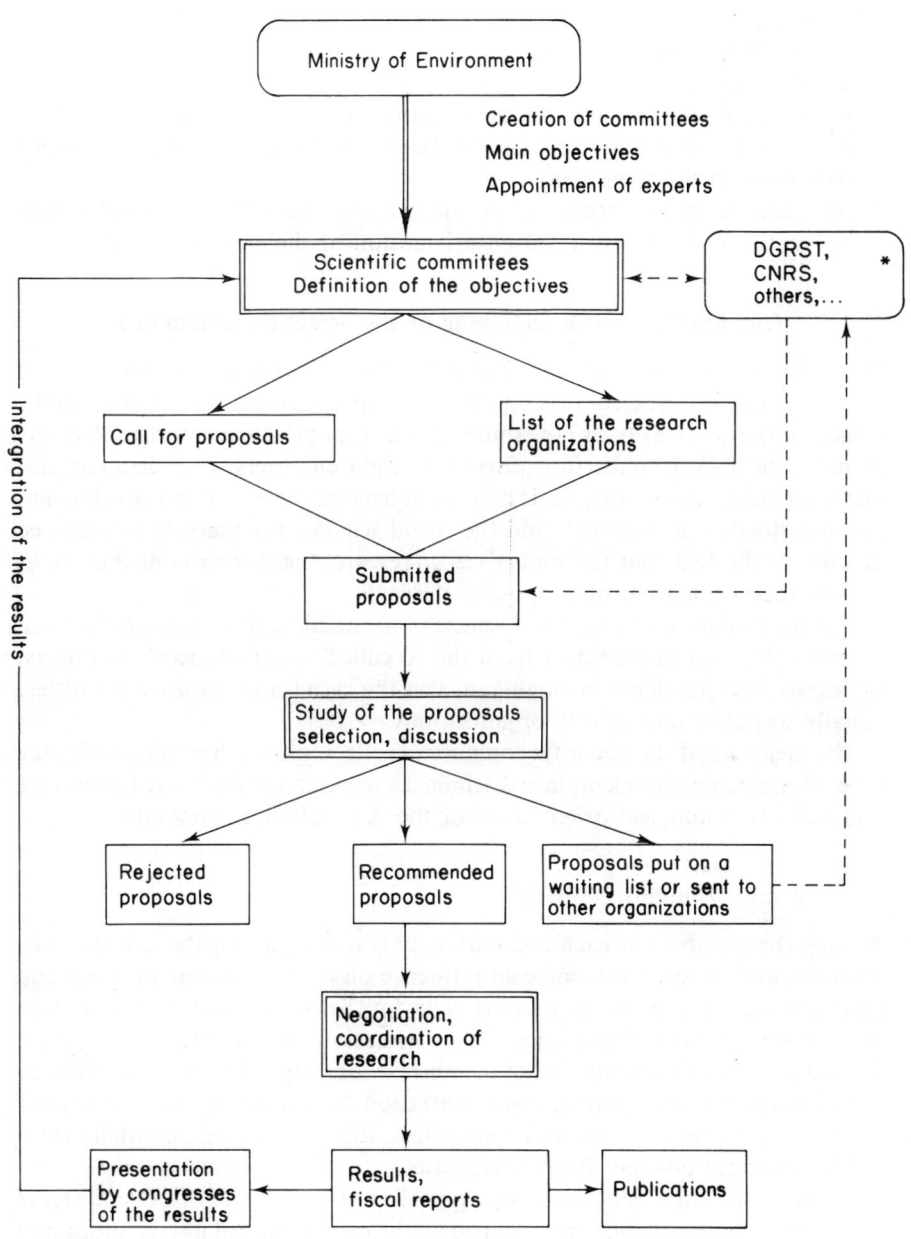

Figure 1

2. A detailed content analysis of the submitted proposals and of the funded research work:
   (a) Topics of research,
   (b) Identity of the applicant,
   (c) Methdology.
3. An analysis of answers to a questionnaire addressed to all research organizations which had not submitted a proposal to the Committee although they work in the same field.
4. An analysis of the programmes funded and the way their results were integrated in the future research orientation of the scientific committee.

Composition and Functioning of the Scientific Committee

Does the composition of the Noise Committee reflect the necessity of interdisciplinary research? Its eighteen members come both from public organizations (university or government) and from private enterprise. They are of different backgrounds: four physicists, eight engineers, four acousticians, one economist, one ethnologist. It must be noted that there is neither psychologist nor sociologist nor architect, and the social sciences are scarcely represented in spite of the fact that the objectives of research need their contribution as well as their evaluation of proposals.

The Air Pollution Committee, because of its mainly technological objectives, is only composed of members from the so-called 'exact sciences': engineers, biologists, and physicists belonging, as was the case for the Noise Committee, equally to public and private organizations.

The members of the scientific committees reflect, although incompletely, the type of research undertaken: interdisciplinary research for the Noise Committee and more technological orientation for the Air Pollution Committee.

How do these committees work?

Among the members of each committee, only a few participate actively in its meetings and consequently have an influence on the functioning of the group (presence and interventions): they are eight for the Noise Committee and seven for the Air Pollution Committee. The orientations of the research therefore depend on a very limited number of members whose importance is not necessarily linked to the part they play in the organization but exclusively to their regular and active participation. In both committees, they are coming essentially from public organizations and from universities.

Globally speaking, what are the types of intervention in both committees? For a better understanding, we grouped all the organizational interventions and the interventions concerning the discussion of the proposals as *administrative activities* on the one hand, and the interventions related to *scientific problems*— research objectives, scientific information—on the other hand. Indeed, the discussion of the proposals may be considered as an administrative activity insofar as the proposals are pre-selected by the sub-group concerned which proposes a certain number of proposals to be retained by the whole committee. Therefore the Noise Committee dedicates more than half of its activities to internal regulation problems. There appear to be neither explicit nor implicit rules of management in it. This absence of rules is probably due to the interdisciplinary composition of the Committee. Is the Air Pollution Committee more active and productive concerning research than the Noise Committee?

The study of the nature of the different scientific interventions in both committees can give us an answer to this question.

We therefore distinguished three types of scientific interventions:

1. General discussion,
2. Research suggestions,
3. Scientific information.

This last type can be considered as an external contribution since it introduces original information into the Committee.

Table 1. Nature of the interventions

	Administrative problems		Research problems		Total	
Noise Committee	265	52%	240	48%	505	(100%)
Air Pollution Committee	294	39%	460	61%	754	(100%)

$X^2 = 22.27$, significant for $p = 0.001$.

Table 2. Importance of the various scientific interventions in both committees

	General discussion		Research suggestions		Scientific information		Total	
Noise Committee	43	17.9%	70	29.2%	127	52.9%	240	(100%)
Air Pollution Committee	160	34.8%	176	38.3%	124	26.9%	460	(100%)

$X^2 = 48.82$, significant for $p = 0.001$.

It can be seen by comparing Tables 1 and 2 that in the Noise Committee more than half of the interventions on research consists of scientific information, while in the Air Pollution Committee the percentage of scientific information represents only one-quarter of the total number of interventions concerning research. The Noise Committee thus receives twice as much external information as the Air Pollution Committee. Consequently we can say that, based more frequently on external contributions, the Noise Committee is more innovating than the Air Pollution Committee. This superiority of the Noise Committee which we can attribute logically to its interdisciplinarity is revealed by some of the topics proposed for submission to the research laboratories:

1. Psychological and biological impacts of noise on man,
2. Noise and education,
3. Social costs of noise,
4. Impulsive noise.

Unlike the Noise Committee, the Air Pollution Committee has without varying been exploring the same topic since its creation.

Therefore it is obvious that interdisciplinary research involves a certain inertia in the functioning (many more interventions on organizational and management problems) but at the same time this makes it possible to bring forth diversified scientific contributions and gives an innovating impulse to research. Is this openness inside the Noise Committee reflected in the proposals submitted?

Response to the Call for Proposals

On the whole, the rate of response given to the calls for proposals is rather low, about 20 per cent. Private organizations are relatively less reluctant to submit a project than public ones: they are more disposed than public organizations (universities in particular) to undertake applied research based on a contract (nearly 30 per cent. of the private organizations working in this field sent a proposal, while only 18 per cent. of the public institutions answered).

With respect to the proposals submitted to the Noise Committee, we investigated which disciplines were involved. Among thirty projects:

11 originated from acousticians, engineers, and technicians;
10 from psychologists, sociologists and economists;
 9 only from associated acousticians and research workers in the social sciences.

From this it appears that only one-third of the proposals meet the required interdisciplinary approach to the problem of noise.

Public research workers, and to a smaller extent private research workers, are reluctant to undertake applied research. Furthermore, only 30 per cent. of the submitted proposals declared a practical and immediate application of their results. The small number of answers from interdisciplinary teams indicates that the submission of projects is being hampered by this requirement of a collaboration between different disciplines. However, is it the only factor responsible for this reluctance of most of the research organizations to submit research proposals?

To find an answer, we sent a questionnaire to all the research organizations which had received the first call for proposals and which had not submitted a proposal. This questionnaire made it possible to identify the laboratories which had not answered and the reasons for their nil response. Three types of reasons were distinguished:

1. Reasons concerning the structure of the laboratory ('the research workers are not available', for instance);

2. Reasons closely linked to the constraints due to research based on a government contract (financial limits, for instance);
3. Reasons concerning the content of the call for proposals ('the laboratory does not work on this type of research', for instance).

It appears that more than 60 per cent. of the non-submission of a project is due to the structure of the laboratory. Most often the reasons put forward are the following:

1. 'Such research work would need extra staff.'
2. 'The research workers are already on defined programmes and are not available.'
3. 'The laboratory has not sufficient funds to launch such a research programme.'
4. 'This would demand a reorganization of the different activities inside the laboratory.'

To these reasons, we can add those concerning structural problems: financial reasons such as the difficulty of getting new finance, etc. The major obstacle seems to be the difficulty of hiring extra staff. The non-availability of research workers and the lack of financial means are impediments to the enlargement of the activities of the various research laboratories. These reasons are mostly set forth by the universities (60 per cent).

More precisely, it appears that it is in the small university laboratories which are carrying out fundamental research programmes that inertia is the greatest. At the same time, those laboratories seem most interested in applied research. Apart from functional problems, they declare themselves competent and interested in the topics exposed in the call for proposals. Most of them are carrying out fundamental as well as applied research.

These laboratories interested in applied research would provide the basis and the knowledge necessary for a high-quality research, but they hesitate to undertake such a research because of too many management, structural, and reorientation problems.

Research Work Undertaken by the Committees

The research work funded by the different committees are a good reflection of the objectives formulated in the corresponding call for proposals.

The *Noise Committee* recommended applied research in three particular topics:

1. Discomfort due to noise in dwellings through the field studies relating noise measures to the level of discomfort felt by the occupants.
2. Study of the social cost of noise by means of epidemiological inquiries.
3. Impact of noise on man: speech disturbance, memorization, personal factors, etc., dealing mostly with concrete cases. Those studies are complemented by

more fundamental researches aiming at extending the present knowledge concerning the impact of noise on sleep.

Most of the studies undertaken are interdisciplinary and associate engineers and acousticians with research workers from the social sciences. They are based on the analysis of the impact of noise on people directly concerned: occupants of noisy dwellings, people living close airports or busy highways, etc. Consequently, more than half of the research workers whose proposals had been accepted meant to get out of their laboratory and carry out a field study. Two-thirds of the studies undertaken put forward essentially the practical interest of the results anticipated.

In other respects, the analysis of the accepted proposals compared to the submitted ones shows that the Noise Committee elicits responses from research teams for which this field is new and which are therefore more likely to bring forward original suggestions to the problems.

This is not the case for the *Air Pollution Committee:* the research is essentially undertaken with the objective of advancing a corpus of knowledge; it is fundamental research. Furthermore, the fact that the members of the Committee come from related disciplines implies that nearly two-thirds of the authors of proposals have links with the committee. It is obvious that research inside this committee is the preserve of an exclusive scientific community which includes the members of the committee and the contracting parties. There is very little room for new staff and consequently for innovation in research.

It follows from all this that the Noise Committee is concerned with a large range of problems as revealed by the successive calls for proposals of this Committee. They express an effort to supply to the decision-makers elements including the various aspects of the impact of noise on man.

Conclusion

The data produced here represent only a description of the functioning of two scientific committees piloting research, the one on the problem of noise and the other on the problem of atmospheric pollution. In a field where research did not exist or was scarcely existent, a study of this functioning makes it possible to formulate two remarks regarding interdisciplinarity and applied research.

1. *Implementation of interdisciplinarity.* We saw that the committees deferred profoundly. The characteristic of the Noise Committee is its interdisciplinarity. It brings in the social sciences to a field where they did not exist before. The Air Pollution Committee involves a field where the members of the Committee, as well as the research workers, form an 'exclusive scientific community'. As we saw, this difference concerning the composition and the objective has an influence on the way the committees work.

   In the Noise Committee, ponderous in its functioning, the members take twice as much time to get mutual understanding. This external contribution is useful: it makes it possible to enlarge the scientific debate and to enrich it with contributions and points of view proceeding from other disciplines.

On the other hand, there is half as much general discussion in the Noise Committee. Research orientation problems do not form the subject of long philosophical debates and the discussion on the general orientations of research deviate very quickly towards comparisons of methods of scientific approaches.

If the Noise Committee, because of a certain inertia in its functioning, seems to be unproductive in the short run, it appears to us that this type of functioning is in the long run the main condition for innovation and the main chance to give rise to real interdisciplinary research, the various fields represented having thus an opportunity to have a direct confrontation.

2. *Applied research.* There are many obstacles in the way of becoming involved in research connected with the environment. We have found that only a limited number of scientists are willing to take part in such research, either as expert advisers or as contractors. In specific terms, laboratories likely to undertake applied research fall into three categories:

(a) Those which undertake it because it will bring in something new to their research interests. This is true of research dealing with the effect of noise on sleep, all of which was engaged in by laboratories concerned with fundamental research on sleep.

(b) Those which, because of their problem-solving environment, are accustomed to change the focus of their interest according to current demand.

(c) Those which accept the challenge of a new demand but only if it fits in with their normal field of research and does not involve any need to adapt, i.e. to acquire new information, to build a new methodology, or especially to recruit additional staff.

The dynamics of the relationship between research workers and decision-makers with respect to matters related to the environment show clearly that the motivations of fundamental research workers are quite different from those which guide workers engaged in applied research. Interdisciplinarity in a committee concerned with fundamental research seems to promote interdisciplinarity in the research it supports, though it has its difficulties. This is not the case for applied research; resolution of this difficulty is essential when the required research is elicited by a problem that is urgent and precise in its specification. It will not be possible to change the reluctance of research workers to substitute the case value of their work for the more familiar motivation of working free of constraints towards fundamental knowledge. However, and this is made clear by the attitudes of those engaged in work on sleep disturbance and the social psychology of disturbance by external interferences generally, being confronted with an urgent practical problem often makes research workers get out of their accustomed grooves and to formulate their fundamental problems constructively.

TEAM-BUILDING AND GROUP PROCESS ANALYSIS IN INTERDISCIPLINARY RESEARCH TEAMS

A. W. PEARSON

R & D Research Unit, Manchester Business School, Manchester, England

Introduction

There has been much debate about the nature of interdisciplinary research and a number of attempts to distinguish between multi- and interdisciplinarity. It has been argued that many of the major problems which we face require an interdisciplinary approach while, for example, many of our academic institutions tend to be organized along single-discipline lines.

In looking at the question of types of differences between multi- and interdisciplinarity it is useful to focus upon aspects of communication. Very briefly, it can be argued that there is the need for a much greater intensity of information-sharing in the interdisciplinary area.

In an earlier study of organizational structure (Gunz and Pearson, 1977) it was found quite difficult to identify the precise nature of matrix organization, given that almost every research establishment had a different structure and that even within a single establishment there were a number of structures operating at the same time. It was found to be more useful to make distinctions based upon the way in which projects were managed. A range of management styles was assumed, the polar opposites of the dimension being coordination versus leadership. It was argued that in some types of projects the major function of the project leader was to make sure that individual activities were carried out at the appropriate time and that the information outputs and inputs between different individuals and/or specialized groups were linked together in the most appropriate manner, taking into account time and cost dimensions. This style characterizes the 'coordination' end of the dimension. The 'leadership' style of management involved a much more interactive relationship between the project manager and the other group members. The project manager was often involved in more detailed discussions of the content of the work and, in many cases, in reprogramming activities on the basis of changes in technical outputs. Clearly there is a continuum and in particular it was argued that the simple coordination mode would not really be possible when there was a heavy pressure on resources, in which case the project leader would have to intervene in many ways in order to make sure the work was progressing adequately. For example, attention would have to be given to maintaining motivation when progress was slow due to factors outside the control of individual project team members.

The key point, then, is information-sharing and here we come up against the question of whether people from different disciplines are not only prepared to share information with each other but whether, in fact, they have enough of a common intellectual background to understand each other's approaches and potential difficulties. The issue of communication between people with different disciplinary backgrounds was mentioned as a major issue, leading to the breakdown of many projects in the First Conference (see Barth and Steck, 1979).

The words 'different cognitive frameworks' have been used to describe this problem. However, this is not the only cause of interpersonal communication difficulties; we are now much more aware of the influence of factors such as personality. For example, recent work which has been looking at the types of people who are involved in problem-solving groups suggests that individuals differ in the degree to which they choose adaptive versus innovative behaviour patterns. Those patterns can have considerable influence on the way in which people react to each other and whether they are likely to be supportive or not of adventurous behaviour in difficult circumstances (see Kirton, 1980). Certainly the recent interest in the different team roles required within a successful team is becoming widely discussed. In a nutshell, research is demonstrating that the difference between more successful and less successful groups can in part be explained by interpersonal and group attitudes and behaviour.

A number of questions must be raised in many R & D situations. For example, how interdependent are the different research activities? Do they require integration into a team or can they be done separately and pooled later? If integration is required, how much is required to turn a group into a team? If a team is needed, what can we do to create one once the members have been assembled?

A number of approaches have been designed and used for developing teams, some of which imply a fairly high level of structure. For example, at the First IDR Conference one approach was described which focuses on (see Pearson, Payne, and Gunz, 1979)

1. Goals,   that is   'What are we doing?'
2. Roles,   that is   'Who does what?'
3. Procedures,   that is   'How do we do it?'

The argument is made by proponents of this approach that if these three issues are tackled in the order specified each step clarifies the problems implicit in the next step and that individual personality problems and commitment issues tend to be reduced in magnitude because they are not exacerbated by problems of unclear goals, roles, procedures, etc. This is a very specific and task-related approach which might have particular relevance to the R & D field where new teams are formed fairly frequently, though it may not be worth the effort if the team has a very short life expectancy.

Are there other alternatives? Can we draw something from other parts of behavioural literature which would help us? A recent workshop on group processes which we conducted with R & D managers suggests certain ways in which this might be achieved and the following brief description of the content of the workshop explains some of the issues and potentially valuable contributions which were highlighted by this approach.

The Group Process Analysis Workshop

A small group of people from different companies, different environments, and different technical backgrounds met together to work with a consultant for two days to learn about group process analysis. From the beginning the point was made that all the individuals must be committed to the idea of sharing experiences in an open way, and from this starting point the group moved into solving an artifically created problem based on survival under adverse conditions (the moon, the desert, a blizzard, etc.). Individuals are asked to specify what their own solutions to the problem were and then to share this with the rest of the group, discussing differences and similarities in solutions and the reasons for choosing the solutions. The group then had to agree as a group what their solution would be. The consultant listened to the discussions and then gave the feedback to the group based on his observations. A number of interesting points were noted. In particular, the average of the individuals' analysis of the survival situation was not seen to be as good as the group's consensus decision using an in-depth analysis by experts as the 'correct' solution. Discussion was also focused upon the way in which differences within the group had been resolved, how individuals had shown particular characteristics in the group (e.g. dominating, encouraging, etc.), and the reaction this had caused among other group members (e.g. withdrawal, antagonism, etc.).

After this another problem was tackled which was much closer to the real world for the participants, focusing as it did on the research and development area. The level of activity, interest, discussion, and disagreement was much higher. It is not perhaps surprising, partly because people knew each other better and partly because it was an issue to which they all had commitment and much background to bring to bear on the problems. Again, the process of discussion and analysis was analysed but this time the group members did it for themselves, making comments about how individual actions had influenced other people within the group and how they felt that the overall performance had been improved or hindered by such actions. An important point to make is that none of the participants had any previous experience of this type of group activity and of feeding back to each other views about personal interaction styles. They were largely from scientific backgrounds, not behavioural orientated, and yet had a quite remarkable degree of agreement about how they had each influenced the group process. Even at this stage they were able, and more importantly willing, to make suggestions for change which they felt would have improved their operation as a group. Many of these suggestions were fairly specific and relatively simple such as 'please don't talk so much' or 'please say more'.

Although these appear to be obvious and even perhaps trivial statements to come out of such a preliminary exercise it was argued that they were not untypical of those that should but did not often get made in the real-life situation. That is, people are often aware of the needs and potential of others but too frequently do not take appropriate steps to do anything about them. This is to the ultimate detriment of the immediate problem and also perhaps as important to the long-term detriment and the development of the individuals concerned and of the project team as a whole—an important point if they are likely to work together again in the future.

This led to some initial discussion of whether some of the behaviour problems exhibited by individual members of the group were ones which they could readily change to advantage, particularly in more difficult situations than those encountered in this artificially created problem setting. Some of the stylistic characteristics appeared to be fairly deep, perhaps part of the personality and probably not easy to change. If this is the case then the results of any process anlaysis exercise might still have considerable implications for selection. This is an important point to be borne in mind, given that not very many people in R & D organizations have the opportunity, as project leaders, to select individuals on the basis of their personal characteristics. Traditionally the first and most important consideration has always been their technical competence.

The next phase of the workshop involved the examination of a case study of a troubled team to which the consultant had been asked to provide advice. The many areas in which actions could be, and had been, taken to improve the morale, motivation, and the performance of this work group were pointed out. It was clear that the group had got to a very low level before the consultant had been called in, raising the important question—would R & D people normally get to the point where they would turn to outside help as it is not frequent for R & D groups to see themselves as being very low on the failure side? Indeed, it is frequently the case, for example, that we must also ask the question whether we have the time because the pressure of work in most innovative-type organizations means that the poorer projects will tend to be dropped and resources reallocated and new groups formed. In such situations it can be argued that there is always the excitement of successful activities to provide real encouragement and support.

A number of points were then raised in discussion. Firstly, do people have the time to pay adequate attention to process analysis? Secondly, under what circumstances is an outside consultant likely to be accepted by R & D groups and how would such a person be 'called in', i.e. by the team itself or by other interested parties, and if so who? Thirdly, who would be involved in any process analysis and at what point in time? These could be advantageous, including a wide range of people including, for example, workshop and other support staff people, by which time the exercise could become very large indeed.

It would not be easy to find a consultant acceptable, and if time is at a premium, all is not lost as it may be possible, and even desirable, for the project leader to take on the role of process analysis. However, returning to the point made at the very beginning about interdisciplinary work, it can be argued that the project leader has already a very difficult task to keep up with the many technical interconnections that are necessary and may not be able, even if equipped to do the job, to cope with the additional effort on the social process, particularly if individual members of the teams are not as concerned as they might be about the group as a whole. Would this sort of activity be dangerous?

The evidence is that it is not, particularly if the leader is well trained and if group members are allowed to back out of it if they choose to.

This raises the question as to whether it might be better to concentrate, in the first instance at least, not on specific teams but rather on the organization as a whole and to make individuals within the organization more aware of the need to consider people and process variables alongside the technical variables. The experience of the participants in the workshop discussed in this paper suggests that this could be done in artificial situations, e.g. through courses and workshops either run at academic institutions or on-site, bringing together people who may well later on be in close working contact. A further development might be for such courses to be built into the educational system for scientists and technologists at the level of higher education. The argument for on-site development rests on an implied need to develop an organizational climate over time in which it is recognized that the interconnections between individuals are likely to have an important effect upon the scientific and technical performance of individual groups and of the organization as a whole. This would clearly suggest that even at the recruitment stage we should be encouraging people to think about this and that induction courses might well include some information about the management of project teams and the roles which individuals at all levels play in their success, the point being made that everybody needs to be concerned about the process and not just the leader.

The final point to make clear is that this is clearly not relevant for all R & D and that there will be some situations and some people who will continue to make significant contributions in certain circumstances in the research and development area by being particularly individualistic and possibly aggressive— the Maverick perhaps. However, it would seem to be that for most people in many organizational settings there could be a great deal of improvement through a better understanding of group process analysis. The experiences from the workshop suggest that individuals with very little background but an interest in this area are able to make judgements which, when fed back to their colleagues in the right setting, can have a considerable beneficial effect on their behaviour in team situations. After all, what is it but development as our own development?

References

Barth, R. T., and Steck, R. (1979). 'Interdisciplinary research groups: their management and organization', *First International Conference on Interdisciplinary Research Groups*, Schloss Reisensburg, Federal Republic of Germany, April 22–28, 1979.

Gunz, H. P., and Pearson, A. W. (1977). 'Introduction of a matrix structure into an R & D establishment', *R & D Management*, 7, 3, 173–181. Blackwells, Oxford.

Kirton, M. J. (1980). 'Adaptors and innovators. The way people approach problems', *Planned Innovation*, March/April 1980.

Pearson, A. W., Payne, R. L., and Gunz, H. P. (1979). 'Communication, co-ordination and leadership in interdisciplinary research', *First International Conference on Interdisciplinary Research Groups*, Schloss Reisensburg, Federal Republic of Germany, April 22–28, 1979.

MANAGERIAL AND ORGANIZATIONAL DETERMINANTS OF EFFICIENCY IN BIOMEDICAL RESEARCH TEAMS

C. PINEAU and C. LEVY-LEBOYER
Université René Descartes, Paris, France

The present research has been undertaken from a decidedly organizational perspective, not only in our approach to the problem (describing methods of training which encourage success in the field of research) but also in our choice of causal variables (work relations, interpersonal relations, style of leadership) and the dependent variable (success defined at laboratory level). We were, moreover, working in a homogeneous and well-defined field of research (biomedical) and our investigations were restricted to organizations belonging to the public sector. Finally, we devoted particular attention firstly to the development of a scheme for rating laboratories in accordance with their level of success and then to the study of the organizational characteristics of these laboratories; this was done in order to avoid confusing the variability of success with the disparity of available funds and human resources. After gaining further insight into the issue, we then set out to discover what it was in the style of leadership that differentiated significantly between the 'good' and the 'less good'. In what follows, we shall describe successively the sample and the method of investigation, the development of criteria for success, and the results obtained.

The Sample and the Method of Investigation

Before describing the sample and the information gathered, it would be worth stressing the exceptionally high percentage of replies obtained. Out of the 155 heads of laboratory included in the initial sample, only four declined to reply. This high rate of response (97 per cent.) may be attributed to the success of the method used, which will be described in greater detail below and which consisted in using the telephone as the means of contact; the success is likewise due to the interest shown by our respondents in the problems raised by our investigation.

Three organizations were selected for this research study: the Institut Pasteur, INSERM (Institute National de la Santé et de la Recherche Médicale), and the René Descartes University. In each instance, the director or head of the establishment was contacted before the study began, the aims of the research were described to him, and his approval was obtained. However, we deliberately did not ask to present our project to the heads of laboratories within the organization itself, for, if this had been done, the study would then have been regarded as an idea inspired by the directors or the management and the replies obtained would have consequently been distorted. We restricted ourselves to asking for a list of the laboratories belonging to these three organizations: the sample used consisted of all the laboratories situated in the region of Paris — 155 in all.

We then sent the head of each laboratory a letter outlining the aims of the research and asking for his cooperation in granting us a telephone interview. Of the heads of laboratory thus contacted 4 refused, 42 indicated that they would prefer a personal interview, and 109 accepted the telephone interview. The interviews varied in length from 15 minutes to 1½ hours (for the telephone interviews) and from ½ hour to 2 hours (for the personal interviews).

The resultant information was then subjected to content analysis using the following item headings: the effectiveness of the research, the organizational variables, the contextual variables, and the heuristic procedures. (They are presented in detail in Annex 1.)

Information was collated from four categories:

1. Data enabling us to establish a criterion for success in research;
2. Information concerning style of leadership and work relations or the working 'atmosphere' in the laboratory;
3. So-called 'anatomical' indications, from which a sort of 'identity file' could be drawn up for each laboratory;
4. Information concerning the objectives and the category of research.

Out of the 151 heads of laboratory questioned, 46 belonged to the Institut Pasteur, 44 to the René Descartes University, and 61 to INSERM. The university laboratories which formed units of INSERM were listed in the sample as INSERM laboratories. In addition, there were fifteen laboratories which also belonged to the CNRS and therefore received support from two organizations. Table 1 shows the fields of research of the different laboratories.

Table 1. Field of research

Field	Number
Immunology	29
Biochemistry	19
Biology	19
Physiology	15
Virology	13
Bacteriology	8
Endocrinology	8
Pharmacology	7
Haematology	6
Surgery and anatomy	6
Paediatrics	5
Neurology	5
Genetics	4
Cardio-vascular diseases	3
Forensic medicine	2
Hydrology	1
Gerontology	1

Clear-cut divisions may be observed in the range of organizations presented, extending from the small laboratory employing a single researcher and two or three technicians to the larger team including thirty researchers and twenty technicians. Altogether, half the laboratories in the sample employed between 11 and 20 people, 20 per cent. employed fewer than 10, and 30 per cent. more than 20.

We also studied the composition of the team: the researchers and technicians at all levels were classified according to eight categories. Table 2 shows their distribution in percentages. The commonest categories were, firstly, the technicians and then persons combining a university position with a medical function; these were followed by university teachers concurrently engaged both in research and in teaching and then by full-time researchers and thesis students. It should be stressed that 20 per cent. of the laboratories examined in the study had no full-time researcher: one cannot help wondering what hopes of success a team may have in which *nobody* is entirely freed from other duties and able to devote himself fully to research.

Table 2. Categories of staff showing frequency in the different laboratories

	Distribution (%)			
	None	1–5	6–10	More than 10
Full-time technicians	8.6	51.6	24	16
Full-time researchers	20.5	43	26.5	10
Thesis students	40.4	49.6	7.3	2.6
Foreign trainees	61	37	2	—
Hospital/university staff	66.2	21.2	8	4.6
Teacher researchers	69	19.2	8.6	3.3
Part-time technicians	91.4	8.6	—	—
Office and caretaking staff	57	40.4	2.6	—

Three other categories figured only rarely: foreign trainees, office staff (non-existent in one case out of two), and technicians employed on a part-time basis. Where no office staff was available, the hospital in which the laboratory was located often provided support. The description 'full-time researcher' corresponds to various situations. It may relate to researchers belonging to the CNRS and working in a university laboratory: 28.5% per cent. of the laboratories had one to three researchers in this situation; 23 per cent. had more than four.

The age distribution conformed to what might have been expected, with the majority being in the thirty to forty age range. A detail worth mentioning, however, is that the average age of the hospital–university staff was appreciably higher than that of the teacher researchers. Mention should also be made of the relative youthfulness of the full-time researchers and technicians (23 per cent. under the age of thirty), a fact which may be attributed to the development of research between the years 1960 and 1970.

Length of service in the laboratory is not always associated with age; it is, in fact, a complex variable. Generally speaking, the figures representing length of service provide an indication of the researchers' mobility, but in the present economic situation, in which there is little recruitment of researchers, instability is rare. Nevertheless, if one compares the researchers' length of service by laboratory, one may agree that it reflects the attitudes of the head (who either attempts to 'keep' his team or else helps it to shape itself by being mobile) and also the attachment of the researchers to their laboratory. Three types of situation may be observed:

1. 'Old' laboratories, in which all the members have at least five years of service. In certain cases, where the laboratory has been active for a long time, a large proportion of the researchers have over ten years of service; in other cases (about a quarter of the sample) those of longest standing have between six and ten years of service.
2. 'Young' laboratories, in which the researchers have less than five years of service. This category represented 18 per cent. of the sample, i.e. nearly one out of five.
3. In the remainder of the sample (somewhat less than ⅔ of the laboratories) the staff had varying lengths of service: either rather young (with some very recently engaged researchers and others somewhat older) or fairly old (with a length of service ranging from two to over ten years).

The technical staff was almost completely female. Among the researchers, there were more men than women in nearly half the laboratories (44.56 per cent.), an equal number in 28.4 per cent. of the laboratories, and more women in 27 per cent. Some of the heads interviewed openly admitted, moreover, that they preferred male researchers as they were less often absent than their female colleagues.

We also interviewed the heads of laboratory concerning the university education of their teams. Their answers are given in Table 3, which shows how many researchers from each category were to be found in the different laboratories. There are four comments to be made on these figures. Firstly, one must note the frequency of researchers with a purely scientific educational background: they were to be found everywhere, and in great numbers. Secondly, graduates of the Grandes Ecoles were not to be found in 88 per cent. of the laboratories were considered. Thirdly, in half the biomedical laboratories there was no doctor. It is true that in most cases the laboratories concerned were carrying out basic research without any clinical aspect; it is likewise true that very often the head of laboratory himself had been trained in medicine. Fourthly, in only one-third of the cases did we find researchers with a double medical and scientific educational background, yet most of the heads interviewed agreed that this was the best background for this type of research.

The heads of laboratory interviewed specified the type of research carried out by their laboratory. One in four described these activities as purely basic and none used the term 'only applied', 18.5 per cent. agreed to describe their research as being more applied than basic, and the remainder qualified their research either as being more basic (17.2 per cent.) or as being equally applied and basic (39.8 per cent.)

Table 3. Researchers' education showing frequency in the different laboratories

	Distribution (%)			
	None	1–5	6–10	Over 10
Grandes Ecoles	88	11.3	0.7	—
Pharmacy	77	17.8	5.3	—
Medicine	49	34.4	16.5	—
Faculty of science	16.6	43.7	30.5	9.3
Faculty of science + medicine	60.3	29	10.6	—

This same tendency towards defining their own work as basic emerged again in the definition of the research objectives. In one case out of two they were described as basic (i.e. analysing biological processes), in 35.8 per cent. of the cases as being oriented towards clinical application and in 13.2 per cent. as towards medical problems, while only 20 per cent. of the laboratories defined their research objective as being the implementation of new techniques and materials.

Among the laboratory heads, there were many who stated that basic research was more attractive and more prestigious; consequently, young researchers are attracted by laboratories where basic research is being carried out. Furthermore, the heads interviewed felt that the basic approach made it possible to achieve results more rapidly.

The conflict between basic research and applied research emerges in the difficult relations between 'basic' researchers and 'applied' researchers. The former consider their activity as being more intellectual, more scientific, and look down with some disdain upon the applied researchers. As one of the laboratory heads expressed it: 'There are two races—the masters and the slaves; the masters are the 'basic' researchers, who develop scientific models, and the slaves are the 'applied' researchers, who are restricted to making up vaccines.'

Some of those in charge of laboratories told us that their team was divided into two groups: non-doctor researchers and doctor researchers who also had hospital duties, each group having powerful internal coherence. However, others ascribed greater value to applied research as it entailed greater responsibility than basic research and made it possible for the results of the work to be seen, and this was its mark of worth.

The Criteria for Success*

Working from the information gathered from the interviews, it was possible to define five criteria for success, representing the activities of the laboratories concerned:

1. The number of times the laboratory was mentioned by colleagues in reply to the question: 'Apart from your own laboratory, could you mention three research laboratories which you consider to be the best in your discipline in France?'
2. The number of invitations to seminars.
3. Participation in international congresses.
4. Publications in international reviews of repute during the previous two years.
5. An assessment by the head of the laboratory of the quality of his researchers (percentage of 'very good' and 'good' researchers).

Mention by peers, while providing interesting information was not totally reliable on account of the rarity of certain specializations. There was, for instance, only one laboratory specializing in hydrology, only one in gerontology, and three in cardio-vascular diseases. These laboratories had clearly little hope of being mentioned by colleagues of the same speciality. These remarks may explain why:

69.5% of the laboratories were never mentioned;
16.6% were mentioned only once;
14% were mentioned two to eight times.

Invitations to attend specialist seminars also revealed a differentiation between the laboratories:

23.2% had not had any researchers invited;
31.1% had received one (or several) invitation for the head;
41.1% had received one (or several) invitation for the head and for other researchers;
4.6% had had all their researchers invited at least once.

Participation at an international congress was a frequent occurrence. Only a minority was not involved in such activities:

6.6% had not taken part in any international congress
9.9% participated if funds were available;
40.4% participated frequently;
32.5% participated with all their researchers taking their turn;

---

*For more details on the criteria definition, see Levy-Leboyer and Pineau (1981).

10.6% participated with all researchers attending congresses devoted to the speciality of their laboratory.

The number of publications varied even more extremely, ranging from zero to thirty for the two preceding years. This figure was, naturally, powerfully influenced by the size of the laboratory; it is, nonetheless, difficult to calculate a percentage (number of publications divided by number of researchers) given the differing status of the researchers. Of the laboratories, 14 per cent. published from zero to four articles, 28.5 per cent. between five and 10 articles, 37.7 per cent. between eleven and twenty, and 19.8 per cent. more than twenty. Among the 'big' publishers (more than eleven articles in the past two years), it was natural that the large laboratories should figure, but there were also interesting exceptions, generally small teams of full-time researchers concerned with basic research.

The global assessment of the researchers was not willingly provided by the heads of laboratory. It was nevertheless possible to classify their replies according to five categories:

Declined to reply: assessment varies with time	21.2%
Nobody 'very good'; most 'good'	18.0%
Some 'very good'	35.0%
As many 'very good' as 'good'	11.3%
Majority 'very good'	14.5%

The first question to be raised if one wishes to use these criteria is whether systematic relations exist between the different indices. We chose first to study the question for indices 1 to 4, as indicator 5 was clearly of too subjective a character. A further difficulty was that all these criteria (except the number of publications) entailed qualitative classifications, which made the calculation of correlations difficult. We adopted the following procedure: the cases corresponding to each criterion were classified from worst to best, with each rating marked by an arbitrary figure, and correlations (r Bravais-Pearson) being calculated between these figures. This method is clearly a simplificaiton of the real situation, i.e. it presupposes that the intervals between the cases are equal in extent. Nevertheless, the results were sufficiently clear-cut to merit attention. In fact, all the correlations calculated were meaningful for $p = 0.001$ or $p = 0.0001$ (Table 4).

Table 4. Correlation between four criteria of success

	1	2	3	4
1 Mention by peers		0.32*	0.42+	0.42+
2 Invitations to seminars			0.36+	0.45+
3 Participations at Congresses				0.33+
4 Publications				

* $p = 0.001$
+$p = 0.0001$

It may be affirmed that there is strong coherence between the four criteria and that they may be used to divide the sample into dissimilar groups. We have thus classified the 151 laboratories into five sub-groups by using two of the criteria (mentions and invitations to seminars):

> Group 1 (22.5% of the sample) comprises laboratories which were never mentioned and never invited.
> Group 2 (18.5%) comprises laboratories which were never mentioned and from which only the head was occasionally invited.
> Group 3 (28.5%) comprises laboratories which were never mentioned and from which the researchers were occasionally invited.
> Group 4 (16.5%) comprises laboratories which were mentioned once and which had various opportunities for being invited.
> Group 5 (14%) comprises laboratories which were mentioned two to eight times and from which either the head or the researchers might be invited.

This classification, clearly, provides a rather crude indication of the success of the laboratories. Errors in classification are indeed possible, owing to the distortion introduced by the size of the laboratories and the field of research. On the whole, however, one may consider group 5 as being superior to the previous ones, and so on down the scale. We shall therefore be able to examine the way in which the information we have collated on the different laboratories is distributed among the five groups, our aim being to discover whether there exist characteristics which would make it possible to distinguish between the highly successful groups of laboratories and those whose success is poor or middling.

Organizational Characteristics and Style of Leadership in the Five Groups

We now have two sets of data at our disposal: the replies given during the interviews by the heads of the 151 laboratories and a classification of these 151 laboratories into five groups from group 5 (the best) to group 1 (the least good). These sets of data have been submitted to systematic comparison for each item of information obtained, the signification of the comparisons being examined by means of the chi squared (X^2) test. In what follows, only the variables which have enabled significant differences to be extracted will be described.

Organizational characteristics

Between the groups, there would appear to be differences of two different kinds:

1. If our typology is sound, it may be expected that the quality—a varying quality—of the laboratories should have an effect upon their activities; thus, for instance, foreign trainees and thesis students will be more attracted by the best laboratories, as will the most highly qualified researchers.

2. Other variables may be organizational causes affecting the quality of the research work. One may, for instance, expect to find that in group 5 there will be a higher percentage of large-size laboratories and of laboratories that are well equipped and well staffed, etc. Assumptions of this kind would not indicate a weakness in the typology. But it must be checked whether the inferred connections actually exist, otherwise possible relations between methods of training and the quality of research may be confused with the relations existing between the method of training and research. Let us assume, for instance, that a high percentage of the laboratories in group 5 are of large size. If this were the case, it would be difficult to know whether the working relations, or the leadership, characteristic of laboratories in group 5 were actually a result of their size or else a cause of their success.

Differences anticipated between the five groups

When a research team sees its work crowned with success, it is in a better position to improve its financial means and its staff resources, particularly by seeking support from various organizations. Indeed, when one compares the body of laboratories belonging to groups 1, 2, and 3 with those belonging to groups 4 and 5, one finds that in the latter body there are far more frequent instances of researchers belonging to several organizations: out of the seventy-eight laboratories with researchers having double affiliation, thirty-two (41 per cent.) belonged to groups 4 and 5; out of the seventy-three laboratories which had no researchers with double affiliation, only fourteen (19 per cent.) belonged to groups 4 and 5 ($X^2 = 12.67$, significant for $p = 0.001$).

Do the best laboratories most often attract foreign trainees? It would seem clear that they do, although one may need to regard the figures with caution since the number of trainees present may vary considerably from year to year. All the same, it must be mentioned that only 12 per cent. of the laboratories in group 1 had at least one foreign visitor and that this percentage increased progressively up till group 5, in which 67 per cent. of the laboratories received visitors from other countries.

Organizational characteristics differentiating the five groups

Appreciable differences were observed in four areas:

1. *Institutional affiliation.* The laboratories attached exclusively to universities were among those with the lowest performance: out of the forty-four purely university laboratories, twenty-two fell under group 1 (50 per cent.), while the same held for only twelve of the remaining 107 laboratories ($X^2 = 26.88$, significant for $p = 0.001$). By contrast, the INSERM laboratories were frequently highly rated: twenty-seven of sixty-one (44 per cent.) belonged to groups 4 or 5 ($X^2 = 9.20$; $p = 0.01$). The distribution of the laboratories of the Institut Pasteur was identical to that of the sample.

2. *Type of research.* We have seen earlier that a quarter of the interviewees described their research as exclusively basic: half the laboratories of group 5 belonged to this category ($X^2 = 86.0$; $p = 0.0001$). Nevertheless, this result would call for more detailed study into what the heads of laboratory understand as the 'basic'. In several cases, in fact, the laboratories concerned were incorporated into hospitals and their activities certainly had a clinical aspect.
3. *Size.* On this point, the differences were clear-cut. Out of the thirty-one smallest laboratories (fewer than ten people), nineteen belonged to groups 1 or 2 ($X^2 = 12.46$; $p = 0.001$). Conversely, in group 5, the number of large laboratories (twenty-one to thirty people) was high: seven out of twenty-six (21 per cent.) as against 11 per cent. (14 out of 125) for the rest of the sample ($X^2 = 4.44$; $p = 0.05$). Size is therefore associated with success. This relation, moreover, admits to important exceptions: in group 3, for instance, half the laboratories and in group 4, 40 per cent, fell into the eleven to twenty bracket.
4. *Composition of the laboratory staff.* In the biomedical field, laboratory technicians play a vital role because many of the experiments involve routine tasks. One should not consider it surprising, therefore, that out of the thirteen laboratories which have no full-time technician, seven belonged to group 1 ($X^2 = 8.0$; $p = 0.01$). By contrast, half the laboratories with ten or more technicians belonged to groups 4 and 5.

Two other more unexpected observations are made: the first concerns the presence of full-time researchers, which would indeed seem to be a cause (or an effect?) of success. Table 5 demonstrates in fact that the presence and the number of *full-time* researchers is also linked to success. Of the thirty laboratories in which there was no full-time researcher, nineteen (61 per cent.) belonged to group 1; conversely, of the laboratories in which there were more than six full-time researchers, seventeen (31 per cent.) belonged to group 5 (in the first case, $X^2 = 33.61$; in the second case $X^2 = 11.77$, the two Chi squared figures being significant for $p = 0.001$). In addition, the distribution of the laboratories among the groups was strongly linked to the number of teacher researchers present ($X^2 = 19.50$; $p = 0.001$). These various figures lead one to think that research done on a part-time basis rarely attains high quality. This is an impression which was, moreover, shared by most of our interviewees who often stated that only those who were able to devote their entire energy to research could achieve very good results. One of the problems which arises, then, concerns the need—mentioned by some—of maintaining contact with the clinic in order to carry out medical research. Might it be said that the ideal situation would be one in which the work was being done by full-time researchers who had previously devoted a number of years to clinical activity? Closer and more detailed research might confirm this hypothesis; let us nevertheless point out here that only half of the laboratories studied had at least one researcher who was a doctor of medicine and that these laboratories were more numerous in groups 4 and 5 (63 per cent.; $X^2 = 3.84$; $p = 0.05$). Even if these figures are not particularly revealing, the problem of the biomedical researchers splitting their time between teaching, clinical activities, and research is clearly of crucial importance. Overspecialization was another matter criticized by all our interviewees, who formulated the question as follows: how can one preserve a realistic view of medical problems and yet simultaneously be able to draw back in order to gain a more general outlook on scientific research?

Table 5. Number of full-time researchers

	Distribution (%)		
	None	1–5	6 and over
Group 5	—	6	31
Group 4	7	17	23.5
Group 3	13	38	25.5
Group 2	19	17	18
Group 1	61	22	2
	100% = 31	100% = 65	100% = 55

Altogether, what can be gathered from the study of the organizational conditions characterizing the five groups? Firstly, the typology we have devised is substantiated by the results: if the laboratories in the two 'best' groups attract more foreigners, more often have researchers with double affiliation, have more staff, and are more often attached to INSERM (where the procedures for testing results are explicit and institutionalized) than to the university (where a laboratory's continued existence does not depend on an institutionalized testing procedure), it means that the classification is adequate—success leading to further success and to the allocation of fresh funds. On the other hand, there are two observations which raise problems that will have to be examined more closely in further research: while the size of a laboratory may be a sign of success it is by no means a condition *sine qua non* of success. This being so, what is the optimal size for a laboratory to be able to maintain its eminence? The engagement of 'full-time' staff would seem to encourage high-quality research. In this case, how is one to reconcile this prerequisite with the need for clinical experience and/or administrative duties?

Style of leadership

The interviews enabled us to gather information on two subjects:

1. The attitudes of the heads towards their subordinates;
2. The social relations within the laboratory.

As before, we shall be describing here only the data which allowed for differentiation between the five groups.

Attitudes towards the subordinates

The interviewees assessed the style of leadership by selecting one of three descriptions:

1. Very free (60% of the answers);
2. Free (33%);
3. Strict (7%).

The percentage of those who rated the leadership as 'very free' diminished progressively from the laboratories of group 1 (76.5 per cent.) to those of groups 4 and 5 (47.6 per cent.). The trend is clear but the difference is just significant ($X^2 = 5.35$; $p = 0.05$).

The picture is the same for the question concerning the control over the researchers' work. We asked the heads of laboratory what kind of reports they required from their researchers, in addition to the compulsory reports required by the various financially supporting bodies. The replies fell into four categories:

1. Regular *written* reports (1%);
2. Only *oral* report (30%);
3. Only *official* reports (22%);
4. *No* report, work being checked 'on the job' (38%).

Oral or written reports were slightly more frequent in groups 3, 4, and 5 (47 per cent. of the cases) than in groups 1 and 2 (27 per cent. $X^2 = 5.9$; ($p = 0.02$).

Social relations

Three questions provided answers which were distributed differently among the five groups of laboratory. There was, moreover, an internal coherence between the differences observed, which revealed that the laboratory's results were better when the social relations between the head and the researchers were based on mutual confidence.

The first point concerns the way in which the laboratory technicians are involved in the presentation of the published results. Table 6 shows the distribution by group of the different possiblities, ranging from 'often sign jointly' (18 per cent.) to 'never sign at all' (44 per cent.), and passing through 'acknowledged in footnotes' (5 per cent.) and 'sign jointly when their contribution is scientific' (35 per cent.). This distribution varies greatly from group to group (cf. Table 6): in group 1, 73.5 per cent. never signed; in group 5, 14.3 per cent. never signed ($X^2 = 16.0$; $p = 0.001$). Although the technicians' job security and career prospects do not depend on publications, one may imagine that their involvement and their motivation will be more powerful when their contribution is visibly acknowledged.

The practice of holding meetings varied considerably, depending on the laboratory. It was rare for there to be 'no meetings' (8.6 per cent); weekly

Table 6. Contribution of the technicians to publications

	Distribution (%)			
		Sign only if contribution is scientific	Thanked in footnotes	Never sign
Group 5	14.3	62	9.4	14.3
Group 4	28	20	12	40
Group 3	20.9	42	4.5	32.6
Group 2	14.4	32	3.6	50
Group 1	12	14.5	—	73.5

meetings were often held (34.4 per cent.); and less frequent meetings (fortnightly, monthly, bimonthly, or irregular) were the rule for one laboratory out of two. But the holding of weekly meetings on a fixed day was clearly an advantage, since the practice was observed in half the laboratories in groups 4 and 5; on the other hand, the complete absence of meetings was a handicap (no such cases were recorded for groups 4 and 5).

The relations between the researchers and the head of laboratory were likewise considered from the point of view of the dialogue between each researcher and the head. Did they discuss career problems: very often (half the replies); occasionally (the other half)? Here again a tendency was observed in favour of the best laboratories (groups 4 and 5) which reached the point of significance ($X^2 = 2.8$; $p = 0.01$). Did they discuss the researchers' personal problems: often (45 per cent); upon request (28 per cent.); rarely or never (27 per cent.). The difference between the groups followed the same lines as before, but without becoming significant. In this connection, it should be noted that there was more chance of a certain intimacy developing in the smaller teams; it should likewise be mentioned that laboratory heads with a medical background found that researchers more often raised their personal problems as they approached the head both as a doctor and as their immediate superior—a double capacity which the heads clearly undertook to assume.

At this stage in the research, several conclusions emerge. As regards the difficult problem of devising criteria of success, the obstacles do not appear to have been insurmountable, on account of the homogeneity among the different criteria. Furthermore, the classification into five groups does not appear to be distorted in relation to the most important organizational characteristics. The one variable, however, which must be constantly borne in mind is that which concerns the large size of the best laboratories, as it may be both a possible cause and a likely consequence of their success.

There are four main aspects of the differences observed between the five groups:

1. The type of research and the objectives were most often described as *basic* in the best laboratories.

2. The laboratories where teacher researchers were working were never among the best; the laboratories in which *full-time* researchers were working had greater chances of belonging to the two best groups.
3. The best laboratories were those managed by heads whose approach was moderately *free* but who did *formally* control their researchers' work.
4. The best laboratories were characterized by *participatory* working relations: more meetings, the technicians were personally involved in the results, and more interpersonal relations between the researchers and the heads.

The two last conclusions clearly bring to mind the classical theories of personnel management, in which the combination of 'consideration' and 'structure' is shown to represent the most effective type of leadership. The data we have thus far obtained introduce an added dimension—participation in decision-making. On the other hand, they provide us with no indication as to the relations between these different variables (free management, formal control, and participation). In order to advance research into this problem it would be necessary to examine more closely the relative functioning of these different variables and to provide answers to questions such as: Do 'structure' and 'consideration' represent two independent forms of behaviour, two possible options in the running of a laboratory? Or, as has already been shown in companies, do they mutually strengthen their positive effects? Does the size of laboratories constitute an important moderating variable? Does the topic of research—and particularly its more or less basic or applied character—necessitate a specific mode of management? These are all questions which we shall tackle using the most finely developed statistical methods.

Styles of Leadership and Situational Variables: Reults of the Correlative Analysis

The results presented above are straight comparisons between the five groups. In order to advance further and discover whether between the variables there exist associations which would enable us to proposed a contingency model (style of leadership/organizational variables/research success), we undertook a correlative analysis following the method of Benzécri (1973). This analysis was carried out on a series of forty variables representing descriptions of the style of leadership. We retained for use the four main axes, accounting for a total of 31 per cent. of the inertia; these will be described below. We then projected twenty-one further variables onto the four axes: the seventeen fields of research and the sizes of the laboratories, representatively grouped into four categories. Finally, the 151 laboratories were also projected onto the axes as additional variables, each laboratory being identified by its code number and by a figure representing the group to which it belonged in the terms of the quality of its research.

Description of the four axes

Table 7 gives details of the variables with an indication of their contributions.

Axis 1 was described as 'participation and control' because at each pole it gathered the variables representing the participation of members of the laboratory in the work performed and also the variables indicating the degree of control over the work. It should be noted that these variables are symmetrically directed towards the two extremes.

Axis 2, 'consideration', also presents a group of variables symmetrically distributed around the two poles of the axis, one end being characterized by frequent contacts between the researchers and their head of laboratory and the other representing rare contacts and a low degree of involvement of the technicians in the results of the work.

Axis 3 is more difficult to decode; the contributions are particularly high on the negative axis and concern variables reflecting a working atmosphere bearing the stamp of formalism: few meetings, official reports, personal freedom for the researchers once their objectives have been defined; the opposite pole of the axis reflects the existence of informal contacts (relating to personal problems) and the absence of meetings geared to professional questions. This is why we have labelled this axis 'formalism'.

Axis 4 gathers together the variables placing stress on competition between the researchers and between the laboratories, and defining a working atmosphere in which personal freedom — even solo work — is encouraged, in contrast to the rejection of competition as a source of stimulus.

These four axes, then, make possible a finely shaded definition of the style of leadership of the heads of laboratory. Before going on to examine the relation between the quality of research (represented by the sub-division of the laboratories into five groups) and the dimensions defined by these axes, it is important to desribe the relation between the axes and the 'anatomic' variables.

Additional variables

The projection of the additional variables helps greatly to clarify the description already acquired using the four axes, and also to elucidate the planes defined by a pair of axes. For the sake of clarity, we shall first consider the axes in isolation, indicating the additional variables which occur in regular patterns on the graph.

Axis 1

The size of the laboratories is distributed regularly over the length of axis 1, the laboratories in the category 'size 1' (fewer than ten researchers and technicians) being characterized by the absence of participation and control,

Table 7. Contributions of the variables distributed over the four axes

Axis 1: Participation and structure

Variables	Positive pole	Negative pole
Meetings	None	Every week
Assessment of work	None	Oral reports
Meetings on reading material	None	Yes
Management	Very free	Fairly free
Personal freedom	—	Restricted to established researchers

Axis 2: Consideration

Variables	Positive pole	Negative pole
The laboratory head discusses his researchers' personal problems with them	Often	Upon request by the researchers
The laboratory head discusses his researchers' career problems with them	Very often	Occasionally
Personal satisfaction is linked to the laboratory's reputation	No	—
Researcher's freedom	—	Very controlled
Laboratory management	—	Fairly controlled
Technicians' signing of publications	—	Never

Axis 3: Formalism

Variables	Positive pole	Negative pole
Meetings	None	Every month
Meetings on reading material	None	Every fortnight
Head of laboratory discusses researchers' personal problems	Often	Rarely
Researchers' freedom	—	Once objectives defined
Research report	—	Official report
Competition	—	Not a stimulus

Axis 4: Competition among researchers

Variables	Positive pole	Negative pole
Laboratory's reputation	Source of satisfaction	Not a source of satisfaction
Competition within the laboratory	Is stimulating in moderation	Is not stimulating
Lone researchers	Exist, but do not disturb	—
Researchers' freedom	Absolute	—
Head of laboratory discusses researchers' career problems	No	—
Laboratory management	—	Fairly free

and those in size groups 3 and 4 (over twenty researchers and technicians) more often having a style of leadership characterized by participation and structuring. Even though the relation is clear, it is not absolute, for one finds small laboratories which are run in a non-liberal fashion and with organized participation. It should be recalled that out of the thirty-one small laboratories (fewer than ten people), nineteen belonged to the least productive categories (groups 1 and 2) and that, by contrast, in the best group (5) there was a high proportion of very large laboratories, although the relationship of success to size was not regular.

Certain research *areas* were also distributed regularly along axis 1, following the pattern below (the figure in brackets refers to the number of laboratories concerned):

Participation and control								Neither participation nor control
Haematology (6)	Biochemistry (19)	Cardio-vascular diseases (3)	Bacteriology (8)		Surgery (6)	Pharmacology (7)	Forensic medicine (2)	

If one examines the way in which these research disciplines are distributed, one may conclude that this axis contrasts relatively empirical research, based chiefly on the analysis of clinical cases, with research of a more basic nature, based on the elaboration of abstract models. Forensic medicine, for instance, analyses specific cases and, working from them, builds up a body of knowledge and rules. Pharmacology, described by the heads of laboratory themselves as applied research, studies the primary and secondary effects of new molecules, the experimental areas being established on the grounds of acquired knowledge, and experimental routine. Surgical laboratories study anatomical data and surgical methods. At the other end of the axis, it is clear that haematology and biochemistry are subjects in which abstract hypotheses and general models are tested in various ways. Cardio-vascular diseases and bacteriology occur between the two tendencies because both aspects (empirical research and the testing of abstract models) can be envisaged in them.

Axis 2

On axis 2, the laboratories do not hold a special position in accordance with their size, but here too the research disciplines are regularly distributed, as follows:

No consideration	Consideration

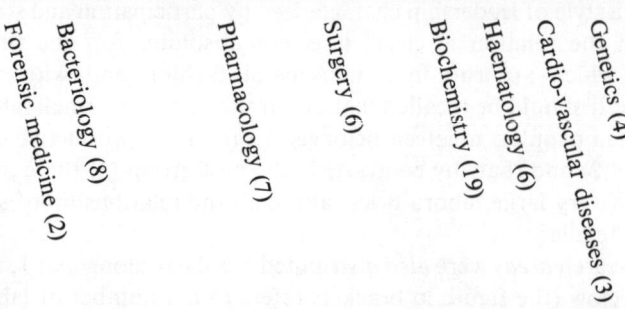

There is one variable which accounts for the position of these laboratories with regard to the axis of 'consideration' and that is the internal distribution of staff among different categories, this being independent of the size of the laboratory. In the disciplines characterized by strong consideration from the head of laboratory (cardio-vascular diseases, genetics, haematology, biochemistry), a greater number of full-time researchers are to be found (an average of seven for the thirty-two laboratories concerned) but few teacher researchers (1.5 on the average) and few thesis students (1.8 on the average). In laboratories where the head's behaviour is characterized by poor consideration, the situation is the reverse: few full-time researchers (an average of two for the twenty-three laboratories concerned) and an equal or higher number of teacher researchers and thesis students (an average of three and four respectively).

This observation may be explained as follows. When the majority of the laboratory researchers are permanently present and have no other affiliation, it may be easily imagined that contacts between the head and the researchers will be more frequent. In this case, the head's behaviour is determined as much by the composition of his team and by the frequency of his contacts with the researchers as it is by his own personality or his opinions concerning the proper way of running a laboratory.

Axes 1 and 2

It should be recalled that the 151 laboratories were projected as additional variables onto the plane described by axes 1 and 2. In addition, each laboratory is presented with accompanying information by which it can be identified. This means that it is possible to discover whether the organizations to which the laboratories are attached play a role in influencing the style of leadership adopted by the heads of laboratory. If such an influence were exerted, one would expect to see the laboratories belonging to the same organizations grouped together at one point or other of the graph, and one would then be able to verify quantitatively the relation thus observed through studying the contribution indices. From this point of view, the results are clear: no coherent grouping is revealed, either along axis 1 (participation and structuring) or along axis 2 (consideration). This fact undermines one of our initial hypotheses, i.e. that there exists a type of laboratory management which is linked to (and explicable by) the constraints imposed by the organization to which the laboratory happens to be attached—and this in spite of the notable differences existing between INSERM, the Institut Pasteur, and the University. This absence of cross-relation becomes even more pronounced when it is compared with the relations observed between the methods of training, on the one hand, and the size of the laboratory and the fields of research study, on the other.

Level of success and position of the laboratories in relation to the different axes

It is naturally possible to situate the laboratories belonging respectively to groups 1 to 5 (from worst to best) on the planes described by the pairs of axes. The only significant grouping, however, occurs on axes 1 and 2. As regards formalism and competition between the researchers, our results reveal no significant connection with the quality of the laboratory's results—as was already the case for the study of the combination of the variables.

By contrast, the role of consideration and of participation and structure as determinants of the laboratories' success already becomes apparent as soon as one proceeds to a simple cross-selection of the variables concerned. The study of axes 1 and 2 confirms this general datum with further nuances and information on the respective roles of the two dimensions. Figure 1 represents axes 1 and 2, with an indication of their poles; for the sake of clarity, only the groups (1, 2, 3, 4, or 5) to which each laboratory belongs on the grounds of the quality of its research have been indicated.

If one examines Figure 1, there are two observations which may be made:

1. The laboratories with good results (4 and 5) are distinctly more numerous around the pole of participation and structure of axis 1.
2. The second axis plays no role except by relation to the first axis; wherever there is little participation and structure, the absence of consideration becomes an aggravating circumstance.

The data of these graphs are confirmed by the figures: the average contribution (representing a correlation between the axes and the variable expressed in 1/1,000) of the laboratories of group 5 (those with the best results) is 199 for the positive pole of the axis, and this average decreases regularly by group, down to group 1 (127). There is, however, one striking exception to to be noted—a group 2 laboratory with a contribution of 486. This laboratory was run with a high level of participation and extremely powerful control by the head. Its field of research—which is wholly original—leads us to believe that it may have been underrated by our method of attributing criteria.

These results are confirmed by the average contributions at the negative pole of the axis (neither participation nor structure), ranging from 259 (group 1)

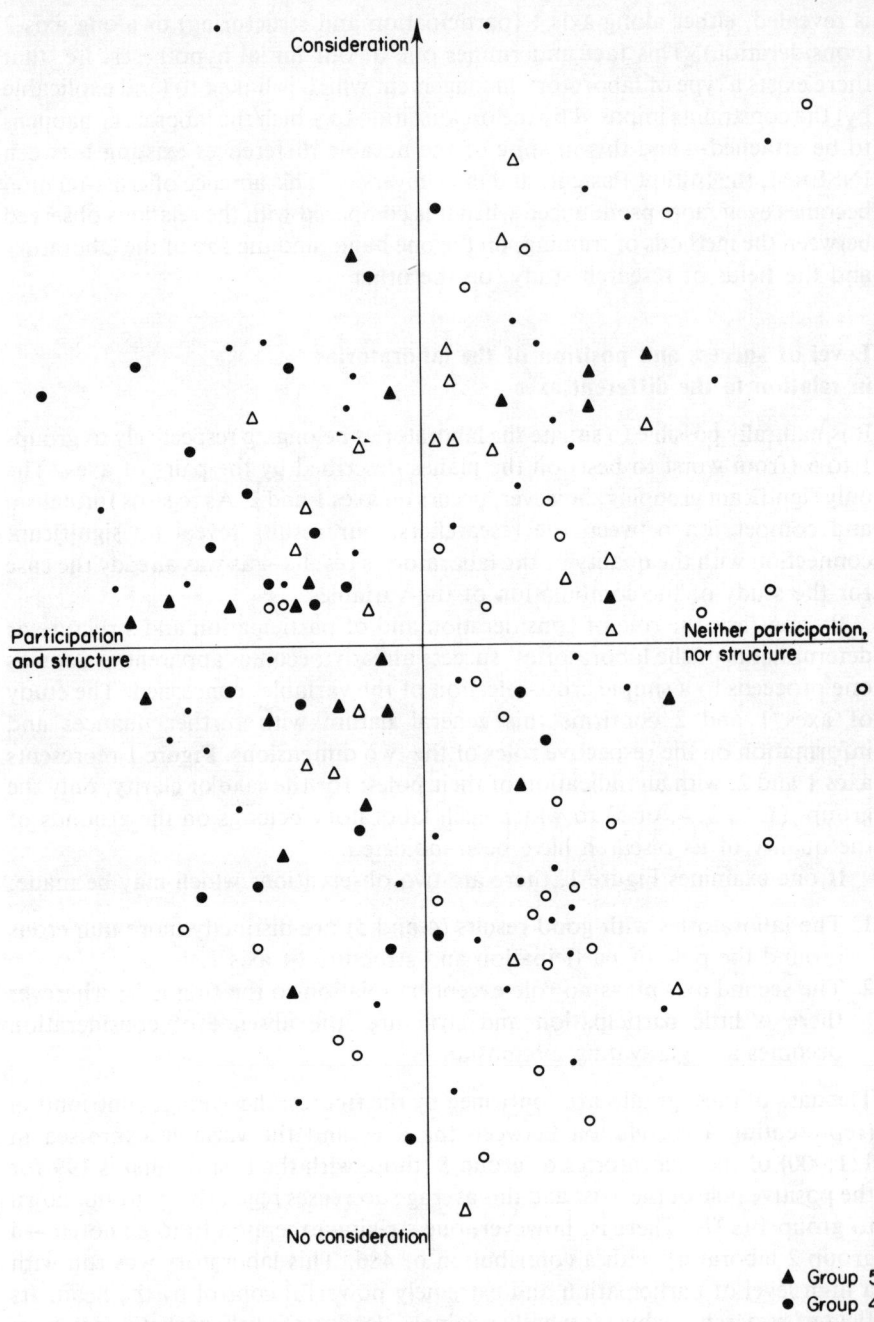

Figure 1. Projection of the laboratories

to 125 (group 5). Here again we have one notable exception: a laboratory classified under group 4, but characterized by weak participation and weak structure. The head who also held important hospital functions, was in fact delegating his authority to 'research team leaders', who undertook charge of control and participation.

As far as axis 2 is concerned, the presence of 'consideration' is not a condition for success: the average contributions of the laboratories at the positive pole vary little and, above all, irregularly for the different groups. Conversely, the absence of consideration (negative pole of axis 2) differentiates strongly among the laboratories (the average for contributions extending regularly from 21 for group 5 to 112 for group 1).

Conclusion

In all, we observed three types of relation, each apparently independent of the other.

Firstly, the organization to which the laboratory is attached determines the quality of the laboratory. This link is further strengthened by the fact that we chose to class under INSERM those laboratories which were also affiliated to the University. It nevertheless remains that the more formalized the control systems are, and the more frequent the work assessments, the higher the quality of the laboratories becomes.

Secondly, there is a relation between the size, the field of research (hence the heuristic process), and the style of management adopted by the head of laboratory. Everything would seem to point to the fact that the constraints deriving from the number of researchers, the diversity of their status and background, and from the nature of the research combine to force the heads of laboratory to adopt more often one style of leadership or another.

Thirdly, there is a relation between the style of leadership (participation, structure, consideration) and the success of the laboratory. It has been seen in fact that the laboratories belonging to the top groups are more often characterized by participation associated with structure and that the lack of consideration for the researchers, which is tolerable when there is 'participation and structure', results in failure when it is associated with weak 'participation and structure'.

These conclusions may be represented by the following diagram:

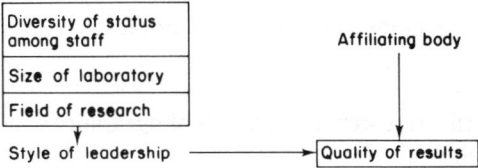

In other words, the smallest laboratories, those whose staff is the least permanent and those specializing in a field of clinical and empirical research, tend to adopt a style of leadership which would seem, among other things, to be ill-suited to the achievement of quality of the results. However, one point must be stressed: there is no systematic connection between the organizational conditions (diversity of status among the staff, size of the laboratory, field of research) and the quality of the results.

What we are dealing with here, then, is not a contingency scheme in which different styles of leadership are effective, depending on the organizational characteristics (as in Fiedler's model), but rather a double connection acting in parallel fashion, the laboratory's characteristics determining the quality of the results obtained by the laboratory.

Annex 1: Headings for the Analysis of Content

Effectiveness of the research
Number of publications (reputable journals) over the past two years
Researchers' participation at congresses over the past two years
Congress papers delivered by researchers over the past two years
Overall assessment of the laboratory researchers
Presence of 'lone' researchers
Staff cohesion
Relations between the researchers and the organization

Organization variables
Meetings with researchers: nature, frequency, aim
Attitudes of the head towards independence and competitiveness among researchers
Researchers' freedom
Reports on and control of work performed
Signing of joint publications

Contextual variables
Size
Research field
Researchers' age
Length of service
Relative percentage of men and women
Functions
Speciality
Relations between the laboratory and other bodies

Heuristic procedures
Starting point of the research (clinical, bibliographical, previous research, theoretical model)
Orientation of the laboratory's research (understanding of biological processes, clinical application, solution of medical problems, development of medical techniques)

References

Andrews, F. and Farris, G. (1967). 'Supervisory practices and innovation in scientific teams', *Pers. Psychol.*, **20**, 497–515.
Bass, B. M., and Valenzi, E. T. (1974). 'Contingent aspects of effective management style', in *Contingency Approaches to Leadership* (Eds J. G. Hunt and L. S. Larson), Southern Illinois University Press, Carbondale.
Benzécri, J. P. (1973). *L'Analyse des Données*, Dunod, Paris.
Kerr, S. (1974). Discussant comment, in J. G. Hunt & L. S. Larson, ed. *Contingency approaches to leadership*, Carbondale: Southern Illinois University Press, 1974.
Korman, A. (1966). 'Consideration, initiating structure and organization criteria: a review', *Pers. Psychol.*, **19**, 349–361.
Korman, A. (1973). 'On the development of contingency theories of leadership: some methodological considerations and a possible alternative', *Jal app. Psychol.*, **58**, 384–387.
Levy-Leboyer, C., and Pineau, C. (1981). 'Caracteristiques organisationnelles, style de leadership et reuscite dans la recherche bio-medicale', *Rev. Psychol. appliquee*, **31**, 201–234.

DIVIDE AND RUIN—A PATHOLOGICAL APPROACH TO FRAGMENTING RESEARCH

N. K. POWELL

Manchester Business School, Manchester, England

Abstract

The author's thesis is that progress of all kinds is being blocked by the fragmentation of the science. He uses the concepts of cybernetics to show that this is a form of degeneration that is inevitable and the resumption of progress depends on science taking the path of integration. The difficulty stems from the fact that reality is an undifferentiated whole but our minds can only grasp it one part at a time. We draw boundaries between fields to enable us to manage them, but cybernetically this is a form of closure. Closure limits the number of control variables at the disposal of the would-be controller and thereby the amount of control that can be exerted on the system. A subtle form of closure is problem definition—the more closely is a problem defined the fewer the solutions that can be applied to it. In fact the worst and, according to the author, a not uncommon manifestation of this tendency is so closely to define a problem that the solution is fully defined as well.

Turning this concept to positive use the author advocates seeing a problem merely as a trigger to set off a wide-ranging creative activity which may in the end lead to a 'solution' that is remote from the problem that gave rise to the work but may be highly relevant to some hitherto unrealized problem. The relevance to interdisciplinary research management is that if several differently trained minds are focused on a problem then the probability that it will be defined out of existence will be much reduced.

THE INTERDISCIPLINARY RESEARCHER: SOME PSYCHOLOGICAL ASPECTS

I. T. ROBERTSON

University of Manchester Institute of Science and Technology, Manchester, England

Introduction

This paper is based on investigations carried out over the last three years or so of over 150 interdisciplinary research projects. The projects studied were being conducted not by teams of individuals from a variety of disciplines but by one person working in a research area where several disciplines overlap (often science, engineering, and social science). In each of the projects the interdisciplinary research was conducted within a manufacturing or service organization and the researchers involved had the dual status of an employee of the organization concerned and a university student (Ph.D. or M.Phil.). The normal duration of each project was at least three years and during this period the researcher worked full-time on his or her project. Some projects finished prematurely, usually when the researcher resigned and took up employment elsewhere, and others ran on well beyond the three-year period. Each researcher reported to a supervisory team (a different team for each project) made up of people from the problem-owning organization and relevant university departments.

One discipline, or combination of disciplines, did not predominate in the projects studied. The list below gives an indication of the range of projects included in the investigation:

1. Computer applications in the drop-forging industry;
2. The application of numerical ideas by Health Service managers;
3. The development and application of a technique for analysing jobs;
4. Improving the development of commercial ideas in a chemical company.

The Research Context

The range of disciplines involved in the projects studied is extensive and although, as noted above, most projects included some social science, science and/or engineering the balance of disciplines varied considerably from project to project. Some projects focused on one discipline very heavily and included others in a peripheral fashion only; others involved a true integration of two or more disciplines. The projects studied for this research were conducted within the context of a particular system of postgraduate education—The Interdisciplinary Higher Degrees Scheme at the University of Aston in Birmingham, England. Further details of the scheme may be found in van Rest (1980) and Robertson (1981). All of the researchers carrying out the projects studied were predoctoral, postgraduate students of the University. Some had several years postgraduate experience and others were recent graduates.

The first degrees were in a range of science, engineering, social science and arts disciplines.

The scheme operates as follows:

1. A company identifies a problem area and contacts the university.
2. Representatives of the company and the university discuss the problem and select a full-time postgraduate researcher to work for two or three years on the problem.

During this period, the researcher becomes a temporary employee of the company (and a full-time research student) and normally spends about 70 per cent. of his time at the company.

3. The researcher is supervised in this work by a team of supervisors from the university and the company. One of the supervisors from the university becomes the 'main supervisor' and the others become 'associate supervisors'.

During the project, the researcher attends relevant course work usually selected from modules of master's degrees within the university, but quite often involving attendance at specially relevant external courses (e.g. psychological testing) or attendance at other universities.

4. The project continues and, while it is under way, frequent reports are produced, new techniques applied, new products developed, etc.
5. When the project is completed, some parts of the work are written up as a M.Phil. or Ph.D. thesis by the researcher. This is one of the benefits to the researcher. Benefits to the Company include the new technique, procedure, or product.

The thesis produced at the end of the project is a case study of practical problem-solving in particular circumstances and attempts to provide an objective review of the project area and place the research conducted within an appropriate academic and theoretical context.

6. After the project is completed, many researchers continue to work for the collaborating organization.

This system of postgraduate education has many unusual features but the two aspects of the most relevance for current purposes are the emphasis on interdisciplinarity and the emphasis on collaboration with organizations outside the university system.

Interdisciplinarity

Researchers are encouraged to take an interdisciplinary approach to problem-solving—an objective which is not by any means easy to attain.

Interdisciplinarity is facilitated by ensuring that supervision for projects is often carried out by members of academic staff from at least two different faculties of the university and that the scheme itself has an organizational base outside the normal faculty structure of the university and does not 'belong' to any single faculty.

To provide an illustrate example of how the emphasis on interdisciplinarity is followed through in practice the following project outline (from Robertson and Cochran, 1980) is given.

Case study

> Collaborating organization: medium-sized manufacturer of hydraulic equipment
> Initial statement of problem: a desire to reduce time taken to translate design concepts into detailed design
> Researcher: engineering graduate
> Summary of work done: after considering technical and non-technical arguments, the researcher decided that computer-aided design offered the best solution. The work concentrated on one particular product range—pumps—and required much technical research and development. By analysing the whole design process and participating in many detailed discussions with those involved in it, the researcher was able to gain considerable insight into how design fitted into the rest of the company activities and the needs of the users of the system. Consideration of these factors influenced virtually every stage from initial planning through design and compilation of the interactive programme to acceptance and installation.

Comment

The discipline of psychology contributed significantly to the project. The researcher was concerned to design a system that would not only optimize the man–machine combination in terms of producing the required outcome but would also be one that the designers would be motivated to use. This may seem obvious to psychologists but not always so to twenty-four year old engineers. The researcher gained a new awareness to relevant aspects of psychology by direct reading and, at one time, by frequent individual tutorials with his supervisor from the Applied Psychology Department.

The system has been installed, accepted, and is working well, so the project succeeded in industrial terms. It cannot of course, be proved that the psychological contribution was essential to the success but we certainly believe it was. What is certain is that the thesis for which the student received a Ph.D., and which indicates academic success, was very different from a normal engineering thesis on computer-aided design.

Action research

As well as being interdisciplinary in nature the research projects studied also had at least one other feature in common—they were *applied* rather than *pure* research and centred on a problem of perceived, genuine importance to an external, host organization. In many cases the problem was an operating problem of the organization and not a 'backroom' research problem.

The distinction between pure and applied research is rather ambiguous so the research typology proposed by Cherns (1979) may help to clarify the nature of most of the research projects included in the sample. Cherns suggested four types of research:

>Pure basic
>Basic objective
>Operational
>Action

Pure basic research

This type of research, originally proposed by the Zuckerman Committee (1961), arises out of the perceived needs of the discipline and is usually orientated towards theoretical problems.

Basic objective research

This kind of research is orientated towards a problem which arises in a field of application of the discipline, although it is not aimed at prescribing a solution to a practical problem. Much of the work currently described as applied research would fall into this category.

Broadly speaking, these first two types of research represent the conventional view of what constitutes doctoral research: i.e. in-depth study of a problem area within a pure or applied field of a discipline with a view to understanding and describing. There is no attempt to tackle or prescribe solutions to practical, *real-world* problems (Minogue, 1973).

Operational research

Research of this type does aim at tackling a real-life problem within some organizational framework. The research is designed to assess, measure, and make comparisons of various aspects of operational problems and to feed back the resulting information to the host organization.

In operational research projects, change may occur as a result of the enquiry and feedback process, but this is not perceived as the aim of the research.

Action research

This may involve a piece of operational research but is distinguished from operational research by the explicit aim of introducing planned change rather than merely feeding back results.

When discussing the action research approach, Warr (1977) makes the following comment:

> Perhaps I should add that action resarchers within say, psychology are still very much the minority in that the prevailing academic culture tends towards a more detached role for the investigator. To exaggerate slightly, the orthodox, psychological research style is one which places the investigator behind a one-way mirror, observing but not intervening in ongoing situations.

This orthodox research style inevitably exerts an influence on the research conducted and seen as valid by researcher workers.

The projects studied all had the characteristics of what Cherns (1979) described as 'action research' or 'operational research'.

Important Variables

Many factors are likely to influence the progress of interdisciplinary research. For example, the original set of symptoms or other information available to the researcher will be interpreted and acted on in a way which depends, at least to some extent, on the characteristics and previous experience of the researcher. The environment in which the research is conducted, the history and nature of the research problem, other people within the research environment, and a large collection of other factors may also be important.

Figure 1 provides a simplified picture of the elements involved in the interdisciplinary research process. (The variables used are for illustration only and are not meant to provide a comprehensive list.) Figure 1 shows that variables may be assigned to one of four categories and each category represents an element in the research and problem-solving process. Some significant features of Figure 1 are:

1. The person (researcher) is embedded within a situation. The researcher's behaviour is determined not by his or her own characteristics alone, nor by the situation alone, but also by the interaction between the researcher and the situation.
2. Various facts, symptoms, etc., concerning the research problem may exist but any researcher will attend to, search for, and interpret information in a way which is influenced by his or her own individual characteristics; e.g. certain features of the problem may be emphasized at the expense of others. The problem as perceived by the researcher is, therefore, dependent on the interaction between the person and the problem — not on the person alone;

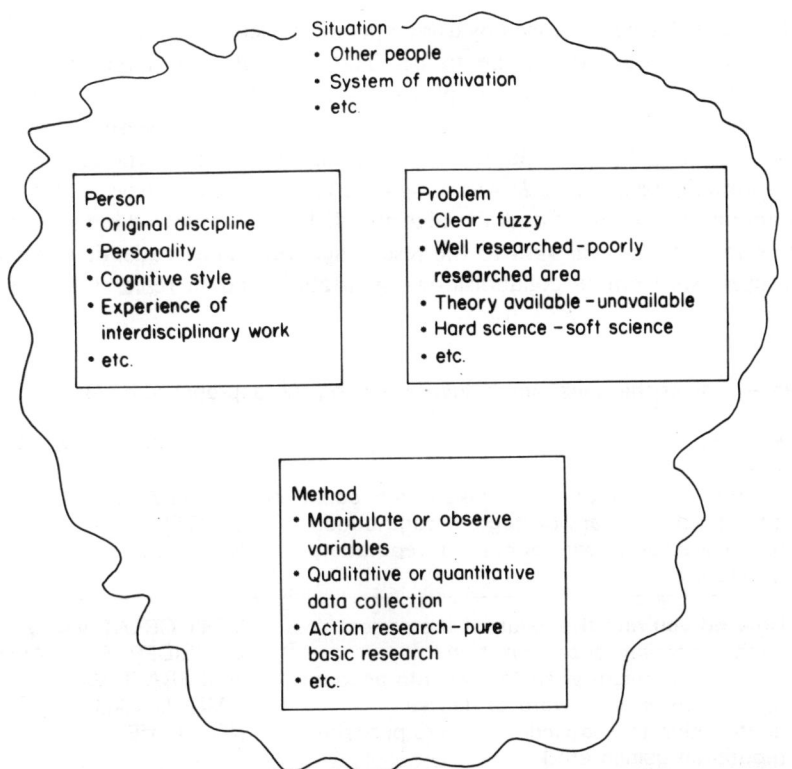

Figure 1. Categories of variables in the interdisciplinary research process

nor on the problem alone. Eden and Sims (1977) have shown how problem definition is influenced by this person–problem interaction and that research problems are to some extent subjectively defined rather than objectively real.
3. From the perspective of any individual researcher other people are part of the situation in which he or she is embedded.

In practice there will be a complex set of interactions and interrelationships between person, situation, problem, and methodological variables and it is not sensible to study one aspect of the research process without at least some awareness of other possibly important factors.

Empirical work

Using these four classes of variables as an organizing framework several linked studies have been conducted over the last two or three years. One study, for example, sought to examine whether the success or value of interdisciplinary projects could be related to certain easily identifiable factors, e.g. class of first degree of the researcher (a person variable), payments made by the organization (a situation variable).

Project value was assessed by asking people closely involved with the project what they thought the value to be. The value derived from this sort of interdisciplinary research is complex and difficult to quantify but opinions on three separate kinds of value seemed to be of interest. They were: (1) academic value, (2) value to the collaborating company, (3) value to the researcher. A questionnaire (see Figure 2) was designed to measure these aspects and also to obtain an assessment of overall value and difficulties involved in the research. The questionnaire was sent to the researcher, the main academic supervisor, the supervisor from the collaborating organization, and the researcher's personal tutor.

Please answer the questions below by ticking the appropriate boxes.

1. How do you rate the value of the project *academically*?
   (Things you might wish to take into account are: award or non-award of degree, contribution to knowledge, papers published, reputation gained etc.)

   VERY GREAT VALUE
   CONSIDERABLE VALUE
   MODERATE VALUE
   LIMITED VALUE
   NO VALUE

2. How do you rate the value of the project to the *company* or *organization*?
   (Things you might wish to take into account are: award or non-award of degree, contribution to knowledge, papers published, reputation gained etc.)

   VERY GREAT VALUE
   CONSIDERABLE VALUE
   MODERATE VALUE
   LIMITED VALUE
   NO VALUE

3. How do you rate the value of the experience to the *student*?
   (Things you might consider are: launching on a rewarding career, ambitions satisfied, nea horizons opened up, sense of achievement, excitement of project etc.)

   VERY GREAT VALUE
   CONSIDERABLE VALUE
   CONSIDERABLE VALUE
   MODERATE VALUE
   LIMITED VALUE
   NO VALUE

4. To what extent did the project create *difficulties*, problems or complications for you, or otherwise demand extra effort?

   VERY GREAT EXTENT
   CONSIDERABLE EXTENT
   MODERATE EXTENT
   LIMITED EXTENT
   NONE

5. How do you rate the *overall* achievement of the project?
   (Interpret this in your own way; maybe just as a summation of the other questions; on the other hand maybe it will include other consideration not covered).

   VERY HIGH
   CONSIDERABLE
   MODERATE
   LIMITED
   NONE

Figure 2. Questionnaire used to collect information on project value

The value of each project was represented (in the subsequent analysis by the unweighted mean for questions 1, 2, 3, and 5 on the questionnaire. This was

Table 1. Summary of relationships between project value and other factors
1. *Statistically significant differences*

		No.	Project value, mean score (min. 0–max. 4)
(a) Sex of researcher*	Male	128	2.4
	Female	19	1.9
(b) Method of payment*	Salary (at or near market rate)	102	2.4
	Scholarship (below market rate)	42	2.1
(c) Academic outcome†	Ph.D.	44	2.7
	M.Phil.	9	2.2
	Ran over time	5	2.2
	Withdrew (first year)	17	1.1
	Withdrew (second or third year)	8	1.8
	Live	63	2.4
(d) Lectures attended by researcher during first two years of research	150 hours or less	91	2.2
	150–250 hours	37	2.3
	250 hours or more	18	2.7

2. *Other variables—no statistically significant differences*
   Previous work experience of researcher
   Public–private problem-owning organization
   Size of problem-owning organization
   Original discipline of researcher
   Researcher and main supervisor matched or unmatched in original discipline
   Educational level of researcher (Master's/Bachelor's)
   Class of bachelor's degree
   Distance between university and problem-owning organization
   Proportion of time at university or organization
   Faculties of university supervisors

*p less than 0.05
†p less than 0.001

based partly on examination of the pattern of intercorrelations between the various indications of project value (but mainly because an average of all of the questionnaire items seemed the most intuitively reasonable overall measure of value). Results from this study are summarized in Table 1.

As Table 1 shows, some statistically significant results were obtained showing relationships between the project value measure and sex of researcher, salary, academic outcome, and attendance at lectures.

Attempts to interpret the results indicate, as much as anything, the dangers of jumping to cause and effect conclusions, e.g. does the payment of a market salary encourage researchers to work harder and, therefore, obtain better assessments of value, or are good researchers more likely to be able to obtain market salaries from their organizations? Similarly, the strong relation between sex of researcher and project value is also related to the greater tendency for female researchers to withdraw early in the research process.

Results such as these led to a more in-depth investigation of some of the variabies involved. Robertson and Molloy (1982) describe a study designed to examine the links between the psychological characteristics of researchers and success in interdisciplinary research. In brief, this study involved obtaining test scores for researchers on three main psychological factors:

1. Reasoning ability—the Watson–Glaser Critical Thinking Appraisal (Watson and Glaser, 1964);
2. Personality (extraversion and anxiety)—the Eysenck Personality Inventory (Eysenck and Eysenck, 1964);
3. Cognitive complexity (indicating the extent to which a person views the world in a complex, multidimensional fashion or within a more simple framework) —the Bieri test of cognitive complexity (Bieri et al., 1966).

Relationships between these test scores and supervisors' ratings of the research abilities of the researchers were then examined. Further details of the rating scale are given in Robertson and Molloy (1982). Table 2 summarizes the results from this study.

Table 2. Correlations between psychological test scores of researchers and supervisors' ratings ($n = 33$)

	Rating
Reasoning	0.04
Cognitive complexity	−0.39*
Extraversion	0.22
Anxiety	−0.50†

*p less than 0.05
†p less than 0.01

As the results show, higher ratings are obtained by researchers who are less cognitively complex and less anxious. Closer inspection of the results for anxiety shows that the relationship between test scores and ratings is more or less linear and as anxiety test scores increase, ratings of ability decrease. For cognitive complexity the relationship is not linear. Although the distribution of scores can be approximated by a straight line and thus produce the correlation coefficient shown in Table 2, the ratings obtained by researchers actually peak at moderate levels of cognitive complexity (see Figure 3)—with high complexity individuals doing worst of all. The researchers who obtained moderate scores (112 to 148) on this scale obtained better ratings than researchers who obtained extreme (high or low) scores.

Some further light can be thrown on the results by examining the progress that researchers have made since this study began and, in particular, by comparing the characteristics of researchers who have successfully submitted their work for Ph.D. degrees with those who have not.

Table 3. Relations between psychological test scores and research progress: *Neuroticism*

	Mean	Standard deviation		
1. Ph.D. ($n=7$)	7.29	2.06		
2. Withdrawn ($n=5$)	12.6	5.32	t 2.53,	$p < 0.05$
3. Fourth year, but not yet submitted ($n=9$)	11.78	5.54		
4. Current ($n=15$)	10.33	4.09		

Cognitive complexity

	Mean	Standard deviation	Number with extreme scores	Number with moderate scores
1. Ph.D. ($n=7$)	132	23.7	4	3
2. Withdrawn ($n=5$)	130	23.7	2	3
3. Fourth year ($n=9$)	133	35.3	4	5
4. Current ($n=15$)	137	28.8	8	7

In fact it seems sensible to allocate the researchers to one of four different categories: (1) Ph.D. awarded, (2) no thesis submitted after four years (or more) of research, (3) withdrawn from the research, (4) in years one to three of research. The award of a Ph.D. is, of course, in some ways an imperfect criterion by which to judge research success but an examination of this factor does at least provide an unambiguous criterion of research progress.

Table 3 shows that, when the researchers in the sample were examined on this basis, the results already obtained, suggesting that low anxiety is associated with success, are supported.

These results cannot be explained without considering the situation in which the researchers worked. Anxiety, for instance, is likely to be a particularly significant personality variable for the group of interdisciplinary researchers studied because they are working in a situation where there are many potential sources of stress, e.g. role ambiguity, work pressure, lack of security. The significance of anxiety as a determinant of success in research may vary as the sources of stress within the situation vary. In a low-stress situation anxiety may

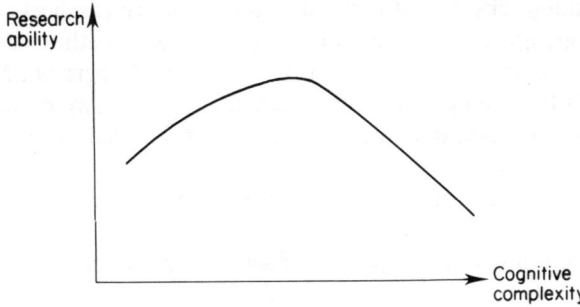

Figure 3. Relationship between cognitive complexity and rated research ability

be associated with success to a lesser degree or in a different way. For example, the slightly increased level of drive associated with anxiety may, in fact, be beneficial in a very relaxed, low-stress situation where internal pressure is likely to be the only source of motivation.

Turning to cognitive complexity, the high-complexity interdisciplinary researchers studied here may be less skilful researchers because they find it more difficult to 'see through' the possible complexities of a problem. This could be brought about, as noted earlier, by a tendency to consider a wide range of possibly important problem features and the development of overelaborate and complex cognitive maps of the problem. Robertson (1978) has shown how high-complexity individuals display broad attention deployment and employ holistic broad-based learning strategies.

Low-complexity students may be relatively more successful because they simplify situations, impose reductions, and proceed in an apparently well-ordered, step-by-step approach. They do seem to impress raters as being more successful than complex individuals, though it is possible that this is a function of the apparent decisiveness and clarity displayed in their approach—a feature which may not, in fact, lead to a better final result.

As with anxiety, the situation in which the researcher works may determine the importance and nature of the relationship between research success (or perceived success) and cognitive complexity. For example, when the situation is extremely complex is it more useful to use many dimensions or would a cognitively simple approach, using relatively few dimensions, be more likely to lead to success?

Situational complexity (variety)

Ashby (1956) introduced the concept of variety as the number of 'distinguishable elements in a system' (p.124). The concept has been taken up by others, e.g. Beer (1972): 'The total number of possible states of a system' (p.307). Although definitions vary, the basic idea seems similar and levels of variety are likely to vary from one research situation to another and the success of any particular researcher may be dependent, to some extent, on the match between his or her cognitive complexity and the complexity (variety) of the situation or problem.

The psychology of individual differences provides many methods and theoretical frameworks for studing differences in researchers, i.e. person variables. As yet, however, there is no suitable system, method, or theory for studying differences in situations. As a starting point Robertson, Molloy, and Cochran (1981) have suggested four dimensions which may be worth taking into account when a research situation is being examined. They are:

1. Stressors (i.e. sources of stress within the situation);
2. Variety;
3. Social interaction variables (i.e. the influence of other people, management style, etc.);

4. Motivational climate (i.e. what behaviour, attitudes, etc., are rewarded/ punished).

In many respects, however, it is inappropriate to consider the situation as if it can be determined in an entirely objective fashion. As James *et al.* (1978) postulate: 'Individuals respond primarily to cognitive representations of situations rather than to situations per se' (p.787). This means, of course, that individuals will construe the same situation differently. For example, underlying differences in cognitive complexity may be reflected in the extent to which a person construes a situation as relatively complex or simple.

On this basis the determinants of successful interdisciplinary research (and many other activities) rest on complex interactions between psychological and situational factors. Disentangling these interactions is beyond the scope of this chapter but is surely an important area for further work.

Interdisciplinary Research

It is not possible to show from the data available whether the specific results obtained and summarized above are related to research in general or to interdisciplinary research in particular or to the sample of researcher studied—and no one else! This question may be properly answered only by further research with other single-discipline and interdisciplinary projects. It is the writer's view that interdisciplinarity is a less significant feature of the projects studied than the fact that the research projects studied were all of an action or operational research nature and were carried out, for the most part, within an environment where pragmatic, action-orientated work is valued highly. The results suggest that in situations where action or operational research is being conducted and there is a fairly high level of stress, low-anxiety, moderate-to-low complexity researchers will be most likely to be successful—or at least be perceived as successful by others.

The research described above has concentrated on a sample of individual interdisciplinary researchers. Problems and opportunities proliferate when interdisciplinary teams are considered. Each member of the team, for instance, becomes part of the situation for every other member—and presumably contributes to situational variety, stress, and other factors. A range of interesting hypotheses emerge, concerning, for example, the mix of cognitive complexity, anxiety, and other personality factors within interdisciplinary teams and the links between the optimum team composition and situational factors. For both the individual and team case the key variables are far from being satisfactorily identified and understood.

Acknowledgements

Some of the research described in this chapter was supported by a grant from the Science and Social Science Research Councils.

I am grateful to Drs A. J. Cochran and K. J. Molloy for permission to use material from research that we conducted together.

References

Ashby, W. R. (1956). *Introduction to Cybernetics*, Chapman and Hall, London.
Beer, S. (1972). *Brain of the Firm*, Allen Lane, London.
Bieri, J., Atkins, A. L., Briar, S., Lobeck, R., Miller, H., and Tripodi, T. (1966). *Clinical and Social Judgement*, Wiley, New York.
Cherns, A. B. (1979). *Using the Social Sciences*, Routledge and Kegan Paul, London.
Eden, C., and Sims, D. (1977). 'On the nature of problems in consulting practice', in *The King is Dead: Long Live the King* (Ed. K. Bowen), Operational Research Society, Birmingham.
Eysenck, H. J., and Eysenck, S. B. G. (1964). *Manual for the Eysenck Personality Inventory*, University of London Press, London.
James, L. R., Hater, J. J., Gent, M. J., and Bruni, J. R. (1978). 'Psychological climate: implications from cognitive social learning theory and interactional psychology', *Personnel Psychology*, 31, 783–813.
Minogue, K. R. (1973). *The Concept of a University*, Weidenfeld and Nicholson, London.
Robertson, I. T. (1978). 'Relationships between learning strategy, attention deployment and personality', *British Journal of Educational Psychology*, 48, 86–91.
Robertson, I. T. (1981). 'Vocational education and the diffusion and application of research-based knowledge, *Journal of Further and Higher Education*, 5, 68–76.
Robertson, I. T., and Cochran, A. J. (1980). 'An interdisciplinary, action research approach to postgraduate education, Paper presented at the Annual Conference on Postgraduate Psychology, University of Lancaster, England, April 1980.
Robertson, I. T., and Molloy, K. J. (1982). 'Cognitive complexity, neuroticism and research ability', *British Journal of Educational Psychology*, 52, 113–118.
Robertson, I. T., Molloy, K. J., and Cochran, A. J. (1981). 'Learning while doing: an investigation of organisationally-based problem solvers', Paper presented at the British Psychological Society Fourteenth Annual Occupational Psychology Conference, University of York, England, January 1981.
van Rest, D. J. (1980). *IHD Thesis Summaries, 1970–1979*, IHD Scheme, University of Aston, Birmingham.
Warr, P. B. (1977). *Action Research*, Social and Applied Psychology Unit Memorandum No. 160, MRC Social and Applied Psychology Unit, University of Sheffield, England.
Watson, G., and Glaser, E. M. (1964). *The Watson–Glaser Critical Thinking Appraisal'*, Harcourt, Brace, Jovanovich, New York.
Zuckerman Committee (1961). *The Management and Control of Research and Development*, HMSO, London.

CROSS-DISCIPLINARITY IN THE BIOMEDICAL SCIENCES: A PRELIMINARY ANALYSIS OF ANATOMY

F. ROSSINI, A. L. PORTER, D. E. CHUBIN, and T. CONNOLLY
Georgia Institute of Technology, Georgia, USA

Introduction and Major Issues

Research which cuts across academic and professional disciplines has often been considered to be predominantly applied, rather than basic (see, for example,

Kelly *et al.*, 1978; Rossini *et al.*, 1978, 1981). This study deals with cross-disciplinary work in a basic science—the biomedical science of anatomy.

In studying cross-disciplinary work we accept as an assumption the claim (Rossini *et al.*, 1981) that cross-disciplinarity is caused by and affects not only the intellectual elements of research but also the social and institutional structures involved in the immediate context of research. It also touches upon larger social, economic, and public policy issues affecting research. This assumption of complex causality means that it is both invalid and misleading to decouple the intellectual treatment of scientific research into such isolated boxes as history, philosophy, sociology, economics, psychology, and public policy. Instead, a systemic treatment is required which involves as causes and effects a variety of entities on differing levels of aggregation. This issue has also been treated, though somewhat more indirectly, by Kuhn (1970) and by Churchman (1971). Suffice it to say that the discussion of an isolated sub-set of elements involved in scientific research almost invariably omits key causal factors, thereby rendering the analysis flawed and suspect.

We also need to draw the distinction between two somewhat different outcomes of cross-disciplinary collaboration—multidisciplinarity and interdisciplinarity (Rossini *et al.*, 1978, 1981). Multidisciplinarity is the result of the interrelation of disciplinary components where they are linked externally only, without any serious attempt to make internal linkages between the various analyses. An example would be a volume about telecommunications with chapters on technology, economics, public policy, and social aspects preceded by an introduction and followed by conclusions. Interdisciplinarity involves the internal and substantive interlinking of the various disciplinary analyses so that each considers the results of the others in its own development, thereby admitting to the analysis the interaction of factors nominally treated by the five disciplines in the illustration. This key distinction, while primarily intellectual, involves institutional considerations as well. In a phrase, multidisciplinary work might be likened to a patchwork quilt; interdisciplinary, to a seamless garment.

Peterson's Annual Guide to Graduate Study succinctly describes anatomy as follows:

> Anatomy today is a discipline concerned not only with structure, but also with the function and the development of the cells, tissues and organs constituting the animal body. Because the anatomy department is usually at the medical school, it also has an important role to play in bridging the gap between the basic and clinical sciences. Gross anatomy consists of that body of information about structures that can be observed at the gross level, that is, with the naked eye by dissection. Research at this level today is mainly carried out by biological anthropologists, some of whom are located in anatomy departments. Microscopic anatomy consists of studies on the structure of cells and tissues using the light and electron microscopes. Research advances in this area have been dramatic in the past two decades. Because the practical resolution of the ordinary

transmission electron microscope is better than 1 nm, molecules can be visualized and the gap between chemistry and morphology bridged (Hay, 1980).

As this description notes, anatomy is moving from a macro orientation to one which is structure-visible microscopically. It has reached down from cadavers to large molecules. The transition from gross morphology in anatomy is illustrated in the autobiographical essay of the anatomist, Corner (1958):

> ... But in biological work especially, the paradoxical situation often occurs that the successful investigator finally cuts off his own ability to advance the subject by carrying his work to the point where further information can only be acquired by new technical methods or new ways of thinking for which he is not equipped. The morphologist, for example, comes to the point at which only biochemistry can help. I have myself more than once wistfully seen my juniors successfully take over problems which I had been keen enough to develop, but was not qualified to solve . . . .

This shift in the field of anatomy is illustrated by the occasional change in the name of medical school units from 'Department of Anatomy' to a label such as 'Department of Anatomy and Neuroscience'. Such a change and its rationale were described by one anatomy department chairman whom we interviewed.

Anatomy is one of the specializations in the developing cross-disciplinary field referred to as neuroscience:

> The simplest and most acceptable definition to its practitioners is that neuroscience is the correlated study of brain and behavior. That definition emphasizes the interrelatedness, the interdependence of cause and effect in the organism's life (Marshall, 1979, p.3).

The neuroscience literature roughly quadrupled from 1967 to 1977, a period during which the scientific literature as a whole doubled. During the same period, membership in the Society for Neuroscience increased by 500 per cent (Marshall, 1979).

Some questions at this point in the research are:

1. What is the current status of cross-disciplinarity in anatomy?
2. What is the general trajectory of cross-disciplinary development in anatomy? What role does the development of neuroscience play in this development?
3. What are the important intellectual and institutional factors which have caused this situation?

To begin to answer these questions, we will first consider some preliminary data.

Preliminary Data

We collected data from two sources—advertisements for faculty positions in *Science* magazine (the primary journal in which heads of anatomy departments advertise for faculty and also a multidisciplinary journal) and interviews with a number of anatomy department heads.

We analysed the position-available advertisement in *Science*, both for anatomists and from anatomy-related units. The first issue of every other month for a twenty-four month period back from August 1, 1980 was studied. The search uncovered forty-six relevant positions. These were analysed by the field of employing unit, the field of person sought, the institutional location of the unit advertising the position (medical school or arts and sciences college), and the type of position (faculty or postdoctoral).

Tables 1 and 2 indicate the result of these analyses. The usual expectation if disciplinary boundaries were to be strictly maintained is that anatomists would be sought almost exclusively by anatomy units. What appears is that only about a quarter of the cases fit this pattern. The cross-disciplinary pattern is more pronounced for medical schools than for arts and sciences colleges, perhaps illustrating greater receptivity in professional schools. It is sharper for postdoctoral positions than for regular faculty positions, possibly indicating greater impetus for cross-disciplinary activities in temporary and research positions than for permanent and instructional positions. Indeed, conversations with chairpersons indicate a general focus on postdoctoral appointments as a means to learn research skills distinct from the area of primary training.

Table 1. Advertisements by field of employer and employee. The top table considers all advertisements. Bottom two tables reflect a breakdown of advertisements from arts and sciences colleges and medical schools

All advertisements

		Employee's field			
		Other	Anatomy	A+O	
Employer's field	Other	0	9	11	
	Anatomy	8	11	2	
	A+O	1	3	1	(n=46)

(Other is non-anatomy; A+O is anatomy and other.)

Arts and sciences colleges

		Employee's field			
		Other	Anatomy	A+O	
Employer's field	Other	0	3	7	
	Anatomy	1	5	0	
	A+O	0	0	0	(n=16)

Medical schools

		Employee's field			
		Other	Anatomy	A+O	
Employer's field	Other	0	6	4	
	Anatomy	7	6	2	
	A+O	1	3	1	(n=30)

Table 2. Breakdown of advertisements by level of position (faculty or postdoctoral)

		Regular faculty positions Employee's field		
		Other	Anatomy	A+O
Employer's field	Other	0	7	10
	Anatomy	5	11	2
	A+O	1	2	1 ($n = 39$)

		Postdoctoral positions Employee's field		
		Other	Anatomy	A+O
Employer's field	Other	0	2	1
	Anatomy	3	0	0
	A+O	0	1	0 ($n = 7$)

The cross-disciplinary developments in evidence in the advertisements were reinforced and expanded by interviews with the heads of eight anatomy departments in medical schools. An initial instrument was pre-tested on department head and was modified as a result for use with the other units. Table 3 lists the units whose heads were surveyed and some of their demographic characteristics.

Table 3. List of anatomy departments surveyed and their characteristics

Anatomy departments surveyed

Emory University
George Washington University
Medical College of Georgia
Michigan State University
University of Arkansas
University of Maryland
University of Texas
University of Vermont

Faculty
Range: 9–22
Mean ± standard deviation: 16 ± 5

Postdoctoral
Range: 0–6
Mean ± standard deviation: 3 ± 2

Graduate students
Range: 5–15
Mean ± standard deviation: 9 ± 3

Most critically, the composition of the faculties is already 45 per cent. non-anatomists, while the postdoctoral positions are held by 75 per cent. non-anatomists. In addition to this information, Tables 4 and 5 also list some of the fields outside anatomy. While most of these fields are in the biomedical area, a few, such as physics and engineering, traditionally stand outside it.

Table 4. Faculty disciplines in surveyed anatomy departments (in a few cases some determinations of the anatomy/non-anatomy distinction were made in accordance with the character of the remainder of the unit)

Disciplines of faculty anatomy departments
Anatomy: 70/127 = 0.55
Non-anatomy: 57/127 = 0.45

Non-anatomy disciplines represented on anatomy faculties
Biology
Zoology
Pathology
Pharmacology
Medicine
Physiology
Genetics
Cell biology
Neurosciences
Biophysics
Physics
Psychology
Biochemistry
Chemistry

Table 5. Disciplines of postdoctoral positions in surveyed anatomy departments (in a few cases some determinations of the anatomy/non-anatomy distinction were made in accordance with the character of the remainder of the unit)

Disciplines of postdoctoral positions in anatomy departments
Anatomy: 5/20 = 0.25
Non-anatomy: 15/20 = 0.75

Non-anatomy disciplines of postdoctoral positions in anatomy departments
Pathology
Biology
Engineering
Physiology
Medicine
Cell biology
Pharmacology
Chemistry

The instructional audience of the anatomy departments includes, in every case, many medical students and relatively few anatomy graduate students (a ten to one ratio is typical). Half of the departments had other student audiences — including dental students, osteopathic students, veterinary medicine students, students of allied health professions (e.g. nurses and medical technicians), and undergraduates.

Research support came to every one of the departments from various Institutes of the National Institute of Health. All had additional support from such organizations as the National Science Foundation, Muscular Dystrophy

Foundation, March of Dimes, various heart associations, the US Air Force, and private firms.

Cross-disciplinary collaboration was present in all units with other medical school units. Three-fourths mentioned cross-disciplinary collaboration within the unit, while one-fourth indicated such collaboration with other institutions. Cross-disciplinary instruction resided mainly in the neuroscience course, required of all medical students. In most instances this course was staffed by faculty from a variety of departments.

Analysis

The data clearly indicate that cross-disciplinary activities (a very wide range was cited by our respondents) are taking place in anatomy departments. At this point in our research there are some things we do and do not know about this situation. We will begin with what we know and develop the rest in the form of a research agenda.

The departments we surveyed varied widely in character. Half were composed predominantly of anatomists while non-anatomists were a majority in others (ranging up to 89 per cent. in one department). Yet in both types of units the heads emphasized the importance of a problem focus in which the researcher follows the problem across disciplinary boundaries using whatever techniques are appropriate. The researcher could either master the appropriate techniques or collaborate with those who already knew them. Thus research on important problems was limited neither by knowledge boundaries nor to specific techniques—in contrast to the historical situation reported by Dr Corner. Resarch is emphasized and, in the words of one respondent, *all* (anatomy department) research is interdisciplinary today—or, as another respondent put it: 'We teach anatomy; we do biomedical research.' This general emphasis leads to interesting practices that differ from much of academia, such as one head's lack of concern with the anatomy background of his faculty. With high-level biomedical research capabilities and outgoing personalities he has found that biomedical researchers can be brought to teach anatomy without any formal background. This also leads to sharp distinctions in research and teaching foci in many cases—as where one does research on neurotransmitters but teaches gross anatomy.

Based on the interviews and the neuroscience inventory analysed by Marshall (1979) we might speculate that the field is in a state of transformation from anatomy to cross-disciplinary neuroscience. The departments we surveyed were distributed along such a continuum. The prospect of studying a field in transition is interesting from a number of perspectives. However, it leaves many unanswered questions.

One major question which requires treatment is to what extent these cross-disciplinary activities are multidisciplinary and to what extent they are interdisciplinary. This will require analysis on a project by project and course by course level.

Several observations can be made in closing. Firstly, it is important to consider what factors are inducing the apparent transformation of anatomy departments. Speculating, there seems to be an interplay (not acidental) between federal research support opportunities, the organization of medical schools, and intellectual challenge driving research towards neuroscience. One side effect of this movement is the possibility of leaving the function of teaching in the lurch. For instance, two of our department titles show a possible evolutionary direction (e.g. Department of Anatomy and Neuroscience). Will this continue to the stage of Department of Neuroscience? If so, what will happen to the teaching of anatomy, already largely a service to the medical school? This question also bears on the individual faculty members. There were indications that those who taught gross anatomy, in particular, tended to be older and less research oriented. Promotion and tenure criteria emphasize research. In the future who will teach the basics needed for clinical practice? One interesting twist was to request clinicians to teach these for the anatomy department (e.g. pathologists to teach histology).

If we are correct in perceiving a transition in progress, how widespread is it? Our pilot survey suggests that it is the dominant, though not exclusive, pattern in anatomy in the United States. We hypothesize that this finding might generalize across the biomedical sciences. We do not know to what extent it crosses the institutional boundaries of the medical school to affect arts and sciences units, nor the importance of research institutes and their roles (e.g. the Brain Research Institute at UCLA). (We have no data from outside the United States on which to base generalizations in that direction, but we suspect this 'interdisciplinarization' to neuroscience to be international in scope). Were one to feel extremely bold, the speculation might extend into the future to project a spreading wave of redirections into other sciences. In particular, the social sciences, stressed by declining student bodies of their own, could mould into a service teaching role for the basics and an applied policy research direction encouraged by federal research support opportunities.

The potential impacts of the transformation of institutional arrangements on the face of science are enormous. Our signals are too preliminary to draw any firm conclusions. Intead, they suggest a research agenda to first define more precisely the past trends of change in the biomedical sciences, then to adduce the critical causal forces, and, next, to project the future directions and impacts of any transformations in progress. Finally, such a study should raise critical issues at stake for the intellectual frontiers in science, moving through cross-disciplinary bounds vis-à-vis the teaching function, and suggest policy actions to direct the evolution in a desirable way.

References

Churchman, C. W. (1971). *The Design of Inquiring Systems*, Basic Books, New York.
Corner, G. W. (1958). *Anatomist at Large: An Autobiography and Selected Essays*, Books for Libraries Press, Freeport, New York.

Hay, E. (1980). 'Anatomy', in *Peterson's Annual Guide to Graduate Study*, 1980 ed. Book 3, *Biological, Agricultural, and Health Sciences* (Eds K. C. Hegener and S. V. Weaver), Peterson's Guides, Princeton, New Jersey.

Kelly, P., Kranzberg, M., Rossini, F. A., Baker, N. R., Tarpley, F. A., and Mitzner, M. (1978). *Technological Innovation: A Critical Review of Current Knowledge*, The San Francisco Press, San Francisco, California.

Kuhn, T. S. (1979). *The Structure of Scientific Revolutions*, 2nd ed., University of Chicago Press, Chicago, Illinois.

Marshall, L. (1979). 'Maturation and current status of neuroscience: data from the 1976 inventory of U.S. neurosciences', *Experimental Neurology*, **64**, 1–32.

Rossini, F. A., Porter, A. L., Kelly, P., and Chubin, D. E. (1978). *Frameworks and Factors Affecting Integration Within Technology Assessments*, Report of National Science Foundation Grant ERS 76-04474, Georgia Institute of Technology, Atlanta, Georgia.

Rossini, F. A., Porter, A. L., Kelly, P., and Chubin, D. E. (1981). 'Interdisciplinary integration in technology assessments', *Knowledge*, June (in press).

PEER REVIEW IN INTERDISCIPLINARY RESEARCH: FLEXIBILITY AND RESPONSIVENESS

M. G. RUSSELL
University of Minnesota, USA

Background

Interdisciplinarity has been one of the continuing forces in the history of knowledge. The earliest communities of scholars recognized the importance of collaborative efforts among academicians in developing the philosophy of science (Gusdorf, 1977). Documentation shows that collaboration served as a basis for professional development as early as the Napoleonic times (Beaver and Rosen, 1978). Later, the technological revolution encouraged the acceleration of knowledge production and provided an impetus for the formalization of various types of collaboration into sub-disciplines and disciplines.

The expansion of knowledge has produced a need for greater diversity in scientific communities and in accountability mechanisms whereby the disciplines monitor their paradigms and progress. Disciplinary frameworks and their refinements have channelled and, in turn, were developed both by the expansion of knowledge and the utilization of knowledge (Sinaceur, 1977).

The disciplinary community has been essential in the transfer of scientific knowledge into educational spheres, into cognitive and social processes, and in training researchers' perspectives. However, interdisciplinary efforts have and continue to characterize not only the research frontier (Blauberg and Mirsky, 1979) but also the utilization of knowledge.

This dynamism of differentiation and integration among scientific disciplines exists in an environment in which one supplements the other and in which each is a pre-condition to the other (Darvas and Haraszthy, 1979). It has been at the points of differentiation among the disciplinary specializations that standards for academic respectability have evolved (Peston, 1978). These standards establish, for each discipline, the criteria for admission into that community of scholars, the range of problems considered important, the approaches considered appropriate, and the criteria for legitimatizing findings as new knowledge through publication. Publication provides the corrective process, the evaluation, and the assent of the relevant scientific community (Price, 1980). There is some evidence that this peer review of scientific inquiry and personnel operates most effectively in disciplines in which there is agreement on criteria and in which the visibility of consequences is high. However, this evidence also supports the view that freedom from the constraints of academic departments which are organized around disciplinary perspectives is associated with more innovative research activities (Gordon and Marquis, 1966).

Two broad classes of criteria for motivating and evaluating research activities emerge. Firstly, the profession of learning stimulates research which advances knowledge by expanding the pool of knowledge. This research is traditionally disciplinary, but is also interdisciplinary in 'the interrelatedness of basic science phenomena' (Huston, 1981b). Secondly, pressures for problem-solving stimulate research efforts which contribute to solutions. Criteria for evaluating disciplinary research focus on the assessment of its scientific soundness and depend on the criteria established by the contributing disciplines (Cotterrell, 1979). The criteria for interdisciplinary research assessment involve these criteria, as well as additional criteria of mission or policy relevance and the utilization of findings.

As interdisciplinary fields become established, the continued external referral to disciplines for validation and assessment eventually grows cumbersome. In some cases, this inconvenience leads to a tendency to de-emphasize the wider theoretical aspects of the interdisciplinary field. Increased consensus in internal criteria develops as the specific interdisciplinary community establishes its own internal standards. The increased focus which results permits the interdisciplinary field to shed some of the reliance on externally established criteria with a minimal threat of isolation from the parent discipline which gave it validity at the onset. Eventually, the infant interdisciplinary effort becomes, itself, a parent discipline. Parent disciplines that continue to produce new interdisciplinary efforts or that maintain sufficient control over their boundaries survive to the next generation. Others do not.

The growth of knowledge and the need for new perspectives to deal with changing complexities have converged in the development of new specializations within the scientific community. Each new phase of specialization has limited the concerns, the perspectives, the paradigms, the methods, and the theoretical frameworks of the succeeding sub-disciplines (Price, 1980). In order to establish standards of academic respectability or negligence, the paradigms for these new sub-disciplines must be articulated. At the same time, the issues identified by sponsors and by socially conscious scientists continue to be broader than any one specialization. These issues call forth research activities which lie outside of the traditional turfs of disciplines and subdisciplines.

It is in this context that the interest in, concern for, and importance of interdisciplinary research, brought about through collaboration, continues to grow. (Several dimensions of collaboration are particularly relevant in considering interdisciplinary research. The administrative, disciplinary, and personnel dimensions of research collaboration are likely to present discrete but interrelated considerations in assessing the goals, processes, and outcomes of interdisciplinary research; Russell, 1981.) The capacity of interdisciplinary research to address very difficult research questions, especially when the procedures and outcomes of the research activities are uncertain, has been acknowledged (Birnbaum, 1981). Yet these very complex problems and responsive procedures resist easy application of the peer review process. The needs and missions from which such problems are identified, the uniqueness of the combination of disciplinary approaches, and the uncertainty of outcomes of such research render evaluation difficult and raise several critical questions:

> Why should IDR be evaluated?
> When is it appropriate to perform the evaluation?
> What aspects of IDR can or should be evaluated?
> Who should perform the evaluation?

Why Should IDR be Evaluated?

Evaluation, of which peer review is one type, is at the heart of quality control in the scientific community. Research results are not considered new knowledge until they undergo critical review and acceptance by the scientific community. This validation of scientific merit is an assessment of quality—of rigour in theory and methodology and of consistency in interpretation. This quality control mechanism serves not only to decide which works merit publication in professional and scholarly journals, but also to control the entry of new members into the community and to identify which members deserve special recognition (Bowers, 1975). As such, this review typically occurs after the research has been completed and written up. The publication of research confirms that it has been performed. The evaluation of research confirms its compliance with standards of respectability.

Funded research, which accounts for much of the large-scale interdisciplinary research, carries with it several additional requirements because fund administrators must account for the money allocated to research activities. How has the money been spent? What did it buy? These are issues that surface throughout the life of the sponsored research project in monitoring systems and at the completion of the project in reporting systems. The missions and goals under which money is awarded to research are, in some environments, broadly defined and in others targeted to specific needs. In either case, evaluation for accountability to the sponsor is required (NCR, 1980).

Evaluation provides information for determining how resources will be used (*ex ante* risk assessment) and how they were used (*ex post* accountability). Through such feedback it permits scientists and administrators to benefit from accumulated experience. The evaluation of interdisciplinary research is, in this context, useful in both *screening* the most promising research proposals and in *strengthening* contributions to the foundation of knowledge. Although responsibility for the screening and strengthening of interdisciplinary research resides with the sponsors, administrators, and editors, inputs for their decisions come from scientists. Several surveys of administrator attitudes towards the critical input received through the peer review of proposals have documented administrator reliance on the critiques by specialists who are informed about the area of study proposed (Cole, Rubin, and Cole, 1978; Vandette, 1977). Thus, the review by knowledgeable peers is a vital input into sponsors' and editors' decisions (Gordon, 1980).

This input is also valuable in addressing administrators' concerns for the organizational processes which permit the conduct of research with the fewest impediments, with harmonious convergence of research results and agency mission, with institutional reputation, and with the response to constituencies. From the sponsor/administrators' perspective, the importance of review for scientific merit and research quality bears directly on the institutions' overall capability to conduct research and the administrations' role in maintaining consistency of funding and continuity in research. This stability is important in avoiding the disruption of productive programmes. Prestige in the public sector institutions and productivity in the private sector institutions are critical to an administrator's ability to assemble a capable research staff (Ruttan, 1981). Critique by peers can estimate the likelihood that proposed research will result in prestige and productivity.

The opportunity to review research also offers benefits to the reviewers. Written reports of proposed, as well as completed, research inform reviewers of new directions in scientific thought, of new applications for existing techniques, and of new techniques. Citations or summaries of related literature provide reviewers with reviews of literature on the proposed issues and thereby serve to maintain reviewers' awareness of the research front.

In this way, the reviewer/investigator relationship is reciprocal. Because most reviewers are also investigators, benefits of the review experience are extended into subsequent research efforts. Thus, peer review serves as a continuing education process for the reviewers and as a feedback device for investigators. *The potential for interdisciplinary research evaluation to expand and refine scientific disciplines lies in the responsiveness of reviewers and scientists to this process.*

When is it Appropriate to Perform the Evaluation?

In the case of federally sponsored research in the United States, it has been mandated that the potential value of research be evaluated before it is funded.

However, among even the most capable researchers, and especially among the most innovative research projects, the outcomes of research are usually known only *after* the research has been conducted. The research front, like other frontiers, consists largely of unknowns. Interdisciplinary research is speculative research and therefore frequently involves higher risk. In order to justify the continued flow of resources into research activities, the administrators of those funds must justify that the money is well spent and that the risks chosen are those most likely to pay off.

This justification includes several types of accountability. Financial and administrative accountability is implemented in-process through incentives and reporting and *ex post* through reviews of expenditures and operations. Scientific accountability is determined before *ex ante* and *ex post* and involves the recommendations of peer scientists to sponsors and editors. Therefore, the involvement of peer scientists plays a major role in deciding what work will be supported, who shall carry out the work, and what inquiry is significant. Sponsors and editors are responsible for selecting scientists who are qualified to make these judgements, and differences in selection qualifications have been noted (Bowers, 1975; Gordon, 1980; Peston, 1978).

Thus the evaluation criteria imposed by peer scientists guide research activities before and after they are conducted. *Ex ante* review of proposed research is directed by the sponsor via the selection of reviewers. *Ex post* review, however, is largely self-enforced in the research community and is conducted without sponsor intervention. This occurs first as editorial boards of discipline-affiliated journals review research results submitted for publication (Gordon, 1980). Through publication, a group of specialists acknowledges an addition to the pool of knowledge affiliated with the discipline they represent.

This review by a group of peers is followed by the review given by an individual scientist in deciding to use and cite that publication. Such a citation extends the verification of the research results and acknowledges that the contribution to the pool of knowledge was worthy of becoming part of the foundation. Indicators of *ex post* review (publications and citations) subsequently become part of the information used to estimate likelihood of success in *ex ante* reviews. The absence of evaluation criteria and the absence of appropriately focused scholarly journals are both problematic in the *ex post* review of interdisciplinary research.

Interdisciplinary research presents additional challenges to reviewers, administrators, and sponsors because collaborative efforts require the coordination of personnel and organizational units (Ikenberry and Friedman, 1972). It is in this context of research management that in-process performance evaluation of ongoing research is significant. In-process evaluation of the leadership and management of the research project provides information about the congruence of intended and realized goals. Much has been said about the unpredictability of the innovation process (Mosteller, 1981; Price, 1977). Evaluation of critical factors related to in-process performance (Birnbaum, 1981) is helpful in guiding the adjustment of objectives and management strategies.

Especially at the frontiers of knowledge, monitoring the progress and process of research activities is essential in recognizing major breakthroughs, avoiding dead-ends, and maintaining appropriate direction.

The in-process review of research performance is also important in allocating institutional rewards to scientists. Evaluation of scientists for tenure and promotion decisions, merit reviews, and special recognitions frequently does not coincide with project completion or *ex post* review. These evaluations are apt to occur at all stages of research activities. Typically, in such assessments, scientific peers apply disciplinary criteria—usually to a single individual scientist. 'The departmental affiliation is the basis for dispersing rewards, considering resource needs, conducting graduate education, achieving professional integrity and allowing others to understand that disciplinary specialty' (Mitchell, 1977). The value of interdisciplinary research efforts may be unrecognized by applying disciplinary criteria. In addition, collaborative accomplishments may be undervalued or considered less meritorious.

To this point, the why and when of interdisciplinary research evaluation have been discussed. *Ex ante* evaluation provides an assessment of risk in allocating funds and reflects the potential contribution of the proposed research to science and also to the identified research issue. In-process evaluation can strengthen research by monitoring its process and progress and providing impetus for redirection when necessary. *Ex post* evaluation is appropriate in validating the scientific merit of completed research as it is submitted as new knowledge to the scientific community.

Two questions remain. What can or should be evaluated by peers in interdisciplinary research? Who are the peer scientists to evaluate interdisciplinary research?

What Aspects of IDR Can or Should be Evaluated

The evaluation of research has challenged scientists, administrators, and sponsors. Research outcomes are varied and they are not mutually exclusive. The same result can be viewed differently, depending on the evaluator. Research outputs have been typified in many different ways: as those which have extrinsic versus intrinsic value (Price, 1977); as representative of scientific activity, scientific production, or scientific progress (Birnbaum, 1981); as fulfilling basic versus applied research goals (Whitney and Frost, 1971); and as representing research productivity versus researcher productivity (Andrews, 1979). It has been noted that the emphasis on more effective monitoring of research output tends to be greatest in those environments in which there is strong clientele pressure (Ruttan, 1980).

Some studies have noted the congruence of ratings of researcher productivity with ratings of research productivity (Andrews, 1979) and the correlation of traditional measures for these attributes with the informal evaluations of colleagues (Whitney and Frost, 1971). Studies of researcher productivity have used measures of publications, citation counts, patents, ability to attract funding, and production of graduate degrees (Birnbaum, 1981; Busch, Lacy, and Sachs, 1980; Evenson and Wright, 1980; Liebert, 1976; Neumann, 1979; Pelz and Andrews, 1966; Price and Gursey, 1976; Salisbury, 1980). Evidence that the peer review system's reliance on these measures has produced biased review selection and favouritism in awarding funds has been presented (Gustafson, 1975; Small, 1974) and refuted (Cole, Rubin, and Cole, 1978; Miner and McDonald, 1981). Variability in selection of reviewers for editorial boards and in criteria used for review has also been documented (Gordon, 1980).

Indicators of research performance have been less systematically studied across all fields of knowledge. However, several critical factors have been identified: the need to distinguish successful from unsuccessful innovations (Mosteller, 1981); the need to develop sponsor agreement on program goals and priorities against which research performance can be evaluated (NCR, 1980); and the need to differentiate between 'scientific merit' — quality of research — and 'scientific contribution' — applicabilty to the discipline (Cutler, Martino, and Webb, 1974). Differences in standards for assessing the economic quality of research and the scientific quality of research have also been noted (Evenson and Wright, 1980). Standards of economic quality involve the assessment of multiple spillover effects (Evenson and Kisley, 1975) as well as the impact of technological change (Price, 1977). These research performance criteria are especially important to sponsor decisions. In order to provide sound advice to sponsors, peer reviewers need to understand both the scientific and economic contexts of research.

The evaluation of interdisciplinary research involves these criteria, but additionally it requires criteria which acknowledge the unique qualities of interdisciplinary research. One such added dimension is the orientation to group output, as opposed to the traditionally used orientation to individual output (Price, 1980; Whitney and Frost, 1971). In-process review of research is considered an unnecessary burden by many scientists. For the interdisciplinary research project, however, the conduct of research is complicated by the need to maintain cooperation and communication towards a common goal.

Evidence exists (Gillespie and Birnbaum, 1980) that effective projects tend to be those in which a leader is defined and in which that leader is able to elicit ongoing evaluation of the type that brings interpersonal and scientific issues into the open for discussion and evaluation. Acknowledgements of the significant impact of research team composition (Gillespie and Mar, 1977), leadership (Pearson, Payne and Gunz, 1979), and organization (Birnbaum, 1981) also offer insight into assessing the potential success of interdisciplinary research and are, therefore, relevant criteria for review.

The challenges in assessing and evaluating research are multiplied for interdisciplinary research for several reasons. Firstly, because interdisciplinary research is frequently undertaken in order to probe new issues, expected outcomes are sometimes ill-defined (Rossini *et al.*, 1981; Wolfe, 1981). Secondly, benefits of interdisciplinary research are occasionally found primarily in the process itself (Lindas, 1979). The influence of collaboration and communication between scientists on research productivity has been documented (Pelz and

Andrews, 1966). Thirdly, successfully completed interdisciplinary research may result in recommendations for several disciplinary approaches to subsequent analysis, or it may reformulate the definition of the problem (Morphet, 1981). Contributions such as these would be absent from traditional measures of research productivity.

Five questions which are relevant both *ex ante* and *ex post* have been proposed for the evaluation of interdisciplinary research (Peston, 1978):

1. Does the project formulated in interdisciplinary terms show a recognition of the existing contribution made by the separate disciplines?
2. Is the interdisciplinarity genuine in the sense that the problems are formulated in terms which enable the different disciplines to get together rather than compete with one another?
3. Is the method of data acquisition likely to be helpful to all the relevant disciplines or is it biased in a particular direction?
4. Does the interdisciplinarity enhance the possibility of hypothesis testing or does it obscure it?
5. What difference will the results of the research make to the policy decisions that will eventually be taken?

Who Should Perform the Evaluation?

The next question which then follows from these is how can all of these perspectives be brought to bear on any specific problem? Regardless of the institutional or project basis for allocating research support (Bredahl, Bryant, and Ruttan, 1980), sponsor, administrator, peer, and client inputs are important in guiding research activities. Sponsor evaluation is most appropriate before the research is begun and after it has been completed, in order to provide an assessment of risk and to account for the allocation of funds. Administrator evaluation can strengthen the conduct of research through in-process monitoring. Evaluation by peer scientists is appropriate in assessing the potential contributions of proposed research, as part of a screening process, and in validating the scientific contribution to new knowledge, again screening but also strengthening the discipline and its knowledge base. Because of the potential for interdisciplinary research outcomes to contribute solutions to identified problems, client or user interest may be appropriate at both *ex ante* and *ex post* phases. Indeed, the documented returns on investment in agricultural research have been partially attributed to clientele involvement in research at both phases through extension programs.

To apply the review criteria identified here, peer reviewers must not only have an intimate familiarity with the disciplinary backgrounds involved but also understand the complex environment towards which the research is focused. Peer review has evolved as an accountability mechanism for disciplines within the scientific community, and it tends to be a conservative influence. 'Peer groups have not rewarded members who apply their training to problems that extend beyond disciplinary confines' (Baram, 1971). It has been argued that peer review teams represent political, rather than theoretical, structures (Morphet, 1981) and that concern for rules and boundaries by the scientific community will heighten when paradigms or models are felt to be insecure or threatened (Kuhn, 1970). Peer review is consequently limited by the restricted vision, which experts who are drawn from the same, self-enclosed pool of scientists tend to maintain. These disciplinary criteria provide the rigour of the disciplines and, at the same time, the barriers to acknowledging the relevance and merit of interdisciplinary efforts.

'Problem oriented research is no respector of disciplines' (Cotterrell, 1979). Yet, for the most part, sponsoring agencies and institutions continue to award funds and incentives along disciplinary structures (Currie, 1976). Disciplinary standards of efficiency and effectiveness are not necessarily consistent with efficiency and effectiveness standards of the scientific community as a whole. The determination as to which of these standards will be applied to interdisciplinary research rests partially in the scientific backgrounds of the reviewers selected and partially in the agency and/or discipline's parameters for review. *It is, therefore, in the flexibility of selecting such reviewers that the optimization and the relevance of the peer review in interdisciplinary research resides.*

It has been suggested that the essential condition for interdisciplinary knowledge is competence in all fields called upon to contribute (Sinaceur, 1977). Additionally, the need for convergence of science-oriented criteria and mission-oriented criteria within reviewers' assessments has been noted (Cutler, Martino, and Webb, 1974). The dynamism of the scientific community's specialization and integration modes calls for reviewers who are specialized in many areas. The continued coupling and recoupling of new and existing specializations require flexibility in the composition of such peer review teams. Yet the maintenance of direction and standards requires stability in the process and criteria. Modification of university reward structures (Currie, 1976), making the rewards for interdisciplinary research more visible (Gordon and Marquis, 1966), and faciliating the use of a common language among reviewers (Gusdorf, 1977) have all been suggested as ways to improve the review process and accommodate the needs for peer review in interdisciplinary research.

An Example

Attempts have been made to operationalize flexibility and responsiveness in review systems. One such system is currently in use by the North Central Region of the Agricultural Experiment Stations.

Agricultural research sponsored by the USDA is accountable to improving the United States' ability to meet food and fibre needs of its citizens. To accomplish this national goal, as well as related goals identified for specific regions and states, basic and applied research efforts are conducted in all states and are aggregated at both regional and national levels. Research activities are

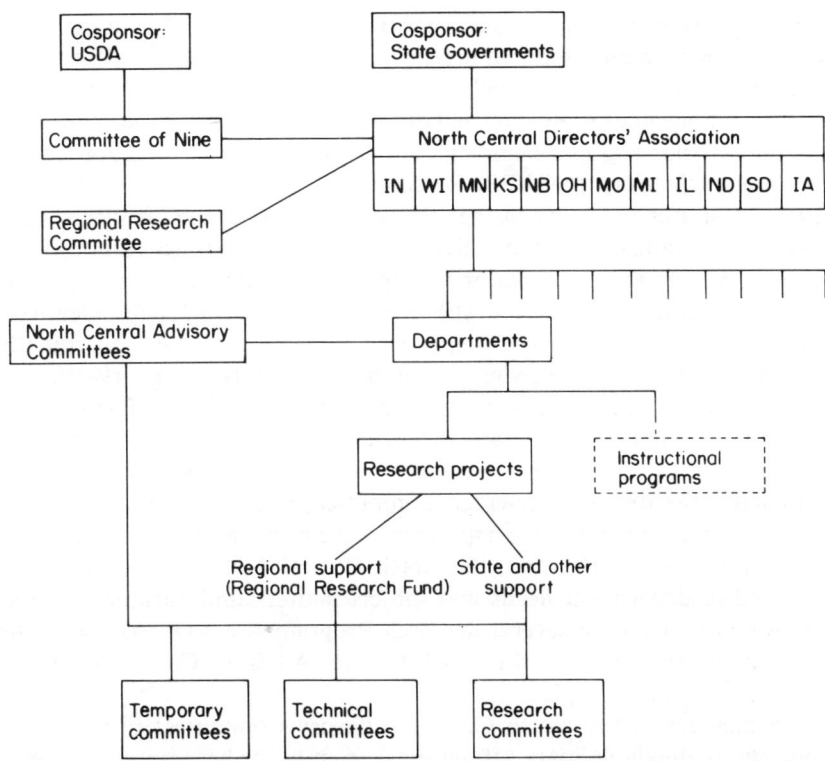

Figure 1. North Central Agricultural Experiment Stations regional planning and priority structure (Huston, 1981b)

sponsored by funds from state, as well as federal, sources and are coordinated at departmental, state, regional, and national levels.

One of several catalysts to integrate regional and national cooperative research efforts is the Regional Research Fund (RRF). The RRF is allocated as part of federal appropriations to the states and is administered through authority delegated by the Secretary of Agriculture (see Figure 1). Control of the RRF funds has resided with the states and represents about 4 per cent. of the total funds in the State Experiment Stations.

Research efforts funded through the RRF are also funded by state and other sources. Through the administration of the RRF, states coordinate their research activities towards regional and national priorities. Many of the regional research teams, organized as committees, are comprised of scientists from different disciplinary backgrounds. Through a regional committee structure, scientists and administrators set priorities for research goals and scientists from various disciplines participate in research endeavours according to their abilities to marshall expertise towards identified objectives. As a whole, this process accommodates both disciplinary and interdisciplinary research efforts and serves as a means to 'continually purge the system of unneeded activities, redirect research effort from low to high priority areas, minimize fragmentation of research efforts, create a sense of urgency, and focus the research effort so that the right resources can be brought to bear on the right problem at the right time, provide adequate evaluation and disseminate the results' (Anderson, 1977).

As one of four regional planning systems, the North Central Agricultural Experimental Stations (NCAES) Research Planning and Priority Structure (RPPS) illustrates flexibility in the selection of reviewers to identify research needs and to evaluate research activities. It also demonstrates responsiveness between reviewer and investigator through the planning and priority setting process. Committees in the NCAES RPPS are the vehicles for identifying research needs and priorities, conducting research activities, coordinating research efforts, and reviewing research progress (Huston, 1981a). The committees are of two types—advisory and management (see Figure 2).

Advisory committees integrate independent but related research efforts through reviews and recommendations. The North Central Advisory Committees, the Regional Research Committee, and the Committee of Nine provide succeedingly broader perspectives in their review of research activities. Closest to the research efforts, the North Central Advisory Committees are comprised of department heads and subject matter administrators and have responsibility for one or several Research Program Areas (RPA). Depending on the nature of the RPA, the North Central Advisory Committee may be disciplinary or interdisciplinary.

Each member of the North Central Advisory Committees brings to that responsibility the disciplinary affiliation(s) from his or her respective research background as a scientist, as well as his or her departmental affiliation. Members of the North Central Advisory Committees are charged with encouraging research endeavours which promote the utilization of knowledge. This they do within the context of research activities which will also contribute to the expansion of knowledge within their respective disciplines. Through such leadership, the criteria for scientific merit are coordinated with the criteria for mission relevance. Recommendations from the North Central Advisory Committees are reviewed by the Regional Research Committee and then may be approved by the Committee of Nine, as delegated by the Secretary of Agriculture.

The Research Management Committees receive recommendations from the North Central Advisory Committees, and they relay information regarding their progress and priorities to the North Central Advisory Committees. These Research Management Committees are of three types. Temporary Committees prepare proposals and project outlines for new projects related to identified RPAs. Technical Committees 'create a formal regional project from which each state participant then creates a state project based on the objectives of the regional effort' (Huston, 1981b). Technical Committees conduct research projects and disseminate findings through publications. Review Committees, on the other hand, informally coordinate research on closely related projects and make recommendations for new projects. These Research Management

Advisory Committees:

Regional Research Committee — 1
Members: 3 Directors (1 alt) and Director-at-Large
Life: 3 years, elected
Role: Reviews proposals and recommends action to the directors on all new and revised Research Program Areas. Evaluates reports of progress of existing projects and recommends their continuation, revision or termination. Coordinates research planning with Advisory Committees. Approves regional publications.

Advisory Committees — 16
Members: Department heads or subject matter administrators
Life: Continuing
Role: Review research priorities and research progress. Recommend new committees and fate of old committees. Responsible for Research Program Areas.

Management Committees:

Temporary Committees — 9
Administered by: 1 Director
Members: Scientists
Life: 1–2 years, until task completed, appointed by Directors.
Role: Prepare proposals and project outlines for new projects.

Technical Committees — 52
Administered by: 1 Director
Members: Scientists
Life: 1–5 years with option for renewal
Role: Conduct regional research project.
Publish findings in scientific literature
May write regional bulletin.

Research Committees — 55
Administered by: 1 Director
Members: Scientists
Life: 3 years with option for renewal
Role: Coordinate state research projects on closely related topics.
May recommend new regional projects.

Figure 2. North Central Agricultural Experiment Stations committee profile for research planning and priority system for regional research funds (Huston, 1981a)

Committees manage the research efforts of individual scientists around priority issues through advocacy, activity, and coordination.

When a new RPA is recommended by an Advisory Committee for approval and is approved by the North Central Directors' Association, Regional Research Committee, and Committee of Nine, the North Central Advisory Committee then selects a Temporary Committee to develop a research plan to address the identified issue. From this point, the North Central Advisory Committee monitors the progress of the Temporary Committee in identifying an approach to the issue and in developing a proposal for the newly identified research area. The proposal is submitted to the North Central Advisory Committee for review. If such a proposal meets the criteria for scientific merit and mission relevance established by that Committee, it is then recommended to the Regional Research Committee and subsequent bodies for approval.

If the proposal is approved, the Temporary Committee is then dissolved and its designated members form either a new Technical Committee or a new Research Committee. Technical Committee members are typically drawn from several specialities and from several states and are themselves collectively engaged in conducting the research. Their contributing components of the research project are conducted at their respective institutions and are coordinated through interdisciplinary or disciplinary interaction within the Technical Committee.

Research Committee members, on the other hand, informally coordinate separate individual projects in various states. Periodic progress of both Technical Committees and Research Committees is reviewed by the respective North Central Central Advisory Committees, and recommendations are subsequently made for continuation, revision, or termination. The coordination of the review process with the planning process makes the NCAES RPPS system simultaneously a screening and a strengthening process. Research projects and programme are reviewed at the onset and termination of research activity, as well as in-process.

'The most important problem in planning for a team attack is to define the objective' (Bush and Hattery, 1953). This NCAES RPPS system allows for regional and national issues to emerge: issues that require long-term efforts of many states, regional issues too large or costly to be accomplished by a single state (but which may be led by a single state), and issues that require immediate solution and in which sizeable inputs from several states are required (Huston, 1981a). These issues may be addressed from a disciplinary as well as an interdisciplinary perspective. Priorities recommended by the committees are based on the integration of efforts of individual scientists from different disciplines, as well as from different institutions. The organizational structure provides stability for the system as a whole. In addition, the composition of committees allows flexibility in disciplinary backgrounds which contribute to the identification of high-priority issues. In this way, continuity in the mission relevance of research activities and flexibility in the utilization of scientific approaches are maintained simultaneously. The ongoing communication between management and advisory committees, between advisory committees and decision-making bodies, and between decision-makers and investigators maintains the responsiveness of the system to science and to mission.

Some research findings contribute to the advancement of knowledge; some encourage the utilization of knowledge; some do both. In this system, research findings are scrutinized for scientific merit and for scientific contribution as results are submitted for publication in disciplinary journals. Additionally, regional publications recognize the contribution of disciplinary, as well as interdisciplinary, findings to regional missions. Thus, the *ex post* peer review of research findings includes both disciplinary and interdisciplinary perspectives on scientific merit and mission relevance.

Research findings useful in accomplishing regional goals are subsequently interpreted for dissemination to clients through state extension programmes. Through this process, the results of research lay new foundations for client needs and knowledge frontiers. These are then incorporated into the next round of research programme planning. (A full discussion of the background, resources, structure, philosophies, and priorities of regional and national research systems can be found in Huston, 1981a.)

This system provides a model for research programme planning and priority setting for a research enterprise with a relatively stable corps of scientists whose research activities address needs identified on a multilevel framework. Other research organizations have used related planning models to implement experience-based resource groups or teams of experts to identify research and development needs, make decisions, clarify problems, and produce group decisions (Denny, 1980). The value of such potential problem analysis resides in its capacity to bring people together to examine concerns in a constructive way, to identify the areas in which benefits are likely to arise, and to estimate the magnitude of them.

> It is not the analytical or decision-optimizing properties of the models that are of value; rather the benefits follow from the fact that the process of using the model forces a conceptual examination of alternative and decision premises, thereby creating important dialogues which may not otherwise take place in an organization (Davies and Pearson, 1980).

It is in the flexibility of being able to identify and utilize the consul of experts for this examination that the benefits of such expertise are captured.

Developing agreement on specifically what is required, for what purpose, by whom, when and why and how, is a very positive outcome of the peer review process. It is this clarification that responsively redirects established disciplines and nourishes emerging disciplines. As proposals are formulated, discussed, reformulated, and finalized (Morphet, 1981) the key issues are highlighted and management's attention is focused on them at an early stage.

Summary

'The interdisciplinary spirit is first and foremost a need for communication' (Gusdorf, 1977). The organizational and communication links between interdisciplinary groups and parent disciplines need to remain strong—as do the links within the disciplines. In order for disciplines to continually reformulate themselves and interrelate with the advance of knowledge, a balance has to be maintained between the support of well-established, high-quality endeavours and the support of new, untried investigators and institutions.

'Interdisciplinary work poses among its many challenges that of obtaining the breadth of vision and range of knowledge necessary to move with confidence beyond orthodox disciplinary boundaries' (Cotterrell, 1979). Especially in viewing the importance of freedom of inquiry in academic environments, interdisciplinary efforts play an important role in maintaining intellectual vitality through encouraging flexibility and responsiveness. They encourage these changes to be made in moderate increments. They also allow the faculty to initiate shifts in direction and anticipate changing organizational goals rather than comply with pressure from outside the programme. Involvement in interdisciplinary research permits scientists to not only pioneer the explorations but also to choose the frontiers.

It has been alleged that peer review is the most important single determinant of funding decisions made by representatives of sponsors (Cole, Rubin, and Cole, 1977) and is a significant factor in editorial acceptance (Gordon, 1980). Yet peer review is rarely the single determinant. Some critics maintain that sponsor/administrator and editor decisions are influenced by political as well as social considerations (Bowers, 1975; Carter, 1979; Liebert, 1976; Symington and Kramer, 1977).

The strength of the peer review system resides in maintaining standards of quality which have been previously agreed upon. This strength is vital to interdisciplinary research at two points. The first is in maintaining the strength of disciplinary backgrounds which researchers take with them into interdisciplinary teams. Strong backgrounds form a strong base. The second is in the development of consensus on new quality standards for the interdisciplinary effort—whether that effort serves the purpose for which it was created and then dissolves or whether it proves sufficiently useful that it is refined and reformulated into a new disciplinary structure.

To the extent that the component disciplines are strong, reviewers can assist sponsors and administrators in assessing the stability of the foundation upon which the interdisciplinary effort intends to build. To the extent that reviewers have a holistic perspective of knowledge creation and use, they can offer their best guesses as to the success of the proposed research and thereby assist in screening projects which are likely to be productive. To the extent that reviewers have the intellectual courage to entertain the unknown, they can help in recommending the best 'next steps' which can be attempted in an effort to advance knowledge. This they do through recommendations for project funding and through approval for publication.

In both the screening and strengthening of objectives and at initial, midpoint, and final stages of research, the potential in using peer review to evaluate interdisciplinary research resides in the creative tension between the parent disciplines and the infant interdisciplines. In an environment of exploration and of inquiry, this potential is realized in its fullest sense when planning and evaluation occur in tandem, when screening and strengthening criteria move the research activities in the same direction, and when both disciplinary and interdisciplinary affiliations and communications are strong for reviewers and for researchers.

References

Anderson, J. (1977). 'Organizing for interdisciplinary team research', *HortScience*, **12**(1), 33–37.
Andrews, F. (Ed.) (1979). *Scientific Productivity*, Cambridge University Press, Cambridge.
Armstrong, D., Laughlin, C., and Ayers, G. (1979). 'Administration of interdisciplinary activities', Mimeographed.
Baram, M. (1971). 'Social control of science and technology', *Science*, **172**, 535–539.
Beaver, D., and Rosen, R. (1978). 'Studies in scientific collaboration. Part I. The professional origins of scientific co-authorship', *Scientometrics*, **1**(1), 65–84.
Birnbaum, P. (1978). 'In-process predictors of research performance', Paper presented at the Joint National Meeting of the Operations Research Society of America and the Institute of Management Sciences, Los Angeles, California, Discussion Paper No.310, Graduate School of Business, Indiana University.
Birnbaum, P. (1981). 'Contingencies for academic interdisciplinary research performance', Paper presented at the Annual Meeting of the AAAS, Toronto, January 7, 1981.
Blauberg, I., and Mirsky, E. (1979). 'Interdisciplinary research groups in the structure of the research front', in *Interdisciplinary Research groups: Their Management and Organization* (Eds R. Barth and R. Steck), First International Conference on Interdisciplinary Research Groups, Schloss Reisensburg, Germany.
Boger, R., and Boyd, V. (1973). 'Institutional policy and operational issues affecting interdisciplinary research', paper presented at the Conference for the Management of Large-scale Interdisciplinary Research, sponsored by the University of Tennessee, Knoxville.
Boulding, K. (1977). 'Peace research', *International Social Science Journal*, **29**(4), 601–613.
Bowers, R. (1975). 'The peer review system on trial', *American Scientist*, **63**, 624–626.
Bredahl, M., Bryant, K., and Ruttan, V. (1980). 'Behavior and productivity implications of institutional and project funding of research', *American Journal of Agricultural Economics*, **August**, 371–383.
Busch, L., Lacy, W., and Sachs, C. (1980). 'Research policy and process in the agricultural sciences: some results of a national study', Bulletin RS-66, University of Kentucky.
Bush, G., and Hattery, L. (1953). *Teamwork Research*, American University Press, Washington, DC.
Carter, L. (1979). 'A new and searching look at NSF', *Science*, **204**(2), 1064–1065.
Chubin, D., and Mitroff, I. (1979). 'Peer review at the NSF: a dialectical policy analysis', *Social Studies of Science*, **9**, 199–232.
Cole, S., Rubin, L., and Cole, J. (1977). 'Peer review and the support of science', *Scientific American*, **237**(4), 34–41.
Cole, S., Rubin, L., and Cole, J. (1978). *Peer Review in the National Science Foundation*, National Academy of Sciences, Washington, DC.
Cotterrell, R. (1979). 'Interdisciplinarity: the expansion of knowledge and the design of research', *Higher Education Review*, **8**(3), 47–56.

Currie, D. (1976). 'Interdisciplinary research and the university reward system', Ph.D. Dissertation, University of Southern California.

Cutler, R., Martino, V., and Webb, A. (1974). 'Biomedical research relevance assessment', in *Health Care Planning* (Eds A. Reisman and M. Kiley), Gordon Breach Science Publishers, New York.

Darvas, G., and Haraszthy, A. (1979). 'Some aspects of interdisciplinary organization of research teams', in *Interdisciplinary research groups: Their Management and Organization* (Eds R. Barth and R. Steck), First International Conference on Interdisciplinary research groups, Schloss Reisensburg, Germany.

Davies, G., and Pearson, A. (1980). 'The application of some group problem-solving approaches to project selection in research and development', *IEEE Transactions on Engineering Management*, 27(3), 66-73.

Denny, F. (1980). 'Management of an R & D planning process utilizing an advisory group', *IEEE Transactions on Engineering Management*, 27(2), 34-36.

Evenson, R., and Kislev, U. (1975). *Agricultural Research and Productivity*, Yale University Press, New Haven, Connecticut.

Evenson, R., and Wright, B. (1980). 'An evaluation of methods for examining the quality of agricultural research', Mimeographed.

Gillespie, D., and Birnbaum, P. (1980). 'Status concordance, coordination, and success in interdisciplinary research teams', *Human Relations*, 33(1), 41-56.

Gillespie, D., and Mar, B. (1977). 'Interdisciplinary team preproposal management', *Society for Research Administrators Journal*, Fall, 33-40.

Gordon, G., and Marquis, S. (1966). 'Freedom, visibility of consequences and scientific innovation', *The American Journal of Sociology*, 72, 195-202.

Gordon, M. (1980). 'The role of referees in scientific communication', in *The Psychology of Written Communication* (Ed. J. Hartley), Nichols, New York.

Gusdorf, G. (1977). 'Past, present and future in interdisciplinary research'. *International Social Sciences Journal*, 29:4, 580-599.

Henley, C. (1977). 'Peer review of research grant applications at the National Institute of Health', *Federation Proceedings*, 36(9), 2066-2068, 2186-2190, 2335, 2338.

Hensler, D. (1976). 'Perceptions of the National Science Foundation Peer Review Process: A report on a survey of NSF Reviewers and applicants. Paper prepared for the Committee on Peer Review, National Science Board, and the Committee on Science and Technology, US House of Representatives.

Huston, K. (1981a). 'Joint planning and priority setting—regional and national systems', Report prepared for the Office of Technology Assessment.

Huston, K. (1981b). Personal correspondence, June 29, 1981.

Ikenberry, S., and Friedman, R. (1972). *Beyond Academic Departments*, Jossey-Bass, San Francisco, California.

Kirschstein, R., *et al.*, (1976). *Grants Peer Review,* Report to the Director, NIH, Phase I, Washington, DC.

Kirschstein, R., *et al.*, (1978). *Grants Peer Review: Opinions on the NIH Grants Peer Review System*, Phase II of the Report to the Director, NIH, Washington, DC.

Kuhn, T. (1970). *The Structure of Scientific Revolutions*, 2nd ed., University of Chicago Press, Illinois.

Lakoff, S. (1977). 'Accountability and the research universities', in Smith, B., and Karlesky, J. (eds.) *The State of Academic Science* (Eds B. Smith and J. Karlesky), Vol. II, Change Magazine Press, New York.

Leopold, A. C. (1979). 'The burden of competitive grants', *Science*, 203, 4381.

Liebert, R. (1976). 'Productivity, favor and grants among scholars', *American Journal of Sociology*, 82(3), 664-673.

Lindas, N. (1979). 'Conclusions from the American Society for Public Administration's assessment of four interdisciplinary research management projects', in *Interdisciplinary research groups: Their Management and Organization*, (Eds R. Barth and R. Steck), First International Conference on Interdisciplinary research groups, Schloss Reisensburg, Germany.

Mayville, W. (1978). 'Interdisciplinarity: the mutable paradigm', AAHE-ERIC/Higher Education Research Report No. 9.

Miner, L., and McDonald, S. (1981). 'Reliability of peer reviews', *Journal of the Society for Research Administrators*, **Spring**, 21–24.

Mitchell, R. (1977). 'The maintenance of personal integrity in the interdisciplinary team research effort', *HortScience*, **12**(1), 36–37.

Morphet, C. (1981). 'Positivist and political approaches to interdisciplinarity', *Science and Public Policy*, **February**, 18–19.

Mosteller, Frederick (1981). 'Innovation and evaluation', *Science*, **211** 4485, 880–886.

NCR (1980). 'Accountability: restoring the quality of the partnership. A report from the National Commission on Research', *Science*, **207**, 1177–1182.

Neumann, Y. (1979). 'Research productivity of tenured and nontenured faculty in U.S. Universities: a comparative study of four fields and policy implications', *Journal of Educational Administration*, **17**(1), 92–101.

Pearson, A., Payne, R., and Gunz, H. (1979). 'Communication, coordination and leadership in interdisciplinary research', in *Interdisciplinary Research Groups: Their Management and Organization* (Eds R. Barth and R. Steck), First International Conference on Interdisciplinary Research Groups, Schloss Reisensburg, Germany.

Pelz, D., and Andrews, F. (1966). *Scientists in Organizations: Productive Climates for Research and Development*, Wiley, New York.

Peston, M. (1978). 'Some thoughts on evaluating interdisciplinary research', *Higher Education Review*, **Spring**, 55–60.

Price, D. (1977). 'An extrinsic value theory for basic and "applied" research', in *Science and Technology Policy* (Ed. J. Haberer), Lexington Books, D. C. Heath & Co., Maryland, pp.25–32.

Price, D. (1980). 'Development and structure', Manuscript.

Price, D., and Gursey, S. (1976). 'Studies in scientometrics. Part I and Part II. Transcience and continuance in scientific authorship', *International Forum on Information and Documentation*, **1**(2), 17–24.

Rossini, F. *et al.* (1981). 'Interdisciplinary research: performance and policy issues.' *Interstudy Bulletin*, 2–5.

Russell, M. (1981). 'Administrative criteria for assessing interdisciplinary research', Manuscript.

Ruttan, V. (1980). 'Bureaucratic productivity: the case of agricultural research', *Public Choice*, **35**, 529–547.

Ruttan, V. (1981). *Agricultural Research Policy*, University of Minnesota Press, Minneapolis, Minnesota.

Salisbury, G. (1980). 'Research productivity of the state agricultural experiment station system: measured by scientific output', Bulletin 762, University of Illinois at Urbana-Champaign.

Sauer, R. (1978).. 'The role of the department head in interdisciplinary research', Presentation at the Fifty-third Annual Kansas Agricultural Experiment Station Conference, January 4, 1978.

Sinaceur, M. (1977). 'What is interdisciplinarity?', *International Social Science Journal*, **29**(4), 572–579.

Small, H. (1974). *Report on Citation Counts for National Science Foundation Grant Recipients and Non-Recipients*, Institute for Scientific Information, Philadelphia, Pennsylvania.

Smith, B., and Karlesky, J. (1977). *The State of Academic Science: The Universities in the Nation's Research Effort*, Vol. 1, Change Magazine Press, New York.

Symington, J., and Kramer, T. (1977). 'Does peer review work?', *American Scientist*, **65**(1), 17-20.

USDA (1981). 'Manual for cooperative regional research', Prepared by Science and Education Administration—Cooperative Research, SEA-CR/OD-1082.

Vandette, E. (1977). 'The issue of peer review: a case study of the agency-to-individual approach to federal funding of scientific research', Ph.D. Dissertation, Michigan State University.

Whitney, R., and Frost, P. (1981). 'The measurement of performance in research', *Human Relations*, **24**(2), 161-178.

Wolfe, D. (1981). 'Interdisciplinary research as a form of research', Presentation at Symposium on Interdisciplinary Research: Policy and Performance Issues, AAAS, Toronto, January 7, 1981.

INTERDISCIPLINARY RESEARCH IN THE UNIVERSITY: NEED FOR MANAGERIAL LEADERSHIP*

B. O. SAXBERG and W. T. NEWELL

University of Washington, Seattle, USA

Interdisciplinary research in the university requires the type of management or leadership that initiates, plans and organizes an interdisciplinary research team which is characterized by collaboration and *esprit de corps* for the duration of the project and beyond. As society frequently provides the major share of universities' resources, it believes it can impose a commensurate claim on the universities in solving society's problems. This in turn is predicated on the institution's willingness and readiness to provide physical space, administrative staff, and other types of institutional support. A problem arises in that societal issues and concerns do not fit existing academic disciplines and departments. Thus, interdisciplinary research depends on a managerial and leadership effort that successfully defines the research problem in terms of a user, attracts faculty from different disciplines, and maintains progress towards the eventual solving of the problem.

Field Study

In the context of a National Science Foundation Research Management Improvement Program grant (NM44380), a research team at the University of

---

*This research was supported by a grant from the National Science Foundation Research Management Improvement Program (NM44380).

Washington did a field study involving a national sample of the major research universities in the United States, including Harvard, Massachusetts Institute of Technology, Pennsylvania, Stanford, California (Berkeley), California (Los Angeles), Southern California, Illinois, Wisconsin, and others besides the University of Washington. Semi-structured interviews were conducted with the institution's central research administrators, directors of institutes and centres, as well as with principal investigators of interdisciplinary projects and their team members.

The interviews were conducted by a team consisting of faculty, doctoral students, and experienced research administrators, including Mr Donald R. Baldwin, Director of Grant and Contract Services at the University of Washington, who was also the coordinator of the research programme. Two series of interviews were conducted. The first involved university research administrators such as vice presidents of research, or deans of graduate schools, and representatives from the offices of grants and contracts. The second series of interviews were conducted with directors of research centres and institutes, principal investigators, and research project team members.

The comments which follow focus on conclusions related to the nature of management or leadership in successful interdisciplinary research in the university setting.

The Role of the Key Individual

One fact emerged forcefully from the field research: the success of an interdisciplinary research project rests on a key individual. Initially such a person must have a strong personal commitment to the importance of the problem and demonstrate a personal willingness to become involved. During the decades of the sixties and seventies, federal funding agencies were frequently under legislative mandate to require interdisciplinary research in the allocation of funds. This provided scope for such key individuals to become directors of interdisciplinary research institutes and centres or principal investigators of interdisciplinary projects.

There have always been opportunities for interdisciplinary research in solving scientific problems (Hagstrom, 1964). In some cases such an effort has required extensive cultivation of a network of interested individuals, going even beyond the confines of a single university. Such an effort has also frequently depended on one or a few key individuals. However, for scientific problems there is the opportunity to have a team of specialists from related disciplines and allow them to contribute as specialists. Their scientific work is not interrupted; they can publish their research in the accepted journals of their discipline's area. Even here the project team may experience difficulties. As one principal investigator pointed out in connection with his research programme: 'You have to keep an eye on the chemists because before you know it they are off on their own investigation and do not provide the answer I need.' To be sure, he was a physicist, and he indicated that a chemist approaches a scientific problem differently, attacks it at a different level, and uses a different methodology.

Our interviews revealed problems of a different magnitude for interdisciplinary teams concerned with societal problems. Applied research is involved in an attempt to improve directly the functioning of society in its sociotechnical, socioeconomic, and sociopolitical aspects. Three kingpins on which interdisciplinary research rests are (1) the user of the data, who frequently directly or indirectly provides the funds, (2) the definition of the problem, which can be successfully attacked only through an interdisciplinary effort, and (3) the academic entrepreneur, who is committed to the interdisciplinary problem and acts as the catalyst and manager of the research effort.

A difficulty arises when interdisciplinary research is assumed to be based on an integrated effort where progress of one part of the research depends and draws on progress in another part. In addition the team is likely to require representation from several totally unrelated disciplines, as defined within the university organization, as was evident for instance in an investigation on air pollution at the University of Illinois involving social scientists, transportation experts, engineers, and physical scientists (Ellis, 1974). The key individual plays a very important role in creating sufficient attraction for the project to collect around him or her colleagues from the relevant disciplines and in assuring that the project moves from the stage of multidisciplinary research, where each contributor is still left doing his own thing, to the stage of interdisciplinary research and the investment by each project member in discussions, meetings, seminars, and so on. The depth of the contribution of each investigator, regardless of his or her speciality, is thus determined by the project.

The interviews also confirmed a general informality in the central research administration in testimony to a strong belief in the faculty member as the originator of research proposals and research results, (Saxberg, Newell, and Mar, 1977). Many university officials were themselves faculty members who had been brought up in this tradition. As a result, the key individual as the initiator of interdisciplinary research saw himself on one hand as an academic researcher in terms of the university's and his colleagues' expectations, and on the other hand as an entrepreneur confronting the university's traditional mode of operations through defined disciplines and departments.

Leadership through Managerial Role

Barth and Steck (1979) have observed that the managerial role comprises its own professionalism. The faculty member who takes on an interdisciplinary project may see this as an opportunity to initiate action, an opportunity which has frequently contained the prospect of some power through command over resources from the outside. At other times managerial responsibilities may have been thrust upon the faculty member as a scientist or technical specialist. The capacity then to move into the managerial role or to delegate its responsibilities successfully to an individual who can meet the demands of that role will determine whether the interdisciplinary team survives. Though our interviews suggested that directors of institutes and centres, as well as principal investigators, were very much aware of the problems they faced in their managerial role, they also volunteered the comment that under normal circumstances they would have little opportunity to discuss the problems they faced in this role.

The managerial role carried a significant problem. There remained a continuous conflict between the demands of the managerial role in comparison with the role of the researcher scientist. As a researcher scientist, the individual enjoyed an orderly sequence of increasing sophistication in education and research or practice. Thus that individual experienced deepening knowledge within an ever-narrowing specialty, enabling him or her to gain status within a group of peers and thus earn not just organizational but also national and even international reputation. This has also provided the individual with access to outside funding sources. As long as resources for research are available, there is an accompanying independence and autonomy, and an expectation of rewards commensurate with the contribution and position in the scientific community.

To become the director of a centre or principal investigator of a project involving a team of researchers was seen as a double burden by many of our interviewees. As scientist or researchers they had strived to earn the hallmark of excellence for their work. Now they faced a range of problems that moved them towards becoming generalists. They still wished to remain scientists in good standing in the discipline, and in order to retain credibility and respect for their scientific judgements and evaluations they needed to stay abreast of progress in their fields. The most successful leaders of interdisciplinary research recognized the need to consider the personalities of their team members reflected in the display of emotions, aggression, idiosyncracies, and unique backgrounds and experiences. They gained their satisfaction from the team's successful performance, even though their personal contribution was no longer distinguishable from that of the research team and its individual members. A large portion of their contribution to the team's success came from their involvement in managerial and human decisions (Barth and Steck, 1979; Nilles, 1975).

In interdisciplinary research it has long been recognized that the relationship between the key individual as the team's manager/leader and the team members is critical (Caudill and Roberts, 1951). It is governed by the personality of the team leader and also involves a potential choice of leadership style (Barrow, 1977).

Relationship between the Leader and the Led

Our field study showed that the director of an institute or a centre or the principal investigator of an interdisciplinary project may either assume a traditional stance and claim authority of position and control of resources or may choose to be concerned about how the team and its members might best be supported to achieve the results they seek. The position of authority is traditionally conveyed through the title which designates that the holder has reached an important position in the organization. Accompanying this, leaders may traditionally believe they are entitled to demand that individuals who depend on them for their support respond to their demands for performance. This is needed because on the organizational ladder there is in turn someone else who expects to review the leader's performance. Instances emerged in the interviews where this somewhat autocratic perspective was seen as a contribution to the institution and protection for the project team members, who frequently gave scant attention to the organizational environment of the university.

As an illustration, at the time of our interviews Stanford University had a chain of command from the University's President, to the Vice President's Provosts, one of whom was the Vice President and Provost of Planning, who oversaw activities labelled Planning, Faculty Affairs, and Research. The research unit was headed by a Vice Provost of Research, to whom reported, for instance, the Institute of Mathematical Studies and Social Sciences, the Institute of Food Research, Hanson Laboratories, and also the Center for Interdisciplinary Research. Stanford University has had a strong orientation towards basic research based on its departmental structure. However, it also desired to provide its graduate students as well as faculty with opportunities for funded research. Though courses and educational programmes may be offered through centres, they must have been approved and authorized by academic departments with whom they must be joint-listed. All academic degrees are conferred through the departments.

In this context the Center for Interdisciplinary Studies had a unique position. Its function had been designed to ensure that research that could not find a home within a department or college, though this would have been preferable, could request a place within the Center. It contained the various research programme units of transportation research, information transmission; telecommunication and television studies; centre for women studies, and centre for drugs, crimes, and community studies.

A focal concern of the Center and its director was the need to review and monitor the quality of interdisciplinary research. The first review of a research project took place after one year of operation. The next review would come within five years, with one additional five-year period permitted after that. The assumption was that by the time the research would have found a natural home within a college or a department, or gained sufficiently in stature to stand on its own feet; otherwise it had outlived its usefulness in relation to the need to adapt to a changing environment and thus changing societal problems and new priorities. The director saw his role in part as one of policing interdisciplinary research in view of the institution's concerns: orientation towards application, exposure to community controversies, the risk of young faculty members jeopardizing their academic careers in their discipline by joining an interdisciplinary research programme, and problems related to evaluation of quality.

In contrast, it is an expression of quite a different and contrary managerial philosophy when a manager steps down from the top of the organizational pyramid and takes on the task of helper, or facilitator, even errand boy, in order to enable all members of the team to realize their potential. In the preferred situation, by opting for collegial authority, the team leader has opted for involvement, participation, discussion, and in many instances raised expectations in the research group of consensual decision-making. However, this assumes that each member is equipped to participate and is willing to participate equally in the decisions of the group.

The early phases of the interdisciplinary research project commonly profit from the knowledge and leadership of the key individual (Smith, 1971; Whyte, 1978). Subsequently, time constraints and personalities may interfere in the creation of participative decision-making. It became quite clear from the interviews that faculty and research staff expect to be involved. Their education and training have instilled in them the belief that they are entitled to be heard, not just because of their specialty but as rational thinking individuals.

The problems faced by project leaders were evident in our study of one large interdisciplinary study, in which the principal investigator outlined confidently the research programme and the role of the various members of the team. However, when the team members were interviewed, they each declared their doubt about their role in the project and their ignorance about the research design, and thus their hesitancy in following through on what they so far had perceived as only a preliminary declaration of interest on their part! In other situations research directors and principal investigators were genuinely concerned about the creation of a team spirit and the fostering of interaction and communication in the research group to preserve the team's fragile unity.

Leadership through Communication

There was unanimity among directors of centres and institutes as well as principal investigators that communication and interaction among the team members form the most critical ingredients in keeping the group and its work on course. The ideal situation was one where the members had their offices physically close together. A number of instances were uncovered where critical equipment had become a focal point for interaction between group members, e.g. project computer (Mar, Newell, and Saxberg, 1976). Other efforts in this vein involved the designation of a coffee lounge where informal discussions could take place. Poor physical space allocation could form a severe barrier to communication, e.g. location of researchers on separate floors or in separate buildings.

Equally important are efforts of the research team to maintain open communication with formal reporting within the group and outside. A number of research teams interviewed maintained weekly meetings at which a member of the research group provided a progress report on the work followed by a give-and-take discussion. Such meetings can also include colleagues from the outside, thus sharing research findings with a larger audience. These efforts may also encourage other faculty members to consider interdisciplinary research and potentially be recruited for the research group.

The field research suggested the use of a wide range of reporting events, from the most informal team interaction and discussion to a formal seminar or symposium to which may be invited interested colleagues from elsewhere. These occasions create the springboard for the writing and presentation of papers which can be given circulation to a wider audience. A network of interested individuals assures informed readership of papers of an interdisciplinary research group that otherwise might not get appropriate distribution.

Recruitment and Retention in Interdisciplinary Research

Interdisciplinary research on a university campus faces a problem in attracting and retaining faculty. Many faculty members become involved in research to solve societal problems because they feel deeply about the need to tackle some of the diffficult issues, such as urban housing, air and water pollution, energy needs, international development, mass transportation, and conservation of resources.

According to our interview sample, faculty engaged in interdisciplinary research are confronted with several criticisms: (1) interdisciplinary research by its very nature is shallow, (2) the researcher's skills and competence are underutilized and so lose their edge, (3) joining an interdisciplinary programme is escape from the rigour of the discipline and thus an indication of failure, (4) the quality of interdisciplinary research is suspect because of the absence of applicable standards of evaluation, (5) interdisciplinary research with an application orientation cannot retain objectivity, (6) in the absence of recognized interdisciplinary scientific journals, research activities will remain unpublished and escape review board evaluations, (7) research activities and findings may generate vocal community interest groups with criticisms of the university's involvement in the project, (8) tenure and promotion prospects become questionable because of senior professors' unfamiliarity with the research, and (9) coauthorship of potential articles, papers, or monographs in some departments may count for less or even not be counted at all in tenure, promotion, and merit reviews. For these reasons, our field research revealed uniformly an underlying recommendation that a non-tenured faculty member should not become involved in interdisciplinary research.

For interdisciplinary research to be successful, managerial leadership is required to counteract the innuendos enumerated above. One highly successful project had to that effect developed initially a board of senior professors who were enticed to join through the efforts of the key individual. They were asked to familiarize themselves with the project and provide counsel, but they were not expected to become involved in the research themselves.

By being able to draw on the support of these highly regarded members of their respective departments, the project harnessed university-wide support, a resource for suggestions for potential faculty members for the project, and protection from unsympathetic senior faculty members in departments from which the project might recruit members. The advisory board was kept informed and met regularly to discuss policy issues. The potential existed that such a group might generate an appreciation in the university for interdisciplinary research and an actively supportive rather than a passively opposing posture to such research (Saxberg, Newell, and Mar, 1977).

There are also positive features generated for the individual in interdisciplinary research: (1) funding for research may be available for time released for research, (2) an approved budget may include allowance for travel to professional meetings, printing costs of journal articles, supplies, computer time, etc., hard to come by within a university's regular operating budget, (3) the opportunity exists to generate papers and articles for publication, (4) tenure, promotion, and merit may be favourably effected by extensive and successful research, (5) new avenues of teaching and research may open up as a result of interdisciplinary involvement, (6) interactions and collaboration with colleagues may prove stimulating and ensure research productivity, and (7) interested graduate students with a commitment may be available and supported to assist in the research project. As a result of these advantages, many faculty members are encouraged to participate in interdisciplinary research. It is up to the managerial leadership to create a positive interpretation of such a decision for an individual's academic career.

Creative Managerial Leadership of Interdisciplinary Research

One of the conclusions emerging from our field research points to the fact that managerial leadership of interdisciplinary research must include a consideration of a political dimension within the university and beyond (Newell *et al.*, 1980). Relationships with existing departments and their faculty are particularly sensitive as interdisciplinary research may loom as a competitor for resources as well as for faculty and students. Almost without fail interdisciplinary research justifies itself in the university only to the extent that it also includes an educational component — mainly opportunities for graduate students to engage in research. The expansion of interdisciplinary research groups into centres and institutes intent on offering courses and establishing degree curricula may create suspicion and outright hostility. By joint appointments and maintenance of departmental course numbers, and forsaking degree programmes, many interdisciplinary research programmes have garnered support and eventually emerged as nuclei of new departments. By deliberately drawing on resources from other departments across the campus and providing full credit to departments for their support and sponsorshop, interdisciplinary efforts enjoy a valued place in the university community.

Creative managerial leadership is also required for the research group itself. As an example, its members must be encouraged to invest in learning each other's terminology and methods of research, which may require extensive sharing of fundamental viewpoints of scientific efforts (Pearson, Payne, and Gunz, 1979).

The challenge of interdisciplinary research in the university setting has been and remains formidable. Thus far universities have not showed much success in claiming victory. Funding agencies harbour serious reservations about the capability of universities to be involved in research with an applied orientation, except as tempted by the funds that are available. As dissatisfaction has been voiced, independent, mostly non-profit research institutes, such as SRI, Battelle, and others, have become increasingly important. They present the universities with the danger that the gulf between theory and practice, research and application, faculty and citizens will grow and endanger the support that the system of higher education requires from society. Thus the managerial leadership of interdisciplinary research and its role in the university is critical in the formulation of the relationship between the universities and society.

References

Barrow, J. C. (1977). 'The variables of leadership: a review and conceptual framework', *Academy of Management Review*, **April**.

Barth, R. T., and Steck, R. (Eds) (1979). *Interdisciplinary Research Groups: Their Management and Organization*, Proceedings of the First International Conference on Interdisciplinary Research Groups, Schloss Reisenburg, West Germany, April 22-28, 1979.

Caudill, W., and Roberts, B. H. (1951). 'Pitfalls in the organization of interdisciplinary research', *Human Organization*, **10** (4).

Ellis, R. H. (1974). *The Planning and Management of Problem-Oriented Interdisciplinary Research at Academic Institutions*, Rensselaer Hartford Graduate Center, July.

Hagstrom, W. O. (1964). 'Traditional and modern forms of scientific teamwork', *Administrative Science Quarterly*, **December**.

Mar, B. W., Newell, W. T., and Saxberg, B. O. (1976). 'Interdisciplinary research in the university setting', *Environmental Science and Technology*, **July**.

Newell, W. T., Saxberg, B. O., Mar, B. W., and Adams, S. A. (1980). *Guidelines for Applied Interdisciplinary Research in the University: How to Manage the University Role in Solving Society's Problems*. Project Report No. 11, The University of Washington, Seattle, Washington.

Nilles, J. M. (1975). 'Interdisciplinary research management in the university environment', Unpublished, American Association for the Advancement of Science, New York, January 29, 1975.

Pearson, A. W., Payne, R. L., and Gunz, (1979). 'Communication, co-ordination and leadership in interdisciplinary research', in *Interdisciplinary Research Groups: Their Management and Organization* (Eds R. T. Barth and R. Steck), Proceedings of the First International Conference on Interdisciplinary Research Groups, Schloss Reisenburg, West Germany.

Saxberg, B. O., Newell, W. T., and Mar, B. W. (1977). *Interdisciplinary Research — A Dilemma for University Central Administration*, Project Report No. 9, Research Management Improvement, The University of Washington, Seattle, Washington.

Smith, C. G. (1971). 'Scientific performance and the composition of research teams', *Administrative Science Quarterly*, **December**.

Whyte, W. F. (1978). 'Extradepartmental enterprise', *Society*, March-April.

A METHOD FOR PEER GROUP APPRAISAL AND INTERPRETATION OF DATA DEVELOPED IN INTERDISCIPLINARY RESEARCH PROGRAMMES

J. M. SHARP
*Gulf Universities Research Consortium,
Houston, Texas, USA*

Introduction

Gulf Universities Research Consortium was conceived and designed as a mechanism for planning, coordinating, and executing multiuniversity interdisciplinary research programmes. In its sixteen years of operation, therefore, it has been concerned with how the various disciplinary components of such a programme can be designed and the results of those components synthesized and interpreted in a manner which is both sound and efficient.

In addressing this need, one quickly becomes aware that IDR is often concerned with the solution (or resolution) of scientific or practical problems composed of disciplinary parts. To an increasing degree, IDR is addressing the scientific aspects of problems that relate directly to the resolution of public issues. Public safety, environmental management, and public health are obvious examples. Consequently, all too often, IDR relating to urgent public issues is forced to be scientifically imperfect; i.e. it requires that conclusions be drawn (or recommendations be made) based on less than conclusive data and, frequently, with less than adequate scientific understanding.

If problem-solving IDR is to proceed systematically and efficiently from concept to scientific publication, in a manner similar to good individual research, there is a sequence of steps to follow. In each of these steps there are basic requirements that must be satisfied if the programme is to be scientifically acceptable *and* the results are to be pertinent to the problem or issue at hand. The peer group procedures discussed have been demonstrated to be an effective way to satisfy these requirements.

In describing these requirements and the means for satisfying them, ecological studies are cited as examples. Ecosystems consist of biological, chemical, geological, and physical components. Ecosystem management, to which much ecological research is related, superimposes social, economic, and even political components. Subsequently, such studies are characterized as being complex and necessarily interdisciplinary. The difficulty in conducting such research has been described by Dr J. W. Hedgpeth, Emeritus Professor of Oceanography, Scripps Institute of Oceanography (Hedgpeth, 1978) as follows:

> We are beset . . . with the problem of studying a complex system in some way that will convince us we know what is going on and that we can predict the effect of our actions on the system.

Hedgpeth eloquently and accurately emphasizes the pitfalls to be avoided in conducting such studies. These are particularly important in the common case where conclusions or recommendations are demanded, the data are sparse, and the pertinent knowledge is imperfect. In particular:

1. Conflicting approaches must not fragment the study. Approaches to such IDR studies range from 'compiling all knowledge and consigning it to a computer to tell us what to think' to the 'notion that one (or perhaps two) numbers from a dying mussel may be all we need'.
2. Discipline-oriented or dominated interpretations of system behaviour are incomplete and can be misleading. A disciplinary, or limited approach, study of an ecosystem is likened by Hedgpeth to the description of an elephant by blind men who feel (and accurately describe) his component parts.
3. 'Considering and representing combined component effects . . . requires access to a computer, and interpretation of the curious graphs produced suggests . . . the need for that most subtle and indispensable of all computers, the old-fashioned naturalist.'

It is precisely these difficulties that the peer group procedures avoid. Specifically, they avoid the fragmented approach and the blind men's description of the elephant by (1) consigning all available and pertinent data (from both organized archives and from the literature) to the computer and, of equal importance, (2) assigning the appraisal, synthesis, and interpretation of these data to a combination of both 'system' generalists and disciplinary specialists. The computer and the methods for its use are, then, only the means whereby these scientists can apply their expertise both individually and jointly in a rapid and efficient manner.

Steps and Requirements

The following are the discrete steps, or milestones, necessary for the proper design and execution of an IDR programme. The requirements discussed are specifically a result of its ID nature:

Problem definition

In the IDR programme, the axiom that an accurate definition of the problem is halfway to the answer is especially true, and even more so when the problem is issue-related. Because the IDR investigation is normally concerned with the testing, synthesis, and interpretation of data and the development of consensus conclusions, this step must include the application of the *collective* knowledge of the coinvestigators to the development of scientific concepts on which the studies will be based. Likewise, this collective knowledge must be applied to the definition of the content, density, and distribution of data that will be required to investigate the concept in a sound and acceptable manner. Using ecological investigations as an example, Hedgpeth's 'old-fashioned naturalist', or the 'system generalist', is a vital member of a group of disciplinary experts in, for example, fisheries biology, seawater chemistry, the physics of diffusion/dispersion processes, and the geochemistry of sediments. Such individuals are not only essential for interdisciplinary communication but, equally, to place the problem, the system under study, and its components in practical perspective as they relate to the objectives.

Access and assessment of extant data

Having formed an interdisciplinary consensus as to the suite of data that are required to support a scientific conclusion, the next step is that of assessing the extant data that apply. There are two primary sources of such data. Firstly, as a result of regulations and associated regulatory procedures, those IDR studies that relate to public issues in developed countries can usually draw on extensive databanks or archives. This is usually 'primary data' in that it relates to both the problem and the geography of interest. Secondly, a great deal of pertinent data can be extracted from the scientific literature and authoritative reports. These references are necessary in any event.

For the very large, disparate, multivariate databanks, archives, etc., that have been accumulated, this step is not at all simple. Once the relatively simple task of accessing these data is complete, it is then necessary that a 'user scientist' who is experienced in structuring, evaluating, and synthesizing data in the problem area of interest (e.g. ecology, epidemiology) carry out the following:

1. Test each databank for consistency as to:
   (a) Time, space, and variable content;
   (b) Comparability, or convertibility, of terminology, units, ranges of variables, etc.; and
   (c) Proper dynamic and statistical behaviour of functionally related variables in time and space (which is also a primary means for data validation that is generally not used or not available).
2. Organize the pertinent data from all sources into a 'program database' in which all elements are readily mergeable and each measurement of each variable in all elements, or any arbitrarily defined combinations and permutations of such measurements, can be immediately retrieved and sorted according to a user-specified hierarchy and format.
3. Develop a 'browsing atlas' of the 'program database' which emphasizes map displays, histograms, etc., for the purpose of permitting rapid assessment of the data content, density, distribution, statistical adequacy, etc., and, therefore, the degree to which extant data may satisfy programme data requirements.
4. Support a peer group assessment in this regard.
5. Document the basis for peer group conclusions.

It is a requirement of this step that those efforts preceding the peer group assessment are performed as a 'service' to the coinvestigators comprising the peer group. It is equally necessary that the combination of the user scientist, who provides these services, and, also, direct support of the group's assessment and documentation effort, and the computer software used for management, analysis, synthesis, etc., be such that a minimum demand is made on the coinvestigators' time in developing their consensus assessment. Finally, this must be accomplished without penalizing each coinvestigator's full knowledge of the data and of the processes by which the group has arrived as its consensus.

Planning the multi component experimental study

Should the extant data be judged adequate by the peer group to support consensus conclusions (not necessarily scientific proof) regarding the programme objectives, an experimental programme is not justified. If not, the first two steps have developed a comprehensive definition of the data gaps to be filled. These gaps are sorted according to disciplinary specialties, and each disciplinary component is defined as to content, schedule, sampling locations, procedures, units, resolution, etc., in order that consistency with the extant data is assured. In ecology programmes, for example, a primary requirement is that all measurement be made according to predetermined grid points and that the measurements be synoptic such that either dynamic or statistical correlative analysis is unquestioned. In any IDR programme, it would appear that correlative and functional analysis of all component data must be performed in order to achieve sound results. If not, then the 'blind men and the elephant' may result and the 'whole is not more than the sum of the parts'. One fundamental requirement for a successful IDR investigation is that the sum of the knowledge produced must be greater than the sum of the parts.

There are two corrollary conditions which should be noted. Firstly, the disciplinary components are an order of magnitude simpler than is the subsequent interdisciplinary appraisal and interpretation. These components can be accomplished adequately—by observers with established competence rather than 'principal investigators'. By their nature, they are directed to answer 'what' questions, rather than 'why' questions. It is the entire suite of measurements which permits the latter. Thus follows the second condition, that the coinvestigators conducting the appraisals and the interpretations need not be responsible for the conduct of the experimental disciplinary components. Rather, they must design and exercise quality control over those components.

Data synthesis and appraisal

If the experimental programme covers an extended period of time (as do many ecological studies), there should be a continuous organized flow of data into the 'program database' from each disciplinary component. Under these circumstances, data synthesis and appraisal should be a semi-continuous process with feedback into the disciplinary components such that data-taking is redirected to improve ultimate data content, density, and distribution for support of the scientific objectives of the programme.

In essence, data synthesis and appraisal is a continuing expansion of the browsing atlas in which content, density, and distribution displays are augmented with, e.g. displays of statistical tests, consistency tests, and intervariable validity tests of specific variables and of related groups, or clusters, of variables. In this step, the coinvestigators work both individually and in conference with the individuals, pursuing their appraisals based on their knowledge of the pertinent disciplines, specific processes, etc. Then, in conjunction with the other coinvestigators comprising the peer group, these appraisals are judged in the perspective afforded by the totality of the data in a sequence of group meetings.

Completion of this step consists of developing a peer group consensus concerning (1) the adequacy, consistency, and validity of the data, (2) the types of conclusions which can be supported from the data, (3) the range of valid application of the conclusions to the scientific problem or public issue at hand, and (4) the selection of those visual displays and tabulations of the data considered best for scientific support and communication of the conclusions.

This process is, again, one in which the peer group is provided with database service according to their specifications. In a major ecological study, the individual and collective directives result in the production of several thousands special displays and tabulations. The peer group controls the tests to be made of the data, the specific protocols to be used in making these tests, and the judgement of the results. For this process to be rapid and effective, there are two basic requirements:

1. The peer group membership must include the perspective of the 'old-fashioned naturalist', or generalist, in its appraisal of the data as they relate to *system* behaviour.
2. Database services must be entirely flexible, imposing no time delays for restructuring of the data base, writing special software for retrieval and sorting, and encompassing all general purpose and special algorithms for computational or statistical treatment of data output considered appropriate for the study by the peer group.

Should the study be of a long-term nature, with continuing expansion or sharpening of objectives based on cumulative results, the efforts of the coinvestigators can be integrated easily and economically by established computer telecommunications networks. This can be implemented using remote terminals and central computing facilities, or it can involve, for example, the geographical dispersion of elements of the 'program database' among the coinvestigators, with these being readily and selectively merged in any of the element facilities to support interelement synthesis and appraisal.

Interpretation

A natural aspect of the synthesis and appraisal of the data includes the coinvestigators looking forward to the kinds of hypotheses they wish to investigate in the interpretive effort in order that the data can be tested for their adequacy to support such investigations. Interpretation, then, consists of the formulation of hypotheses by the group and its members, and the iterative judgement and reformulation of these hypotheses in the process of converging on those that are based on sound science and are supported adequately from the totality of the data. Completion consists of the derivation of consensus conclusions and recommendations, and the selection of those compressed data displays and tabulations which demonstrate their support from the data. The requirements for effective completion are the same as those for synthesis and appraisal; i.e. efficient and flexible database services, the continued emphasis on the use of *all* of the pertinent data in the testing of the hypotheses such that all disciplinary component data consistently supports the judgement made, and the continued application of system perspective.

Publication

Whether the objectives are issue-related or not, the end product of the IDR programme is publication in a refereed scientific journal. This is neither simple nor cheap. A single publication, covering all aspects of the IDR study, and including publications from the scientists conducting the disciplinary components, is essential if the results are to be useful for either scientific or management purposes. In IDR programmes of even modest complexity, the publication absorbs an entire volume of the journal selected. For complex programmes, one or more volumes may be necessary.

The pitfall to be avoided is that of permitting disciplinary component publications *in advance* of the formulation of the consensus IDR interpretation or, preferably, in advance of the publication covering the total programme. Since the components are directed primarily to describing *what* is observed, rather than *why* it is observed, the publication relating to 'why' based on a single component is the most likely to be incomplete or misleading and the single component content may not be judged suitable for publication.

Examples of Applications

Space does not permit examples of applications of these procedures to be presented in this paper. Two comprehensive applications where the author participated are reported in Sharp and Appan (1982) and Ward, Bender, and Reish (1979).

Summary

The procedures for peer group IDR investigations

The peer group IDR procedures described are shown diagrammatically in the lower part of Figure 1, 'interdisciplinary research programme'. The purpose of the figure is to discriminate between (1) those 'interdisciplinary research programmes' in which each disciplinary component *relates* to the others, but in which synthesis and interpretation consists essentially of summing the disciplinary results, (2) the 'polydisciplinary research programme' in which components are interdisciplinary but limited in scope and are related, but in which synthesis and interpretation is, again, a summation of component results, and (3) the 'interdisciplinary research programme' conducted according to the peer group method in which there is total *data* synthesis and interpretation, rather than a summation of component results. The latter programme is possible *only* if adequate *correlatable* data are obtained, and the database services facilitate unrestricted and rapid peer group appraisals of the data.

Requirements for effective peer group method application

The preceding discussion is based on eight years of practice in the synthesis and interpretive procedures and four years of experience utilizing the peer group method of analysis whereby diverse and dispersed scientific expertise is applied to the solution of specific social or scientific problems. This experience has demonstrated the feasibility of the peer group method *provided* the three primary conditions are satisfied; i.e. (1) database support is fast and flexible, (2) database services are cast in the mode of knowledgeable and experienced scientific use rather than computer science mechanics, and (3) the 'generalist(s)' are an influential guiding element of the interdisciplinary peer group.

Applications

Four implications regarding the use of the peer group procedures described are important to the advancement or improvement of IDR:

1. A properly structured peer group is essential to both the scientific soundness and the credibility of the consensus conclusions. Not only must the appropriate mix of disciplinary and generalist skills be included, but such skills must frequently be drawn from sources representing different biases or convictions relating to the issue to which the IDR programme is related.
2. The data bases, the appraisals, the hypothesis investigations, the interpretations, and the scientific support of each are examples of interdisciplinary problem-solving efforts which illustrate the means by which both generalists and disciplinarians can integrate their experience and knowledge to develop sound and documented interdisciplinary answers. Such

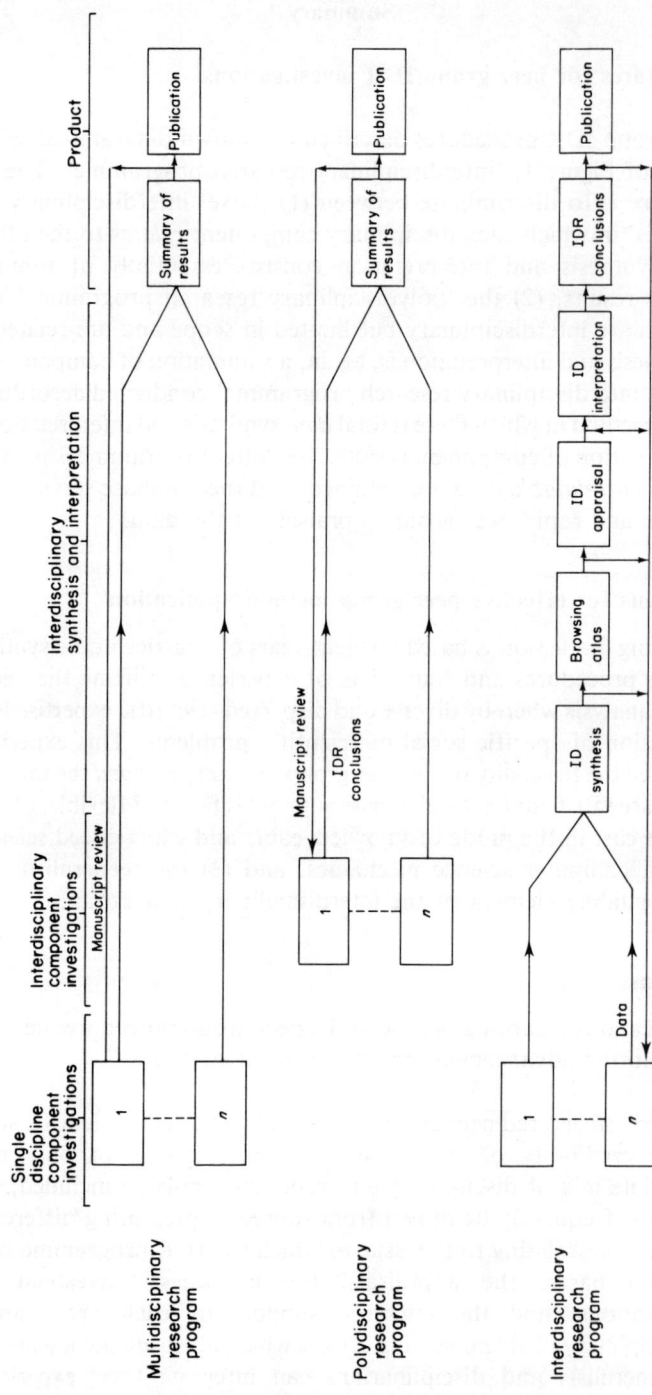

Figure 1. Comparison of alternative research schemes

information can be organized readily and recorded on computer tape together with instructional narrative. These tapes can be mailed, telecommunicated, etc., for widespread use in the teaching of interdisciplinary subjects— such as ecology—and of methods for interdisciplinary problem solution—such as policy research.
3. The procedure provides a mechanism for more rapidly achieving scientific recognition of the 'bridge', 'systems', or 'general' scientist by reducing the time and cost of deriving a totally interdisciplinary conclusion and the subsequent scientific publication of these conclusions, thereby enhancing the probability and rate of academic recognition and advancement.
4. The peer group procedure makes it possible to practice the 'imperfect' science that has become necessary because of the demand for 'the best possible appraisal and interpretation' of extant data and knowledge to support policy, legislative, regulatory, and management decisions.

References

Hedgpeth, Joel W. (1978). 'As blind men see the elephant: a dilemma of marine ecosystem research', *Estuarine Interactions* (Ed. M. L. Wiley), Academic Press, New York, pp.3–15.
Sharp, J. M., and Appan, S. G. (1982). 'The cumulative ecological effects of normal offshore petroleum operations contrasted with those resulting from continental shelf oil spills', *Phil. Trans. Roy. Soc. Lond.* (June issue in Press).
Ward, C. H., Bender, M. E., and Reish, D. J. (Eds) (1979). 'The offshore ecology investigation: effects of oil drilling and production in a coastal environment', *Rice University Studies*, **65** (4 and 5), 589.

DEVELOPMENT OF A SPECIAL PURPOSE, INTERDISCIPLINARY RESEARCH INSTITUTE IN AN ACADEMIC SETTING: A CASE STUDY
R. J. TRYBUS
Gallaudet Research Institute, Washington, DC, USA

The Host Institution: History, Mission, and Characteristics

Gallaudet College was established as a liberal arts college for deaf people in 1864, under congressional legislation approved by President Abraham Lincoln. The very existence of the college was in the nature of an educational experiment, since it was based on the previously unaccepted premise that deaf persons were capable of higher educational attainment, providing that a situation was provided in which deaf persons could communicate by means of their sign language and in other ways bypass the effect of their hearing loss. For most of its first century of existence, Gallaudet remained a very small undergraduate liberal arts institution. However, beginning in the early sixties, the College embarked on a substantial expansion of its services, its personnel, and its physical plant, so that at the present time the institution functions as a small university—in fact, if not in title. In particular, research programmes began to be developed in the early sixties in a way and on a scale beyond anything which had occurred previously. Several major research groups were established during these years, including a Linguistics Research Laboratory, a Sensory Communications Research Laboratory, and an Office of Demographic Studies.

The Gallaudet Research Institute

Institutional self-study and reorganization, 1976-1978

In 1976, Gallaudet College began a year-long process of self-study, to determine its strengths and weaknesses and to set its goals and objectives for the next decade. After completion of this institutional self-study, a document entitled, *New Challenges, New Responses* was developed, stating sixteen goals for the institution for the coming years. One of these goals was to significantly expand and improve research at Gallaudet, so that it would become a nationally and internationally recognized centre for research on deafness.

History of research at Gallaudet College

Because of Gallaudet College's character as a small liberal arts institution, research was an activity on a limited scale and was not of particularly high priority. A few individuals over the course of the first century of its existence distinguished themselves in scholarly or research activities, but these were clearly the exception rather than the rule. As indicated earlier, several significant research groups began operating in the early to mid sixties, and represented the beginning of organized, long-term research at Gallaudet on problems of deafness. In addition to the research groups mentioned above, when Gallaudet began to operate the national demonstration elementary and secondary schools for deaf children authorized by the US Congress, each of the schools was provided with a research group, the purpose of which was to study major issues pertaining to the education of deaf children. However, the efforts of these units, as well as the others which pre-dated them, were not coordinated or integrated and proceeded as separate and independent activities, with very limited contact among themselves.

Purpose and mission of the new research institute

In response to this state of affairs and to the new goal declaring a desire for expanded research activity, the institution established a Gallaudet Research Institute as part of its reorganization in 1978. The purpose of the Research Institute was to develop a comprehensive rationale for research relating to deafness, develop clear priorities for such research, and manage the development and implementation of these new lines of research, drawing first of all upon the pre-existing research groups and making major efforts to expand the quantity and improve the quality of research on the campus.

Organizational position of research at the College

Although at present the Gallaudet Research Institute is of relatively modest size (annual budget approximately $2 million), the intention of the College was clearly to give a high visibility to research activities. Consequently, in the administrative reorganization of the institution, research was given the status as one of five major divisions of the institution, headed by a Vice President for Research. The other divisions of the institution were Academic Affairs, Pre-College Programmes, Public Services and Continuing Education, and Business Affairs.

The Development Process—Major Issues and Tensions

From periphery to mainstream in the institution

Although research had existed at Gallaudet for at least the last twenty years in an organized form, these research activities and most of the researchers engaged in them were far from the main-stream of institutional life. This was reflected very glaringly in the fact that most doctorate holders engaged full-time in research were not permitted membership on the College's faculty, with the corresponding responsibilities, rights, and benefits. Therefore, one of the early responsibilities of the newly established Research Institute was to develop and obtain approval for a procedure whereby appropriately qualified research personnel would hold faculty rank with all of the rights, privileges, and responsibilities which are entailed. This was a difficult process, but it was finally resolved after two years of discussion, in the summer of 1980. The decision, however, went contrary to the recommendations of most authors (e.g. Ikenberry and Friedman, 1972) who have studied ways in which research institutes can be made viable institutions at colleges and universities. That is, research persons may hold faculty membership through one of the teaching-oriented departments, by contributing at least one-sixth of their working time to departmental activities. The department, however, is not required to pay one-sixth of the individual's salary. This continues to be paid from research funds.

The place of research in a liberal arts college

Although the question of faculty affiliation for researchers was finally resolved, there is not yet an accepted understanding throughout the institution of the place of research in a liberal arts college. Most of the academic deans and other administrators support an increasing level of involvement in research on the part of their faculty, but many faculty members disagree with this point of view, indicating that their preference and their understanding of the conditions under which they were hired was that their efforts were to be devoted to teaching and not to research. At the present time, outside the staff of the Gallaudet Research Institute, probably less than 10 per cent. of the faculty have any involvement, however slight, in research activities.

Cultural membership and political influence in the deaf community

Like many minority groups, the members of the deaf community have recently become aware of their cohesiveness and their potential political power within institutions and in society at large. A fair number of faculty and staff members of Gallaudet College are themselves deaf and are members of the deaf community, wielding significant influence in the local and national trend of events affecting the deaf community. By contrast, very small numbers of deaf persons have acquired the higher educational credentials as well as the necessary interest to move into the research programmes of the College. Therefore, the faculty and staff of the Research Institute, as a whole, have less political influence and are less accepted as a part of the culture than are other groups of personnel within the institution.

Advocacy versus investigation as institutional roles

Given the point of view of the deaf community as a cultural minority in the United States, there has been a significant trend for Gallaudet College to function as a public advocate on behalf of deaf people and the deaf community. With the exception of some broad general positions, this advocacy point of view is very much at odds with the objective investigation point of view typical of researchers. In addition to the cultural differences, therefore, there are also fundamental intellectual differences between the research personnel and other significant persons throughout the institution on the issue of advocacy versus investigation. The researchers' approach of questioning all accepted orthodoxies and demanding empirical evidence for the validity of the policies, procedures, and advocacy positions espoused by the College administration consitutes a continuing irritant to members of the deaf community and the College administration. This poses significant problems since these same officials are responsible for authorizing funding for the research programmes.

'Hard' money versus 'soft' money

Most of the work of the Gallaudet Research Institute is supported by so-called 'hard' money, in the sense that it is part of the institution's operating budget, a large minority of which is provided by congressional appropriation. At least several of the senior researchers came to Gallaudet because of this 'hard' money position, with the feeling that they could spend their time doing research, rather than writing grant proposals trying to generate 'soft' money to support their work. As the institution moves more and more to a posture of seeking external sources of support for research, the issue of 'hard' versus 'soft' money assumes greater importance.

Management and serendipity

Another issue on which there are significant differences of opinion within the Research Institute itself is the issue of the extent to which research activities can be managed or directed, as opposed to the extent to which significant advances must depend on serendipity, on the random strokes of genius of individuals left largely to their own devices. The current direction the Research Institute is taking is towards a more management-oriented focus, on the grounds that even genius and serendipity must have clearly defined boundaries to focus the activity. This, however, remains a significant point of difference of opinion among various sub-groups of personnel within the Research Institute.

'Small is beautiful' versus economies of scale

Another major trend in the development of the Research Institute is the amalgamation of previously very small working units (e.g. one professor with a part-time secretary) on the grounds that the intellectual activity of researchers can be improved by more contact with colleagues across disciplines, as well as on the more common ground that joint activities can result in significant economies of scale, as equipment, supplies, and support personnel are shared. However, since a number of the research personnel have worked for five or more years under a very different mode of operation, they tend to feel strongly that any level of management or organization beyond the individual researcher with minimal necessary support is unnecessary and counterproductive.

From a secure present to a risky future

Although the organized research programmes have collectively not been able to increase their share of the College's operating budget significantly, they have made some minor advances over the years in the level of budget support they have been able to obtain from the College's appropriated budget. While this level of support is below that which might be desired, it has been at least a secure and predictable base from which to operate. The notion of dreaming large dreams and planning for major expansion in the years ahead has provoked a significant concern about the risks of such an activity, and a substantial proportion of the personnel of the Institute are not convinced that the risks of such an expansion are worth the potential benefits.

Last among equals

At a recent review of research activities by the College's Board of Trustees, the decision was made that research should expand in major ways but that the financing of this expansion should not be primarily from the College's basic operating budget. Instead, funds are to be obtained from both governmental and private sources other than the usual appropriation channels. This has resulted in a situation in which, even though research is supposed to have high priority, it has very low priority for internal allocations of funds, staff positions, and physical facilities.

Mechanism and Machinery for Integration

Monthly seminars

As one way of fostering discussion and interchange across units, a 'scientific and professional issues series' has been established. This monthly meeting takes on different formats according to the nature of the topic—this includes lectures, panel discussions, brainstorming sessions, problem-solving round tables, and the like. This has provided an opportunity for researchers at the College to obtain an evaluation of their past work and critical input in their plans for the future. On occasion, the series involves invited presentations by prominent researchers from elsewhere in the country or from other countries.

Physical facilities

Unlike the other divisions of the College, the Research Division has its physical facilities scattered in eight different locations across the campus. All other units are located in a single building or in close proximity to each other. This scattered physical situation reinforces the interpersonal and disciplinary separateness of the researchers and their research programmes, and is a major obstacle to be overcome. Plans are currently underway to attempt to assemble significant quantities of usable space, in temporary buildings and the like, in reasonably close proximity in one section of the campus. This is viewed as a significant potential method for reinforcing the integrated nature of the work which is supposed to emerge from the Research Institute. Some researchers object to this increased contact across disciplines, however, going so far as to say that it endangers their 'ideological purity'. Most members, on the other hand, indicate a sense of excitement about potentially stimulating new perspectives coming from other disciplines now beginning to address their familiar problems.

Intellectual challenge as administrative style

Since most of the researchers on campus have been in their positions for a significant length of time, they have continued to develop their lines of research and have been relatively less active in generating new ideas for new directions. Therefore, one of the major elements of the administrative style of the Dean who heads the Research Institute is to operate by intellectual challenge, i.e. by challenging particular researchers and particular groups to respond to areas of concern relating to education of deaf persons, linguistics, etc., which they are not apparently considering seriously. This poses a significant challenge to the administrator himself, who must remain sufficiently knowledgeable and current in each of the fields of research within the Institute to be able to provide some level of intellectual challenge of this sort.

Redefinition of peer groups

Another aspect of the development of the Institute is a new way of looking at who constitutes peers for each person. The general tendency of our current researchers has been to consider an extremely small number of persons, perhaps only one or two, as professional peers, and to restrict major communications to these few individuals. Part of the intention of the operating style of the Research Institute is to redefine the peer groups as larger networks of individuals pursuing work in related or potentially related fields. This redefinition is being reinforced by such mechanisms as involving this larger peer group in annual evaluations of the work of individuals, as well as involving the larger peer group in the review and critique of proposed new areas of research.

Centralized management, decentralized action: can it work?

Another major theme in the development of the Institute has been that, while management and accountability need to be centralized to a far greater extent than has been the case, the final action or implementation of research can and should remain largely decentralized. We are committed to the notion that it can work, although not all personnel within the Institute accept this point of view. What this means in fact is that, while research groups and their directors have significant leeway in how they actually conduct their research and in determining the nature and extent of their work from day to day and from week to week, such functions as budget planning, expenditure of funds, equipment acquisition, etc., require significant contact with the central administration of the Research Institute.

Plans for the Future

Large-scale growth — its pains and pleasures

During 1980–81 the administrative personnel of the Research Institute were involved in a major planning activity, which was expected to lead to a major statement of the vision or mission of the Research Institute, its available and future needed resources, a restructured organizational pattern, and a new series of work assignments for research personnel. This process initially captured the interest of a small number of the current researchers and research directors, but was viewed with a much less enthusiastic eye by the other members of the Institute. By the conclusion of Spring 1981, a consolidation plan was developed and approved by a large majority of research personnel as well as by the College's administration. This plan calls for consolidation from eight units to three and for a shift to a project-oriented (rather than organizational unit-oriented) planning and budgeting system. Project proposals involving credible interdisciplinary research approaches will receive higher priority for funding.

Relationships with the host institution

Although this question is not really on any public agenda at the moment, a review of the literature (e.g. Daniels *et al.*, 1977) indicates clearly that many universities have found it necessary or desirable to incorporate their research activities in a separate research institute or research foundation, which is heavily overlapping with and controlled by the host institution but which forms a separate legal corporation. This procedure is employed to facilitate handling of funds and hiring and compensation of personnel. Although this item is not presently being considered in the case of the Gallaudet Research Institute, it is highly probable that if the Institute succeeds in achieving a significant amount of growth, the external donors providing funds to finance this growth will be interested in assurances, such as might be given by a separately incorporated structure, that their contributions will go specifically to support research programmes and not for more general support of the institution.

New funding patterns

As indicated previously, the major funding of current research activities comes from the operating budget of the college, which is appropriated by the US Congress annually. In addition to these base funds, relatively limited amounts of grant funds have been obtained in the usual away from the National Institutes of Health, the National Science Foundation, and other sources of research support. These sources of support will continue to be sought, but in addition the Board of Trustees has issued a strong call for a major effort to seek foundation and corporate funding for a large-scale integrated programme of research in areas related to deafness. Because of the unfamiliarity of this approach to funding, all participants in the process find themselves with some level of uncertainty and anxiety about the actual prospects of achieving such funding.

Organizational self-identity redefined

At the present time most research personnel, whether at the doctoral level or at support levels, tend to identify themselves as working for a particular sub-unit, such as for the Linguistics Research Laboratory or for the Signed English Programme—to take two examples. There is relatively little identification when working for the Gallaudet Research Institute or seeing oneself as a part of this larger set of activities. A clear direction in which management will be attempting to move in the future is a shift in this pattern of self-identification, so that a year or two in the future a larger proportion of personnel will identify themselves with the Gallaudet Research Institute as a whole, and not only with particular units or programmes within it.

How to tell success from failure

This item is not entered in jest, since there is a significant opinion within the ranks of researchers that mere expansion cannot be taken as success, but that the level of productivity and ingenuity displayed must be considered more important than quantitative expansion. Fears have been expressed that success will be claimed, even though all that happens is that there is an increasing flurry of activity such as administrative reports, conferences held, and the like, without evidence that this activity has in fact generated significant improvement in our understanding or handling of problems in deafness. We do not at present have a clear resolution to this issue, but as part of the planning process we must redefine or perhaps define for the first time what will be taken as evidence of success in achieving our goals as we move towards them in the years ahead.

References

Allen, T. (1978). 'Cross-impact analysis: a technique for managing interdisciplinary research', *Journal of the Society of Research Administrators*, **X**(1), 11–18.
Andrews, F. (Ed.) (1979). *Scientific Productivity: The Effectiveness of Research Groups in Six Countries*, Cambridge University Press, New York.
Bowonder, B. (1980). 'The research manager and his roles', *Journal of the Society of Research Administrators*, **XII**(1), 17–24.
Daniels, R., Martin, R., Eisenberg, L., Lewallen, J., and Wright, R. (1977). *University-Connected Research Foundations: Characterization and Analysis*, The University of Oklahoma, Norman, Oklahoma.
Fenn, M. (1978). 'Management of Change', *Journal of the Society of Research Administrators*, **IV**(4), 21–28.
Ikenberry, S., and Friedman, R. (1972). *Beyond Academic Departments*, Jossey-Bass, San Francisco, California.
Karger, D., and Murdick, R. (1980). *Managing Engineering and Research: The Principles and Problems of Managing the Planning, Development and Execution of Engineering and Research Activities*, Industrial Press, New York.
Meechan, C. (1978). 'Interdisciplinary problem solving: some actual teaming experiences', *Journal of the Society of Research Administrators*, **X**(1), 19–25.

INTERDISCIPLINARY IN-SERVICE TRAINING IN THE URBAN REALM
F. VIDOR
Hungarian Academy of Sciences, Budapest, Hungary

Abstract

Urban planning is an area in which considerable changes are taking place in response to public demand. Consensus within the community on the desirability of any proposed development is essential but because of the conflicting interests and values very difficult to obtain. Resolution of the conflicts depends on the adoption of an interdisciplinary approach to planning such developments.

The paper contains a brief historical overview of the trends in urban planning, from the mediaeval walled city to the open industrialized city of the early nineteenth century to the segregated industrial and residential areas typical of the unplanned cities that grew up in the early twentieth century. The present trends in urban planning in which geography and economics are no longer the only element of importance and where avoidance of sprawl and enhancement of the quality of life are powerfully demanded implies the broadening of the training of urban planners to enable them to make these new features a natural part of their approach to their professional work and to the public they serve.

FUTURES RESEARCH AS A FRAMEWORK FOR TRANSDISCIPLINARY RESEARCH
R. WAŚNIOWSKI
Technical University of Wroclaw, Poland

Introduction

The development of human knowledge has brought about its own fragmentation into strictly specialized disciplines. An enormous cohesion of methods, notions, and detailed information has been divided up and distributed among defined groups of scientists, possessing the status of professional specialization. These specialists, having in mind their own interests, jealously protect their realm from intrusions by other people. The state of affairs results in the isolation of particular disciplines which are separated into their 'own' colleges, institutes, departments, etc., but at the same time there appears a growing number of problems in society which cannot be solved by means of one discipline of science. Much attention is being paid to this problem by the strategists of social life, publicists as well as many scientists who, within their possibilities and interests engage themselves in more than one field of science. In order to meet the necessity for science to participate in solving the problems of social development, centres are being organized which group the specialists from several disciplines of science.

The establishment of such centres requires a new organization, and time will be needed for the specialists from various disciplines to build communication before their activities can bring valuable effects.

In this paper are presented the experiences concerning the functioning of the Futures Research Centre of the Technical University of Wroclaw, a scientific centre grouping the scientists from many disciplines of science. We intend to show the metamorphosis of the group of people employed in this centre from multidisciplinarity through pluridisciplinarity, cross-disciplinarity and interdisciplinary to transdisciplinarity.

Need for Interdisciplinarity in Futures Research

The use of the term 'futures research' gives rise to much misunderstanding. In the literature the terms 'prediction' and 'forecasting' are also used. In the sense of prediction or forecasting it means the assertion that a particular event will inevitably occur in the future with a high probability.

Futures research has a broader sense. It means the attempt to foresee the future of various systems. This is also used in the prescriptive sense implying whether a given, desired future is inconsistent with mechanisms believed to operate in the real world and what actions are recognized to make the occurrence of that future more likely.

Futures research is also extended in the centres involved in futures research; this is why we have it concentrated in a specific centre, i.e. the Futures Research Center (FRC) of the Technical University of Wroclaw. FRC was established in 1971 as an organization for systematic and complex studies on the development of science and technology in their social and economic environment. The Center carries out futures research, studies on long-term planning and technology assessment, courses on forecasting, staff education, and scientific conferences.

At present the programme of research includes:

1. Methods and techniques of futures research and technology assessment including an application for the purposes of formulating development strategies on the national, regional, and departmental levels (e.g. electronic industry, petro-chemistry, construction materials, etc.).
2. Methods and techniques of modelling and analyses of the process of education and intellectual potential. This research is directed towards identification of possible trends of development and may be used to formulate policy in the range of planning on a higher level.
3. Techniques, procedures, and algorithms for the selection, planning, programming, and controlling of research programmes. This research also includes the application of various techniques for control of the research in a university and conducting a well-developed cooperation with industry.

In all these directions subjects for the government agencies, industry, and research institutions are conducted by the interdisciplinary team consisting of forty persons. There also participate specialists temporarily engaged from other institutions in the country and from abroad.

At the initial stage of FRC functioning three types of contributions of various disciplines in the research were observed:

1. Several disciplines involved, usually at the same hierarchical level, but no integration and no co-operation between them, i.e. multidisciplinarity. Papers were written on futures research, considered from the point of view of particular branches of science.

2. Interaction between disciplines but no coordination, i.e. pluridisciplinarity. Forecasts were written concerning such problems as constructional materials.

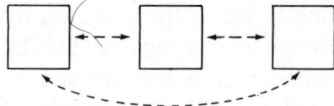

3. Undirectional cooperation and coordination in which the goal of one discipline is imposed upon the other discipline, implying polarization towards a specific disciplinary approach, i.e. cross-disciplinarity. In this way forecasts for such subjects as biochemistry were developed.

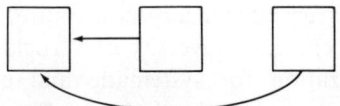

In the Centre undertaking research concerning the future development of science and technology, development compelled the staff to more intense cooperation. Then formation of interdisciplinary research teams could be observed in which disciplines of at least two hierarchical levels were involved and interacted with each other. Cooperation introduced a sense of purpose (problem-solving research).

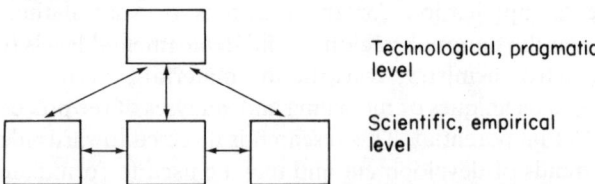

A schematic diagram of the various disciplines of science and methodology participation in future research is presented in Figure 1. In order to examine systematically the influence of one discipline upon another (mutual interaction) and to follow carefully the changes of the influence in the course of time a decision was made to carry out a study based on interpretative structural

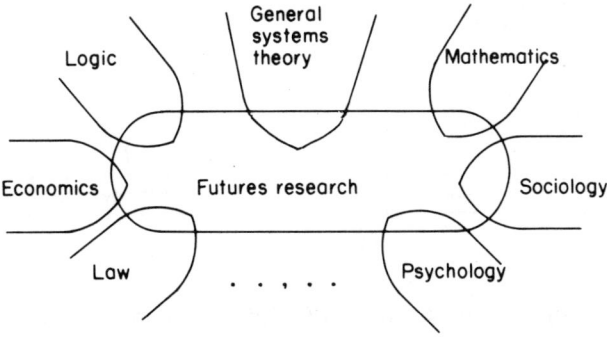

Figure 1. Futures research as interdisciplinary research

modelling (Warfield, 1976). For these investigations it is necessary to have the data about the influence of one discipline upon the other for a given group of scientists in a form of matrix components.

	D_1	D_2		D_j		D_n
D_1						
D_2						
D_j				a_{ij}		
D_n						

$D_1, D_2, \ldots D_n$ are disciplines such as: biology, sociology, psychology, history, economics, computer science, physics, mathematics, chemistry, cybernetics. The matrix elements are integrated as follows:

a_{ij}
- 0 no influence
- 1 weak influence
- 2 moderate influence
- 3 strong influence
- 4 very strong influence

After receiving this information from experts (in this case from the staff members of the Centre) and by means of the structural modelling method, the result shown in Figure 2 was obtained. The presence of the representatives of systems science (persons possessing a specific point of view, techniques of procedures, and capable of grasping skilfully complex phenomena and analysing complex problems) turned out to be especially useful in the practical realization of research projects.

It is as well to emphasize that the use of the systems approach in the course of the research enriched particular branches of science not only with new theoretical solutions but also with new research methods and empirical investigations. The systems approach brought language as well as additions

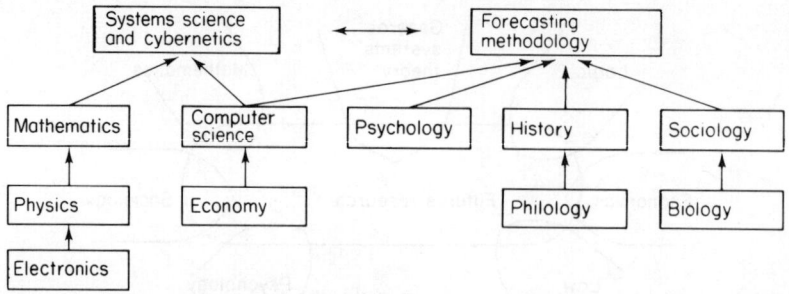

Figure 2. The structure of disciplines of science in futures research of FRC (1978)

to the techniques found useful for research. In many cases the application of such notions as system, sub-system, and appropriate block diagrams was very effective. In time the following important and interesting projects were developed: forecasting intellectual potential, regional development, models of goal-oriented management, and many others.

New Stage in Futures Research—Transdisciplinarity

The experience from recent years, designated in the field of organization of futures research as interdisciplinary research, has revealed a number of advantages. For example, a hierarchical structure of research in which some persons were engaged in the problems of the model of needs, system of values and others on the problems of satisfying definite needs by technological means has been developed.

As the result of the above-mentioned phenomena we could observe multilevel interactions, and horizontal and vertical coordination of disciplines leading to an entire common purposes system. A feedback mechanism between basic sciences, applied sciences, and decision-making in innovative pattern emerges.

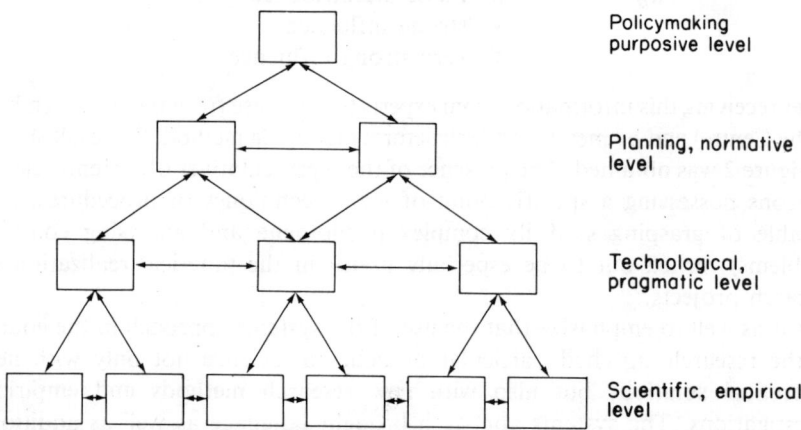

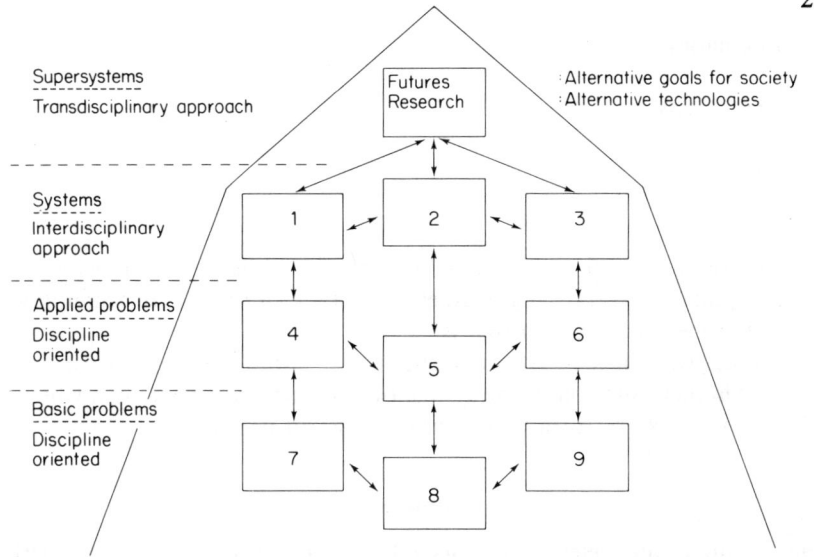

Figure 3. Scheme of the place of futures research as transdisciplinary research

Phenomena such as more intense cooperation of teams, implementation of tasks in a hierarchical system with a division into the policymaking level, planning level, technological level, and scientific level were favourable for undertaking more complex problems of social and economic systems development. The contribution of particular fields and research trends, taking into consideration cooperation with the specialists from other scientific institutions, from the Technical University of Wroclaw, and from Poland and abroad, gives the shape shown in Figure 3:

1. Technological systems
   food production
   waste disposal
2. Sociotechnological systems
   controlling the environment development
3. Social systems
   developing countries
   factory
4. Engineering
5. Assistance in decision-making
   analysis of decision
   methods of forecasting
6. Sciences on behaviour
   law
7. Physics
   structure of life
   geology

8. Mathematics
   logics
   theory of sets
9. Social science
   sociology
   history

The experience acquired has enabled us to undertake projects within transdisciplinary research, e.g. studies in the field of the role of technology in the advancement of social progress.

For some years, in socialist countries, extensive studies have been carried out aiming at implementation of the system of goal–program control in which the main social goals are formulated based on social needs.

Comments

Summing up, futures research appears to be a cognitive trend with clearly defined specific areas of interest, but by nature is bound to cooperate with other sciences. Futures research concentrates on fundamental problems connected with the future development of society, economy, technology, etc. The latter predisposes futures research to the role of a peculiar bond between the isolated specialists, initiator of research, contacts, confrontation of achievements, and exchange of experiences. Futures research opens broad possibilities for transdisciplinary research. The information obtained during the course of the research constitutes, as a rule, interesting material for various fields of science, their needs in the spontaneously created organism, and the mutually penetrating circle of common interests. This denotes permanent, natural integration and thus greater practical utility of the research.

References

Blauberg, I., and Mirsky, E. (April, 1979). *Interdisciplinary Research Groups in the Structure of the Research Front*, First International Conference on Interdisciplinary Research Groups, Schloss, Reisensburg, FRG, April, 1979.

Jantsch, E. (1972). *Technological Planning and Social Future*, Cassell Business Programmes, London.

Linstone, H. A. (1969). *A University for the Post-Industrial Society*, Vol. I, *Technological Forecasting*.

Nikolajew, V. (1980). 'Application of systems analysis as a framework for interdisciplinary research', Prace Naukowe OBP PWr, No. 13/7.

Nilles, J. M. (1978). *Communication versus Interdisciplinary Research*, University of Southern California, Office of Interdisciplinary Programs.

Pelc, K. 'Futures Research in a University', Manuscript.

Potucek, M. (1980). 'Form and utilization of teleonomic explanatory schema in social development models', Prace Naukowe, OBP, PWr, No. 13/7.

Rivett, B. H. P. (1979). 'Futures literature and futures forecasting—a critical review', *OMEGA*, 7(1).

Rossini, F. A., and Porter, A. L. (1979). 'Frameworks for integrating interdisciplinary research', Research Policy No. 8. Georgia Institute of Technology, Atlanta, U.S.A.
Schultze, D. (1980). 'Some theoretical and organizational aspects of interdisciplinary research', Paper presented on Fourth International Conference on MR and E, Wroclaw.
Warfield, J. N. (1976). *Societal Systems*, Wiley, New York.
Waśniowski, R. (1979). *Management of Interdisciplinary Research Programs in a University*, First International Conference on Interdisciplinary Research Groups, Schloss Reisensburg, FRG.
Waśniowski, R., and Blach, L. (1980). 'A Framework for national science and technology policy and strategy analysis', *Proceedings of the Fourth EMCSR*, Vienna.

List of Papers Presented at the First International Conference on Interdisciplinary Research

(Extracted from
Interdisciplinary Research Groups: Their Management and Organization
edited by
R. T. BARTH and R. STECK, 1979)

Interaction of Cognitive and Social Factors in Steering a Large Interdisciplinary Project	J. Barmark and G. Wallen
Some Behavioral, Managerial and Research Perspectives on the Organization and Management of Interdisciplinary Research: An Overview	R. T. Barth and G. E. Manners, Jr.
Determination of the Research of Computer-Based Technologies for Urban Traffic Systems	D. Bents and W. Horsmann
Research Team Composition and Performance	P. D. Birnbaum
Interdisciplinary Research Groups	D. Blaschke, S. Heeg and R. Steck
Interdisciplinary Research Groups in the Structure of the Research Front	I. Blauberg and E. Mirsky
Problems of Interdisciplinary Co-operation as Applied to Pharmaceutical R & D	J. S. G. Cox and P. Neuwirth
Technological Economics at Stirling: An Approach to Interdisciplinary Research	M. F. Culpin

A Policy Perspective on Interdisciplinary Research in US Universities	R. S. Cutler
Some Aspects of Interdisciplinary Organization of Research Teams	G. Darvas and A. Haraszthy
The Use of Support Groups in Handling Interfaces in Multidisciplinary R & D Projects	G. B. Davies
Corporate Strategy, R & D Structures and the Occurrence of Interdisciplinary Sciences in the Telecommunications Industry	F. Hagemeyer
An Assessment of the Present State of Research on IDR Management	L. H. Hattery
Conclusions from the American Society for Public Administration Assessment of Four Interdisciplinary Research Projects	N. Lindas
Communication, Co-ordination and Leadership in Interdisciplinary Research	A. W. Pearson, R. L. Payne and H. P. Gunz
Informational Network for International Team Research	W. D. Rauch
Frameworks and Factors Affecting Integration within Technology Assessments	F. A. Rossini, A. L. Porter, P. Kelly and D. E. Chubin
The Integration of Interdisciplinary Research with the Organization of the University	B. O. Saxberg, W. T. Newell and B. W. Mar
A Goal-oriented Pharmaceutical Research and Development Organization: An Eleven Year Experience	J. C. Stucki
Trends in the Organization of Academic Research: The Role of ORUs and Full-time Researchers	A. H. Teich

Organization and Management of   R. Waśniowski
   Interdisciplinary Research Groups

Meshing Interdisciplinarity with   B. Wilpert
   Internationality

Bibliography

Aimetti *et al.* (1979). 'The utility of using different typologies of research units to understand their functioning and management', *R & D Management*, **9**, Special Issue, 193-206.

Aldrich, H., and Whetten, D. A. (1981). 'Organization-sets, action-sets and networks; making the most of simplicity', in *Handbook of Organizational Design*, Vol. 1: *Adapting Organizations to Their Environments* (Eds P. C. Nystrom and W. H. Starbuck), Oxford University Press, New York.

Allen, T. J., and Cohen, S. I. (1969). 'Information flow in research and development laboratories', *Admin. Sc. Quart.*, **14**, 12-19.

Belbin, R. M. (1981). *Management Teams—Why They Succeed or Fail*, Heinemann, London.

Birnbaum, P. H. (1981). 'Progress report on the organization and management of interdisciplinary research, *Interstudy*, **2**, 6.

Brooks, H. (1977). 'Office of technology assessment invites comments on health of science', *FAS Public Interest Report*, **30**(1), 6.

Brunsson, N. (1982). 'The irrationality of action and action rationality: decisions, ideologies and organizational actions', *Journal Management Studies*, **19**(1), 29-44;

Campbell, J. P., and Pritchard, R. D. (1976). 'Motivation theory in industrial and organizational psychology', in *Handbook of Industrial and Organizational Psychology* (Ed. M. D. Dunnette), Rand McNally, Chicago.

Carlisle, J., and Leary, M. (1981). 'Negotiating groups', in *Groups at Work* (Eds R. Payne and C. L. Cooper), Wiley, London.

Cooley, C. H. (1902). *Human Nature and the Social Order*, Scribner, New York.

Fineman, S., and Payne, R. L. (1981). 'Role stress—a methodological trap?', *Journal of Occupational Behaviour*, **2**, 51-64.

French, J. R. P., and Caplan, R. D. (1973). 'Organizational stress and individual strain', in *The Failure of Success* (Ed. A. J. Marrow) Amacon, New York.

French, J. R. P., Jr., and Raven, B. (1959). 'The bases of social power', in *Studies in Social Power* (Ed. D. Cartwright), ISR, University of Michigan.

Gerwin, D. (1981). 'Relationships between structure and technology', in *Handbook of Organizational Design*, Vol. 2: *Remodeling Organizations and Their Environment* (Eds P. C. Nystrom and W. H. Starbuck), Oxford University Press, New York.

Janis, I. L. (1972). *Victims of Groupthink*, Houghton Mifflin, Boston.

Jönssen, S. (1982). 'Cognitive tuning in municipal problem solving', *Journal Management Studies*, **19**(1), 63-74.

Kirton, M. J. (1980). 'Adaptors and innovators in organizations', *Human Relations*, **33**, 213-224.

Lambright, W. H., and Teich, A. H. (1981). 'The organizational context of scientific research', in *The Handbook of Organizational Design*, Vol. 2: *Remodeling Organizations and Their Environment* (Eds P. C. Nystrom and W. H. Starbuck), Oxford University Press, New York.

Lane, H. W., Beddows, R. G., and Lawrence, P. R. (1982). *Managing Large Research and Development Programmes*, State University of New York Press, Albany, New York.

McCann, J., and Galbraith, J. R. (1981). 'Interdepartmental relations', in *Handbook of Organizational Design*, Vol. 2: *Remodeling Organizations and Their Environment* (Eds P. C. Nystrom and W. H. Starbuck), Oxford University Press, New York.

McGrath, J. E. (1976). 'Stress and behaviour in organizations', in *Handbook of Industrial and Organizational Psychology* (Ed. M. D. Dunnette), Rand McNally, Chicago, pp.1351–1396.

Miles, R. H. (1980). 'Boundary roles', in *Current Concerns in Occupational Stress* (Eds C. L. Cooper and R. Payne), Wiley, London.

Mintzberg, H. (1979). *The Structuring of Organizations*, Prentice-Hall, Englewood Cliffs, New Jersey.

Moch, M. K., and Morse, E. V. (1977). 'Size, centralization and organizational adoption of innovations', *American Sociological Review*, **42**, 716–725.

Ouchi, W. (1980). 'Markets, bureaucracies and clans', *Admin. Sc. Quart.*, **25**(1), 129–141.

Pugh, D. S., and Hickson, D. J. (1976). *Organizational Structure in Its Context: The Aston Programme 1*, Saxon House, Farnborough.

Pugh, D. S., Hickson, D. J., Hinings, C. R., and Turner, C. (1968). 'Dimensions of organization structure', *Admin. Sc. Quart.*, **13**, 65–105.

Sayles, L. R., and Chandler, M. K. (1971). *Managing Large Systems*, Harper & Row, New York.

Stankiewicz, R. (1979). 'The effects of leadership on the relationships between the size of research groups and their scientific performance', *R & D Management*, **9**, 207–212.

Starbuck, W. H. (1982). 'Organizations as ideological systems', *Journal Management Studies: Special Issue*, **19**(1).

Tushman, M. L. (1977). 'Special boundary roles in the innovation process', *Admin. Sc. Quart.*, **22**, 587–605.

Watzlawick, P., Weakland, J. H., and Fisch, R. (1974). *Change: Principles of Problem Formulation and Problem Resolution*, Norton, New York.

Index

Academic research, 12
Accountability, 186, 188, 191
Action research, 167, 168
Adaptation, 121–122
Adaptors, 30
Adhocracies, 29, 30–34
Administration, 204
Administrative function, 32
Administrator evaluation, 191
Advisory committees, 194, 196
Aggression, 140
Agricultural Experiment Stations, 192
Agricultural research, 192
Air Pollution Committee, 128–135
Aircraft windshields case study, 118
Anatomy
   discipline of, 177–178
   macro- and micro-, 177
Anatomy departments, 178–183
Anatomy faculties, 181
Androgogic approach, 98
Applications, 216, 217
Applied research, 204
Assessments, 192
Aston University, 19
Atmospheric pollution, 16
Atomic bomb, 13

Basic objective research, 167
Behaviour, expectancy theory of, 107–108
Behaviour problems, 139
Bieri test of cognitive complexity, 172
Biomedical research teams, efficiency in, 141–163
Biomedical sciences, 176–184
Biotechnology, 15
Bridge-scientist, 19–20, 41, 219

Center for Interdisciplinary Studies, 206
Cognitive complexity, 20, 172, 173, 174

Cognitive factors, 97, 98
Cognitive frameworks, 92, 98, 100, 137
Cognitive tuning, 36
Collaboration, 184, 186, 190
   between universities, 105
Commitment, 35, 38
Communication, 35, 36, 190, 207–208
Communication patterns, 40
Community factors, 97
Community identification, 94, 100
Community services, 94
Competition, 155
   between universities, 105
Computer technology, 18
Computer telecommunications networks, 215
Conflict resolution, 48
Consideration, 155, 158
Consulting, 6, 7, 88, 90, 96, 100, 102, 106, 139
Contextual variables, 162
Contracting, 6, 7, 90, 97, 99, 100
Cooperation, 35
Corporate policy, 104
Correlative analysis, 154–161
Criteria for success, 146
Cross-disciplinarity, 6, 7, 9, 10–20
   and basic research, 10–12
   and innovation, 15–16
   and organizational forms, 21–37
   and technology assessment, 16
   approach to applied R & D, 12–15
   in biomedical sciences, 176–184
Cultural factors, 24–25

Data access and assessment, 213
Data interpretation, 211–219
Data synthesis and appraisal, 214–215
Databanks, 213
Databases, 213, 215

Deaf community, 219, 222
Decentralized organizations, 24
Decision making, 33–34, 207, 232
Deep ocean mining, 82
Dependent variables, 53
Diagnosis (specifying the needed input), 97, 99
Disciplinary differences, 12, 95
  effect on intra-group interactions, 95
Disciplinary differences and barriers, 91–92
Disciplinary identification, 100
Disciplinary socialization, 100
Disengagement/closure (using the input), 99–100

Ecological studies, 211
Ecosystems, 211
Editorial acceptance, 198
Effectiveness, 47, 162
Effectiveness levels, 24
Efficiency in biomedical research teams, 141–163
Engineering disciplines, 15
Entry phase, 96
Environmental effects, 8
Environmental problems, 127–135
Environmental Protection Agency, 63
Environmental research in France, 127
Evaluation, 185, 186, 187, 189, 191
Evolution of new scientific disciplines, 11
Expectancy theory, 107–108
Experimental conditions, 93
Exploration environment, 199
External constraints, 31
Eysenck Personality Inventory, 172

Feedback loop, 87
Feedback mechanism, 232
Field research, 202–203, 208
Financial resources, 23–25
Financial rewards, 34
Fishery industry productivity, 17
Flexibility, 36, 184–202
Formalism, 155
Fragmentation, 163, 228
France
  environmental research in, 127
  noise research in, 127–135
Freshwater diversion project, 71–78
Funded research, 186–187
Funding agencies, 210
Funding decisions, 198
Futures research, 228–235
  as transdisciplinary research, 232–234
  need for interdisciplinarity in, 229–232
  new stage in, 232–234
Futures Research Centre, 229

Gallaudet College, 26, 219–227
Gallaudet Research Institute, 220–224
Genetic engineering, 15, 123–127
  consequent institutional developments, 125–126
  contemporary context of, 123–124
  interdisciplinary implications in, 124–125
  potential applications, 124
Global assessment, 147
Group cohesion, 40
Group creativity, 15
Group dynamics, 16
Group leadership, 100, 103
  see also Leadership
Group process analysis, 136–140
Group process analysis workshop, 138–140
Group size effects, 21–34
Gulf Universities Research Consortium, 211

Health and Safety at Work Act, 65
Heuristic procedures, 162
Historical investigations, 12

Ideology, 32–34
Implementation, 38
Independent variables, 52
Individual interdisciplinary research, 164–176
Individual role, 209
Industrial/government cross-disciplinary groups
  small, 30–32
  large, 32
Information provision, 24
Information-sharing, 136
Innovation, 15–16, 41, 121–122, 188
Innovators, 30
Inquiry environment, 199
INSERM (Institute National de la Santé et de la Recherche Médicale), 141
In-service training, 228
Institut Pasteur, 141
Institute of Research, 26
Institutional affiliation, 149
Institutional setting, 22–23
Integrated research, 4
Integration, 3–5
Interaction mode, 91
Interaction patterns, 87
Interdependence, 32–34

Interdisciplinarity
  approach to problem-solving, 43, 165
  categories of variables in, 169
  challenge of, 210
  comparison with multidisciplinarity, 177
  complementarity with multidisciplinary 39–40
  criticisms of, 208
  formation of fields of science from, 66–71
  higher degrees scheme, 19
  impact of, 122–123
  implementation of, 134
  implications in genetic engineering, 124–125
  indicators of, 66
  individual characteristics, 19–20, 42
  multidisciplinarity plus integration, 3–5
  origins of, 12
  peer review in, 184–202
  productivity, 86–101
  psychological aspects, 164–176
  rapprochment, 123
  research scheme, 218
Interinstitutional collaboration, 16
Interinstitutional groups, 34–37
Internal structure, 28–30
International congress participation, 146
Interuniversity–industrial projects, 17

Key individual role, 203–204, 207
Kirton Adaptation–Innovation Inventory, 122

Laboratory efficiency determinants, 141–163
Laboratory heads, interviews with, 142–145
Laboratory size effects, 150
Laboratory staff categories, 143–144
Laboratory staff composition, 150
Laboratory technicians, 152
Leadership, 136, 190, 208
  attitudes towards subordinates, 152
  by objectives in R & D, 46
  creative managerial, 209–210
  group, 100, 103
  managerial, 202–210
  relationship with led, 205–207
  through communication, 207–208
  through managerial role, 204–205
Leadership styles, 151–154
  and situational Variables, 154–161
Liaison bureau, 102
Liberal arts, 219–227

research, 221
Line personnel, 32
Location problems, 25
Long-term research performance, predictors of, 47–59

Management, centralized, 225
Management committees, 194
Management implications, 38–45
Management process, 71–78
Management roles in matrix system, 13
Managerial determinants, 141–163
Managerial role, 204–205
Manhattan Project, 13
Manpower resources, 31
Marine Resources Project (MRP), 19, 79–85
Marine Technology Directorate (MTD), 78–85
Matrix management, 122
Matrix organization, 136
Matrix system, management roles in, 13
Medical Research Council, 27
Mineral resources project, 19
Mississippi and Louisiana Estuarine Areas, 76
Mississippi River, 72
Mississippi Sea Grant Program, 71
Monitoring, 189, 206
Motivation, 35, 36, 107–108, 185
Multicomponent experimental study, 214
Multidisciplinary, 3–5, 39–40, 177, 218
Multiple regression analysis, 53

NASA, 32
NCAES RPPS, 196
Neuroscience, 178, 182, 183
Neuroticism, 173
New disciplines, 11–12
New technologies, 40
Noise and Vibration Committee, 128–235
Noise control progress, 62
Noise control R & D, 59–66
Noise control research, 14–15, 16
Noise control technology, 61–64
Noise research in France, 127–135
Noise Technology Support Unit (NTSU), 59, 64, 65
Normative factors, 93, 97
North Central Agricultural Experimental Stations (NCAES), 194
North Sea oil, 80
North Western Universities Consortium for Marine Technology (NWUCMT), 78–85

Nuclear science and technology, 13
Ocean thermal energy conversion (OTEC), 82, 83
Office of Interdisciplinary Research, 26
Operational research, 167 168
Organization, 5–8
Organization of Petroleum Exporting Countries (OPEC), 80
Organization process, 71–78
Organization variables, 162
Organizational characteristics, 148
Organizational determinants, 141–163
Organizational forms, 21–37, 39
    taxonomy of, 21–23
Organizational logic, 38
Organizational structure, 136
Organized research units (ORUs), 26–29

Participation and control, 155
Participation and structure, 161
Partnership, 6, 7, 89, 100
Pedagogic needs, 11
Peer assessments, 115
    different techniques (methods) and purposes of, 109–110
    in industrial R & D departments, 108–117
Peer group appraisal, 211–219
Peer group consensus, 215
Peer group investigation procedures, 217
Peer group membership, 215
Peer group method application requirements, 217
Peer group procedure applications, 217
Peer group redefinition, 225
Peer nomination, 109
Peer ranking, 109
Peer rating, 108, 109, 112
    contamination by friendship bias, 112
    for appraising scientific personnel, 110–115
    interrater agreement in, 112
Peer review, 184–202
Performance, 5–8, 47, 190, 206
Performance criteria, 57
Performance index, 56
Performance levels, 24, 25
Personal freedom, 155
Personal identification, 36
Personal interviews, 142
Personal traits, 20
Personality, 172
Petroleum resources development, 18
Pilkington Brothers Limited, 118
Planning process, 71–78

Policy Research in Engineering Science and Technology (PREST), 81–82
Political logic, 38, 40
Polydisciplinarity, 218
Polymath, 19
Postgraduate degrees, 19–20
Pragmatic problem-solving, 34
Precision, key to, 5–8
Predictors of long-term research performance, 47–59
Problem-definition, 19, 212
Problem-oriented research, 192
Problem-solving, 211
    interdisciplinary approach to, 43, 165
Problem-solving community, 43
Problem-solving styles, 121–122
Problem-solving systems, 36
Process analysis, 139
Productivity of interdisciplinary groups, 86–101
Productivity ratings, 189
Professional performance, 112
Profitability, 105
Programme design, 19
Project organization, 20
Project value, 170, 171
Psychological aspects, 164–176
Psychological test scores, 172, 173
Psychology in interdisciplinary research, 166
Public policy formulation, 14
Publication(s), 147, 152–153, 185, 188, 216
Pure basic research, 167

R & D
    applied, 12–15
    complexities of, 8
    industrial, 12
    leadership by objectives in, 46
    mission-oriented, 13
    noise control, 59–66
Random sampling, 49
Reasoning ability, 172
Recruitment and retention, 208–209
Regional Research Fund (RRF), 193
René Descartes University, 141
Research ability rating, 173
Research and problem-solving (RPS) group, 86, 99, 100
Research and problem-solving network, 87–91
    model of individual transaction in, 88–91
Research committee, 196
Research findings, 197

Research institutes, 210
Research needs, 11
Research organizations, 32
Research Planning and Priority Structure (RPPS), 194
Research programme design, 211–219
Researchers' education distribution, 145
Resource barrier, 24
Response (producing and evaluating the needed input), 98–99
Responsiveness, 184–202
Review committees, 194
Review criteria, 191
Review systems, 187–190, 192, 198, 206
Reward structures, 42, 192
Risk assessment, 18

Salford University, 14, 26, 105, 106
Salford University Industrial Centre Limited (SUIC), 105, 106, 107
Science and Engineering Research Council (SERC), 64–65, 80, 102
Scientific activity, 47, 48
Scientific contribution, 190
Scientific merit, 190
Scientific production, 47
Scientific products, 48
Scientific progress, 47
Scientific quality, 190
Seafood industry, 71
Seminars, 224
Sequential patterns, 87
Shirley Institute, 16, 117–121
Situational complexity (variety), 174
Slack resources, 31
Social implications, 18
Social relationships, 22, 152
Societal problems, 204, 208–209
Socioeconomic aspects, 204
Sociopolitical aspects, 204
Sociotechnical aspects, 204
Southern Mississippi University, 71
Specialist seminar invitations, 146
Sponsor evaluation, 191
Sponsor's role, 27–28
Sponsored research, 187
Sponsorship, 40
Standards, 185, 192
Stanford University, 206
Sub-disciplines, 185
Subject matter factors, 92–93, 98
Success criteria, 146–148
Success level, 159
Success requirements, 208, 227

Tasks, 5–8
  cross-disciplinary, 6, 9,
Teaching-learning phase, 99
Team-building, 20, 136–140
Team composition, 41
Team research, 49
Technical committee, 194, 196
Technical logic, 38
Technological developments, 18
Technology assessment (TA), 16–19
Technology group leaders, 103
Technology transfer, university-based, 102–107
Telephone interviews, 142
Temporary committee, 196
Traffic management system, 18
Training efforts, 100
Transdisciplinarity, 232–234
Triplex Safety Glass Co. Ltd., 118
Turnover, 48

UK Atomic Energy Authority, 13, 122
UMIST, 14, 105, 106
UNESCO, 10, 66, 67
Universities, 13–14
  as problem solving communities, 43
  collaboration between, 105
  competition between, 105
  interdisciplinary research in, 202–210
University-based groups
  large, 26
  small, 23–26
University-based technology transfer, 102–107
University company, 102, 103, 104
University of Manchester Institute of Science and Technology (UMIST), 14, 105, 106
Urban planning, 228
US Air Force, 14, 105–106, 112
US National Science Foundation, 26

Value judgements, 93

Watson-Glaser Critical Thinking Appraisal, 172
Wroclaw Technical University, 229